Politics, Sociology and Social Theory

POLITICS, SOCIOLOGY AND SOCIAL THEORY

*Encounters with Classical and
Contemporary Social Thought*

Anthony Giddens

Stanford University Press
Stanford, California

Stanford University Press
Stanford, California
© 1995 Anthony Giddens
Originating publisher Polity Press, Cambridge
  in association with Blackwell Publishers
First published in the U.S.A. by
  Stanford University Press
Printed in the United States of America
Cloth ISBN 0-8047-2622-1
Paper ISBN 0-8047-2624-8

This book is printed on acid-free paper.

Original printing 1995
Last figure below indicates year of this printing:
08 07 06 05 04 03 02 01 00

Contents

Preface

The articles which compose this book have been drawn from several sources. The first article in the collection, 'Politics and Sociology in the Thought of Max Weber', was originally published as a separate booklet. The remainder of the selections come from two further sources: *Studies in Social and Political Theory*, originally published by Hutchinson, and *Profiles and Critiques in Social Theory*, published first of all by Macmillan. In choosing papers from these two books, I have been guided mainly by the criterion of contemporary relevance. I hope that the reader might agree that the articles reprinted here retain their interest today. I have made minor alterations to some of the articles included herein and have cut down on surplus notes. However, most of the substance of the articles remains unchanged.

I am grateful to various people who have helped me in preparing this book for publication. Thanks in particular to Katy Giddens, Don Hubert and Nicola Ross.

Introduction

This book offers a series of integrated reflections upon a set of topics in classical social theory and more recent schools of thought. At the time at which the first several articles in this volume were first written, the state of thinking about the sociological 'classics' was rather different from what it is now. Two decades ago the 'classics' were not what they have since become. At that time, sociology in the English-speaking world was dominated by American perspectives, particularly in respect of theoretical work. The agenda was set by Talcott Parsons's *The Structure of Social Action*, which first appeared in 1937 but did not achieve a substantial influence until considerably later in the post-war period. Parsons it was who sought to establish what would later be called a 'paradigm' in sociology and who drew up the writings of European thinkers of the nineteenth and early twentieth centuries to do so. Parsons's work from the beginning was vociferously criticized and continues to be the subject of critical debate down to this day.

Whatever the merits or otherwise of Parsons's path-breaking book, it was one of the main influences bringing into common currency the idea that there was a distinctive 'generation' of thinkers who in some sense established sociology, and to a degree the other social sciences too, as viable enterprises. That generation, the '1890–1920 generation', according to Parsons, had broken in a definitive way with the more speculative forms of social interpretation which preceded them; and that generation had done most of the ground-clearing for the later emergence of a properly founded theoretical framework for social science.

Of course, Parsons was not alone in suggesting these ideas, but his influence was none the less quite profound. Parsons helped initiate the idea that there were distinctive founding fathers in sociology – a notion to which Parsons's student and intellectual colleague R.K. Merton gave further flesh. Parsons's *The Structure of Social Action* was important in another way too. For it was Parsons, more than any other author, who introduced Max Weber to an Anglo-Saxon audience as one of the principal founders of sociology. Parsons translated *The Protestant Ethic and the Spirit of Capitalism*, he produced the first English translation of segments of *Economy and Society*, and he propelled into public view the sociological aspects of Weber's work.

Parsons's interpretation of Weber was idiosyncratic, because Parsons wished above all to make use of Weber to develop his own doctrines. Yet whatever objections others might have made to 'Parsons's Weber', there is no doubt that Parsons was the main scholar who early on helped make Weber a figure of such extraordinary stature in English-speaking sociology. This might have happened anyway, but before Parsons came along Weber was thought of by Anglo-Saxon authors mainly as an economic historian and theorist of jurisprudence. This was the way, for example, that Weber had been interpreted by R.H. Tawney and again by Frank Knight, the translator of the texts which appeared in English under the title of *General Economic History*.

Parsons did not have as much influence over the reception of Durkheim in the English-speaking world. Several of Durkheim's works had become accessible before those of Weber; and Durkheim was a self-professed advocate of sociology, whose thought had from the beginning had some impact upon both sociology and anthropology in Britain and the United States. Nevertheless, apart from its reception in anthropology – particularly in the writings of Radcliffe-Brown – Durkheim's thought was only poorly understood among Anglo-American sociological authors. Many thought of Durkheim as a theorist of a metaphysical collective consciousness – someone who thought the 'collective' always superior to the 'individual'. Parsons's work on Durkheim had many shortcomings, but it did serve to elevate the critical analysis of Durkheim's works to a new plane of sophistication.

When I wrote my own book, *Capitalism and Modern Social Theory* (1971), and some of the later pieces included in this collection, Parsons's influence was at its height. Few people at that time, though, curiously, thought in terms of the triad of classics which later became such a central part of the received wisdom in undergraduate courses in sociology. *The Structure of Social Action* included only a few brief pages on Marx, whom Parsons regarded as a utilitarian forerunner of the 1890–1920 generation.

There were many authors who sought to use Marx to counteract what they saw as certain one-sided tendencies in Parsons's thought – Ralf Dahrendorf, John Rex, David Lockwood, among others. Most Marxists, however, had little truck with either Weber or Durkheim, and saw the development of sociological thought mainly in terms of a line of continuity from Marx and Engels through to the various schools of Marxism which developed over the following century or so.

Even as late as the 1960s, the idea that there were distinctive founding fathers of sociology, and that they were to be found specifically in Europe, had barely taken hold. British sociology up to that period tended to be strongly empirical – dominated by Fabianism and an orientation towards questions of social welfare. The writings of T.H. Marshall represented perhaps the leading example. Theoretical thinking in sociology was overshadowed by anthropological thought. Sociology had no one to compare with the dazzling group of anthropological authors which, besides Radcliffe-Brown, included Bronislaw Malinowski, E.E. Evans-Pritchard, Edmond Leach, Raymond Firth, Meyer Fortes, Audrey Richards and many others. With the exception of one or two émigré authors, such as Karl Mannheim – whose work was in any case slightly earlier – indigenous social theorists were not in the same league. They looked mainly to previous British thinkers, such as Spencer or Hobhouse, rather than to continental thought for their inspiration: the work of Morris Ginsburg is an example.

In the United States, the majority of sociologists at that date traced back their ancestry to indigenous sources – symbolic interactionism, the Chicago School and so forth. As a result of the influence of Albion Small, the writings of Georg Simmel – or some of them – had for some while been better known in the US than those of either Weber or Durkheim, let alone the work of Marx. Not just the efforts of Parsons, but those of a sizeable group of immigrant authors, served in the end to alter these emphases. Writers such as Hans Gerth, Reinhard Bendix and Lewis

Coser were critical of Parsons and put forward their own interpretations. Yet their collective influence served strongly to reorient American interpretations of the past history of sociology towards Europe.

In *Capitalism and Modern Social Theory* I included sections on Marx as comprehensive as those concerned with Weber and Durkheim. I sought to question Parsons's idea of the 1890–1920 'breakthrough' generation, as well as some of the specifics of his interpretations of Weber and Durkheim. I also tried to show that Marx anticipated some of the key theorems worked out by Weber and Durkheim; the influence of Marx on Weber was something which appeared only in muted form in Parsons's account, and I wanted as well to make clear how thoroughly Weber was indebted to Marx. The idea of the trio of founding fathers thereafter became fairly strongly established – a phenomenon which I had not fully anticipated and to which I did not want particularly to contribute.

The past few years have seen basic changes affecting the status of the three main sociological classics. Important debates have occurred in intellectual history – debates which bear upon the interpretation of the past history of all intellectual disciplines, but which have been extensively pursued in the area of sociology. In addition, all of a sudden, the 'holy trio' are a trio no longer – because of what seems like the final disappearance of Marxism. In the eyes of many we are more or less back where we started when Parsons first came on the scene. The collapse of Soviet Communism, and the disintegration of socialism as a model for an alternative social order, mean that Marx should again be erased as equivalent in status to Weber or Durkheim. I shall come back to the issue of the current status of Marx later; first of all, however, I shall look at the debates about the status of the sociological classics in general.

What should we mean by the 'classics of sociology'? Does the term 'classical social theory' have some real force, or is it just a vague label of convenience? And are 'classics' the same as 'founders'?

I would take it, first of all, that every intellectual discipline, including sociology, has itself a sociological or, if one prefers, a constructed history. The idea that there was a certain Archimedean point at which a discipline became founded – begotten by its founding fathers – does not stand up to scrutiny. Thus Parsons claimed that the 1890–1920 generation established a 'great divide' from what went before. The serious history of sociology, in other words, can be dated from that period. But this claim is a contestable one, to say the least. It accepts at face value the claims of the 1890–1920 generation to have established a new discipline. If we look back to prior periods in the evolution of social thought, we find that a succession of thinkers claimed to have put behind them the lapses of their forerunners and to have instituted a new science of society for the first time. Durkheim argued as much in respect of Marx. Yet Marx believed that he had superseded Comte and Montesquieu; Montesquieu in turn believed the same of his predecessors. Even earlier, Vico thought of himself as the first founder of a 'new science' of the social (perhaps in this case, he actually was).

I would suggest that all intellectual disciplines have their commonly recognized founders, but only in some are the works of those founders widely thought of as 'classics'. All disciplines have their founders because they are part of their myths of origin. There are no more natural divisions between disciplines than there are between countries on a map. Every recognized intellectual discipline has gone through a process of self-legitimation not unlike that involved in the founding of nations. All disciplines have their fictive histories, all are imagined communities which invoke myths of the past as a means of both charting their own internal development and unity, and also drawing boundaries between themselves and other neighbouring disciplines.

Although it might not follow any natural features at all, the territoriality of a nation may gain immense symbolic value. It is at once often the source of devotion and of schism. Much the same is true of the intellectual disciplines, which depend for their identity and their differences upon teaching curricula. Even the terminology is rather similar: a state has a territory and a discipline marks out a 'field'; in each case the larger area is also mapped into sub-regions, which can sometimes prove a threat to the unity of the whole.

The fictive histories which inform the imagined communities of intellectual domains – just as in the case of national ideologies – are highly selective. What counts, obviously, is not only what is 'institutionally remembered' and commemorated in some sort of

ritual sense, but what is forgotten in the reshaping of the past.
Marx, Durkheim, Weber, Simmel and others are remembered and
still read. But who now remembers, let alone reads, Schäffle,
Worms or Le Play? The founders have a distinctiveness in retrospect which is at least partly the result of selective remembering; it
does not normally correspond to how the individuals in question
were thought of by their contemporaries.

As in the case of nationalist ideologies, the ways in which the
great figures of the past are viewed are not static. They are interpreted and reinterpreted in the light of changing events, fashions
and imperatives. Wolin has argued that the legitimating of founders 'has both a *political dimension* and a *politics*'. Founding is
'political theorising' precisely because principles inferred from the
work of founders legitimate basic dimensions of intellectual activity. For some ideas to 'win' in this retrospective battle, others of
course must lose. Political action in this context means the more
or less constant struggle between different forces over the legitimate constitution of an intellectual arena. The 'politics' of intellectual inheritance becomes obscured from view to the degree to
which successful monopolizing claims are registered: dominant
presuppositions thereby become taken-for-granted ideas and
procedures.

The question is: how arbitrary are the frameworks which
thereby become legitimated? If history had in some way taken a
different course, *would* we now have books by Schäffle, Worms
and Le Play on our bookshelves, instead of Marx, Durkheim,
Weber and the others? Have they withstood a 'test of time' which
has a kind of quasi-evolutionary value? Here we make the transition from the notion of founders to that of classics. All intellectual disciplines have founders, but it tends to be only the social
sciences which recognize the existence of 'classics'. Classics, I
would take it, are founders who still speak to us in a voice which
is held to be relevant. They are not just antiquated relics, but can
be read and re-read with profit as a source of reflection upon
today's issues and problems.

Probably several reasons exist as to why this sense of the 'classical' has a particular force in the social sciences. One is methodological. There is a logical gulf between the natural and social
sciences; in the social sciences there is not the same kind of cumu-

lative knowledge which can be claimed for natural science. Second, and related to this, is the inevitable reflexive engagement of sociology and the other social sciences with the subject matter – human actions as historically constituted – which they seek to analyse or explicate.

Two somewhat paradoxical consequences follow. On the one hand, ideas and findings can become banal as they are 'swallowed up' and incorporated into the everyday knowledge of actors in society itself; as contexts of action change, they can come to seem archaic or trivial. On the other hand, there are, as it were, wisdoms in the work of some authors which speak to long-standing aspects of human social existence.

Wolin's 'epic theorists' are individuals whose work contains just such wisdoms. Epic theorists, Wolin suggests, are not just legitimated as such by retrospective invention, but earn their status through their deeds. Such deeds are heroic endeavours on the level of thought: they involve essentially the invention of novel perspectives upon states of affairs which were previously looked at in a different way. Some epic theorists, therefore, weather the 'test of time' just because of the sheer scale of their achievements, when compared either to prior or to subsequent thinkers. The judgement of 'history' undeniably has a certain arbitrariness about it, as well as having a mobile character. Yet epic status has to be earned; it cannot merely be dispensed.

Suppose one were to ask why sociologists now still read Weber, but do not read Sombart. In his day, Sombart was probably the more famous of the two, and his writings ranged very widely. Yet Sombart's work is largely forgotten, whereas the lively dialogue with Weber continues. I think that, were one to undertake a systematic comparison of the achievements of Sombart and those of Weber, one would have to conclude that the forgetting of Sombart is to some degree an arbitrary matter. That is, one could imagine a possible world of intellectual development in which Sombart continued to figure as an author of continuing relevance. At the same time, looked at dispassionately, one would also conclude that Weber was an epic theorist on a scale beyond anything that Sombart managed to achieve. The same conclusion would be reached were one to make a comparison between the works of

Durkheim and those of Schäffle, Worms, Le Play or a host of other comparable authors whose works have long ago ceased to command a wide audience.

Since I first started writing about Marx, Weber, Durkheim et al., various controversies have arisen about the proper status of intellectual history. It is plain enough that the history of sociology encapsulates what it is about. Problems of the interpretation of meaning, intentionality and the historical character of cultural creation are not simply discussed in sociology texts, but have to be coped with when analysing the significance of those texts themselves. Puzzling through the implications of this phenomenon has produced quite widely different standpoints; and, of course, different standpoints in turn reflect wider theoretical variations in views of the issues involved.

I shall not try to deal with this diversity here. One approach which has been particularly debated, however, is that suggested by Quentin Skinner and others. The so-called 'historicists' criticize both Whig versions of intellectual history and the more relativistic positions taken by some influenced by structuralism or post-structuralism. Intellectual history, they suggest, should be written with due sensitivity to context. The uses which we might make of the 'classics' in the present day, for example, might be quite different from the impulses which originally drove the production of a given set of ideas in a particular context. 'Context', in this style of reasoning about intellectual history, must be given precision. It does not mean just situating ideas or writings in a wider framework of intellectual production. We have to investigate thoroughly, the historicists say, what authors were intending when they wrote their texts, what kinds of audience they wrote those texts for and what sorts of problem or question they had in mind in generating them. Works can be understood as embedded in a nexus of illocutionary acts – acts that are always practical and constitutive as well as sheerly intellectual.

Thus Robert Jones has argued that to understand Durkheim one must grasp Durkheim's intentions in producing his texts under descriptions which the author himself would have accepted as authentic. Durkheim 'cannot be said to have meant or *done* something if *he* could not, at least in principle, have accepted the statement as an accurate account of what he was saying or doing'. It is easy to see how closely such a view of an author reproduces more general aspects of hermeneutics. The principle is more or less the same as that enunciated, not so much by J.L. Austin, as by Wittgenstein. To know what an agent is up to, an observer or interpreter must know what the agent knows and applies in relation to his or her actions. A description of an action which ignores this quality of 'adequacy' is liable to be mistaken.

Historicism has been widely criticized, both in the version developed by Skinner and in its more sociological guise. It has been pointed out, for instance, that many authors – and this would apply with particular force to the 'epic theorists' – do not in fact orient their arguments only to the local contexts of their activities. Authors may not only write with an indefinite future audience in mind, but also see themselves to be dealing with very general questions which form part of overall intellectual traditions. 'Context', which seems to be a way of narrowing down and delimiting the audiences to whom works were addressed, becomes then widened out again and reconnected with overall parameters of culture.

The main thesis of the historicists is not refuted by such an observation, although it does lose some of its apparent hard-headedness. The issue of understanding an author's intentions in context remains important; if it is philosophically valid, as I think it is, it provides a firm bulwark against the eccentricities of relativism.

Consider the various interpretations I offer of Weber and Durkheim in the opening chapters in this book. There I discuss the socio-political contexts in which Weber and Durkheim developed their sociological ideas. These contexts are interesting in and of themselves, but, crucially, they allow us to gain a greater sense of what led the two authors to write in the way in which they did. When we get to know more about the context in which Weber and Durkheim wrote, we can infer more about their intentions; and inference from their intentions in turn allows us to elucidate further the contexts of their writing.

The implications of these observations should be made clear. The point is not that an author has in some sense a final say – or would have, were he or she to be available for interrogation – over what a text means. The author has no such ultimate privilege. What is at issue, instead, is grasping what an 'author' is. We are all the authors of our own actions, no matter whether there be influences which affect us which we do not fully understand, or whether there be consequences of our activities which we do not in any way anticipate.

To be an 'author' of a text has a connection with being the author of an action. Foucault and others argue that an author is a kind of assemblage of 'discursive' qualities. But this is not so; to write something, just as to do anything, implies agency, reflexivity and the meshing of intentions with longer-term projects. In intellectual history – as opposed to the latter-day use of works as classics – authorship is essentially interrogated just as actions, no matter how trivial or large, can be interrogated in the contexts of everyday life. In everyday speech and action, we do not allow an individual ultimate control over the meaning of what he or she says or does; but we do accord the speaker or agent special privileges of explication.

When someone says or does something which appears initially incomprehensible, or with which we want for some reason to take issue, we do ask for a story of intentionality and we grant the individual in question special access to that intentionality. However, we also assess the guiding threads of what an individual says or does, on the level of intentionality, in terms of wider criteria than the individual is likely to be able to supply. We look to slot particular actions, or sequences of actions, into a wider biographical interpretation. What we do in casual everyday inquiries bears a logical similarity to what goes on in the 'interrogations' of intellectual history or of the writing of biographies. Why are biographies normally only satisfactory if they are rather detailed? The reason is that on the whole the more we know about someone, the more we are able to grasp the 'author' who stands behind the 'life'.

The articles comprised in this book do not concentrate solely upon classical social theory, but try to strike a balance between the classical and the present-day. The chapter which discusses Auguste Comte and the origins of positivism provides a useful link between the nineteenth century and our current preoccupations. A dictionary of modern culture recently gave this tongue-in-cheek definition of post-modernism: 'Postmodernism: This word is meaningless. Use it often.' Much the same could be said of 'positivism', save that it has become more of an epithet than a word used in an approving way. Yet, defined with some rigour, the idea of positivism traces the main connecting thread of sociology from the mid-point of the nineteenth century to at least three-quarters of the way through the twentieth.

For Comte, positivism meant both a logic for the social sciences and a practical programme of social reform. Comte's version of the religion of humanity might have been bizarre, but the outlook he developed, on the level of both logic and practice, anticipated many later developments. Comte had a directly political influence too. For a while his followers in political associations in Europe and in the Americas outstripped those of Marx.

Most of the methodological debates in sociology of the past century and a half have in some sense concerned the relation between the natural and social sciences. Until some twenty or thirty years ago two main lines of orientation could be distinguished. The positivists looked to natural science as an exemplar for sociology – along the way, of course, drawing upon various models of the logic of natural science. The traditions of interpretative sociology, particularly hermeneutics, on the other hand, have mostly seen natural science as more or less irrelevant to the study of human institutions and human social action. Curiously enough, it is scholars from the second of these traditions who have been most concerned with the impact of science and technology on society – presumably in large part because for them these are more 'alien forces' than they are for the positivists.

Something of a new chapter was opened in social theory when, over about the last twenty or thirty years, the division between positivism and hermeneutics began to be questioned. A diversity of figures were involved in such questioning, including Jürgen Habermas, Michel Foucault, Pierre Bourdieu and many others – and a diversity of standpoints has resulted. At one time it looked as though sociology would dissolve into a welter of conflicting theoretical perspectives, none of which could properly communicate with the others. I do not think that this is in fact what has happened. The questioning of the opposition between positivistic views and the perspectives of hermeneutics has proved both important and fruitful in reorienting social and political theory.

Rather than standing apart from mainstream sociological thinking, hermeneutics and ordinary language philosophy have increasingly been absorbed into it. This also applies to structuralism, even if there remains a certain lunatic fringe of post-structuralist think-

ing. There is no 'orthodox consensus' today to replace that which
used to hold sway until sometime in the 1970s. Yet there is nothing
like complete disarray either. The philosophy of language, particularly those approaches which stress language as praxis, has
made a major contribution to this reorientation. 'Society' is not
like a language, yet none the less can be conceptualized in terms
which borrow something from language practice. In other words,
'society' is not an entity, and does not have a time-space presence;
it exists only as social practices reproduced in an indefinite diversity of milieux.

Of course, some of the major recent debates which have re-
shaped the social sciences have not been particularly concerned
with methodological questions. They have been bound up above
all with the reinterpretation of modern society, its trajectory of
development and its likely future. A certain terminological shift
has occurred which symbolizes a movement in intellectual
orientations. Whereas some decades ago most discussion concentrated upon notions of 'industrial society' or 'industrial capitalism', now the more usual terminology is that of 'modernity' (or
'post-modernity'). Not long ago, all the talk was of 'industrial
society' versus 'capitalism'. The difference between the two, by
and large, corresponded to an opposition between orthodox and
Marxist sociology. To speak of 'capitalism' was not simply to
identify a particular type of socio-economic system; it signalled a
recognition that capitalism could, or should, be superseded by
socialism. The proponents of the notion of industrial society, by
contrast, from Saint-Simon through to Dahrendorf, Bendix and
Lipset, already had their own version of the end of history – and,
explicitly, of the end of ideology. For them, 'industrial society' was
a more inclusive notion than 'capitalism', which it subsumed; and
industrialism created a set of institutions which rendered the aspirations of socialists either futile or dangerous.

Now all this has changed. In the real world, capitalism, as
it were, is everywhere, while socialism is dead on both the level
of theory and that of practice. Many now speak of a post-
industrial society, rather than sheerly an industrial one; curiously,
however, 'capitalism' as such in sociology seems to be spoken of
less and less. The reasons seem to be either that it is so ubiquitous
that it barely needs mentioning, or that it was mainly applied in
the past as part of a critical discourse of socialists.

'Modernity' is taken by most who use it, including myself, to refer to an historically specific socio-economic and cultural formation whose claims to universality are questionable. As I would understand it, modernity is not the end of history; but the modern has not dissolved into an amorphous, fragmented, non-linear post-modernity. For me the idea of the 'post-modern' implies transcendence, not simply 'modernity come to its senses' or being forced to face up to its limitations. I would not write off the possibility of a post-modern order in the sense I have just mentioned; but this would not, and could not, come about through the mechanisms of socialism.

It is not the crisis of capitalism as a rational mode of economic management which has come to dominate our era. Rather, it is the ecological crisis around which most tensions – but also most future possibilities – today are grouped. The ecological crisis is a crisis of a 'damaged modernity', but should not be identified solely with environmentalism. Modernity is indeed running up against its limits. Yet these limits do not only, or even primarily, concern the physical 'limits to growth'. What is at issue, rather, is coming to terms with the 'social repressions' upon which modernity is built. Not physical ecology but an 'ecology of life' is what has to be confronted and elucidated here. A society where most things have become 'plastic' – open to human intervention, but not actually subject to universal human control – is one where political initiatives are called for which owe little to classical conceptions of socialism.

And this is a point at which we can return briefly to Marx. Should Marx now be seen as a founding father whose legacy has turned out to be dross? To this I would certainly say no. Some years ago, I often felt myself to be swimming against the stream when suggesting that Marx's writings showed fundamental flaws. Now, when even Marx's most seemingly devoted supporters have melted away, it is time to swim the other way. As a system of economic management, socialism is no more. Much of what Marx fought to achieve, therefore, no longer holds much sense for us. Yet in a world where many sorts of disaster threaten, and where the possibilities of a good society remain to be fully elucidated, critical theory still retains its importance. Marx's weaknesses lay at those very points at which he thought himself strongest and most original: his reflections on the transcendence of capitalism by socialism. Marx's most enduring contributions, which ensure that he will remain a 'classic', with whom a continuing dialogue is carried on, lie in his analysis of the order of industrial capitalism, which he wrongly imagined would be short-lived.

1 Politics and Sociology in the Thought of Max Weber

The aim of this chapter is to elucidate some of the connections between Weber's political writings and his more academic contributions to the social sciences. As a preface to the main part of the discussion, it will be useful to mention a few of the important moments in his political and intellectual career.

Max Weber was born in 1864, the son of a prominent politician, a member of the National Liberal Party. In her biography of her husband, Marianne Weber described in some detail the richness of the influences which the young Weber experienced in his father's home. From an early age he came into contact with many of the leading figures in the Prussian political and academic worlds, including Treitschke, Knapp, Dilthey and Mommsen. His childhood spanned a period of years which was of decisive significance for German political development: the crucial phase in German history at which, under the leadership of Bismarck, the country at last became a centralized nation-state. The German victory over France in 1870–1 had an effect upon the Weber household which left a lasting emotional impact upon Max, although he was no more than six years old at the time.[1] While he never obtained political office, there was no point in his life at which political and academic interests did not intertwine in his personal experience. His youthful impressions of politics, filtered first through his father's circle and, as a young man, through the influence of his uncle, Hermann Baumgarten, produced in Weber an ambivalent orientation towards the achievements of Bismarck which he never fully resolved, and which lay at the origin of the whole of his political writings.

Weber's earliest academic writings concerned legal and economic history. What appeared to be purely technical, scholarly works, however – such as the dissertation on land tenure in ancient Rome, which Weber wrote in 1891 – actually held broader social and political implications in his thinking. In the thesis, Weber rejected the view, taken by some scholars of the day, that the economic history of Rome was a unique set of events, totally unamenable to analysis in terms of concepts derived from other situations; and he perceived in the social and economic structure of Rome some of the characteristics later to be discerned in the formation of capitalism in post-medieval Europe. Moreover, although he refused to accept some of the more specious comparisons which others had attempted to draw along these lines, the tensions which developed in the ancient world between the agrarian economy of large landed estates and emergent commerce and manufacture seemed to him to illuminate some of the problems facing contemporary Germany. He had the opportunity to confront these problems directly in a study, published in 1892, of the Junker estates to the east of the Elbe. This work formed part of a larger piece of research sponsored by the Verein für Sozialpolitik, investigating the conditions of land tenure in several main regions in Germany. Through his affiliation to the Verein, a group of 'academic socialists' concerned with current social and political issues, Weber was able to participate in discussion and interchange of ideas with a number of younger economists and historians interested above all in the problems facing Germany in its transition to industrial capitalism. While the founder members of the Verein, the 'older generation' of economists such as Wagner, Schmoller and Brentano, were interested primarily in questions connected with formulating policies of partial state intervention in economic life, the 'younger generation' – including, besides Weber, such authors as Sombart, Schulze-Gaevernitz and Tönnies – concerned themselves more broadly with the nature and origins of capitalism, and were heavily influenced by Marx.

Weber was appointed to a professorship of economics in Freiburg in 1894, and the following year delivered his *Antrittsrede* (inaugural lecture) there.[2] In the lecture, Weber developed some of the conclusions which he had reached in his study of agrarian conditions to the east of the Elbe, and related them specifically to the political and economic problems of Germany as a whole (see below, pp. 20–23). He gave particular attention to the so-called 'boundary problem' in the east. East Prussia, the homeland of the Junker landowners, had provided the springboard for the unification of Germany, and was the ultimate basis of Bismarck's power. But the position of the landed estates was being undermined by a burgeoning emigration of agricultural workers to other parts of Germany, attracted by the expansion of industrial production there. This situation was causing an influx of Polish workers from the east, which, according to Weber, threatened the hegemony of German culture in those very areas where it had been strongest. Hence the influx of Poles had to be stopped, and the eastern boundaries of Germany made secure. For Germany, he concluded, political and economic questions were inextricably linked; the country had forged its unity in conflict with other nations, and the maintenance and furtherance of its culture depended upon the continued assertion of its power as a bounded nation-state.

Weber did not develop the full implications of these views until later. For a period of several years, from 1897, he was incapacitated by an acute depressive disorder which forced him to abandon academic work altogether. While he did not return to university teaching until much later on in his life, he was able to resume his scholarly activities shortly after the turn of the century. This period was the most productive of his career. He continued his studies of the Junker estates, but he was able for the first time to work out what had been latent in his earlier writings: a broad treatment of certain fundamental aspects of modern capitalist development, which found an initial statement in *The Protestant Ethic and the Spirit of Capitalism* (1904–5). At the same time he wrote and published essays dealing with the epistemology and methodology of the social sciences. These works undoubtedly both influenced and were influenced by a clarification of his political views which he attained during this period. In his *Antrittsrede* he had already set out a preliminary version of the 'leadership problem' facing Germany. The country had achieved unification in the political sphere while beginning to experience a rapid period of industrial development. Junker power had provided the main foundation for the achievement of political unity, but the future of Germany as a 'power-state' in Europe depended upon its becoming an industrialized country. Thus Junker domination, founded upon landownership, had to be replaced by a new political leadership. But, as Weber had stated in 1895, neither the bourgeoisie nor the working class was as yet capable of providing that leadership. Bismarck had systematically fragmented and weakened the liberals; and he had stunted the leadership potential of the labour party, the Social Democrats, by passing the anti-socialist laws which, until they were repealed in 1890, had effectively placed the working class outside the political structure of the German state.

It became increasingly apparent to Weber, after the turn of the century, that the immediate future of Germany had to lie with a sharpening of the political consciousness of the bourgeoisie. An important underlying motif of *The Protestant Ethic* was certainly that of identifying the historical sources of such a 'bourgeois consciousness'. The essays in epistemology and methodology which he wrote at this time also reflected political problems with which he was concerned, on a personal as well as an intellectual plane. Throughout his life, Weber was subject to two conflicting impulsions: towards the passive, disciplined life of the scholar, and towards the active and practical vocation of the politician. On the intellectual level, he sought to draw a clear-cut distinction between these two competing inspirations, recognizing an absolute dichotomy between the validation of 'factual' or 'scientific' knowledge on the one hand, and of 'normative' or 'value' judgements on the other. Hence, while the activity of the politician could be guided or informed by scientific knowledge of the kind established by history, economics or sociology, such knowledge could never ultimately validate the goals after which the political leader strove. This position had the effect of distancing Weber from the two major political movements competing with the liberals in Germany: the Conservative nationalists on the right, and the Marxist Social Democrats on the left. Each of these, in Weber's view, adhered to a 'normative' conception of history which they introduced into politics, claiming historical 'validation' of their right to rule.

In 1906 Weber also wrote two long essays on Russia, assessing the chances of the development of liberal democracy there following the first Russian Revolution. The so-called 'constitutional' government in Russia seemed to him as much of a sham as that in Germany, and for not altogether different reasons: in Russia, as in Germany, a politically conscious bourgeoisie had not yet emerged, and the country was still dominated by the traditional, agrarian elite. The question of the nature of the constitutional reforms required in Germany, if the necessary bourgeois political leadership were to be forthcoming, increasingly occupied Weber's attention during the years of World War I, especially as it became apparent to him that Germany's military fortunes in the struggle were declining. In the period immediately before the outbreak of hostilities, and in the early part of the war, he wrote voluminously, producing his long essays on the 'world religions', Hinduism, Confucianism and Judaism, and a draft of *Economy and Society* (which was not published until after his death). But the war years brought to a head the tensions in German society which he had begun to analyse two decades earlier, and he gave over much of his time to the examination of political issues. He had for some while been strongly critical of what he once referred to as the 'hysterical vanity' of William II, and later on in the war changed from his previous advocacy of constitutional monarchy to arguing in favour of republicanism. In the two years prior to his death in 1920, he took up an active role in both the academic and political worlds. He accepted a professorship at the University of Vienna, and gave a series of lectures – a version of which was subsequently published as *General Economic History*[3] – in which he attempted to sum up the major themes in his sociology of economic life and capitalist development. Weber made a number of important political speeches during the period of the German Revolution of 1918–19, and narrowly missed selection as a parliamentary candidate for the newly formed Democratic Party. One of his last political activities was as a member of the commission which drafted the Weimar Constitution.

Main themes in Weber's political writings

The following analysis is divided into three principal sections. This section analyses the main elements in Weber's political standpoint at the various stages of his career. The next section examines the influence of his political involvements upon the structure and substance of his more academic works. The final part 'reverses' this perspective, in order to specify how far his assessment of German politics was itself conditioned by the framework established in his other works.

Weber's writings in both politics and sociology had their roots in an attempt to analyse the conditions governing the expansion of industrial capitalism in Germany in the post-Bismarckian era. The background to this is well known to anyone with a cursory knowledge of German social history. For the greater part of the nineteenth century, Germany lagged behind both Britain and France in definite respects – especially in terms of its lack of political unification and, as compared to Britain particularly, in its relatively low level of industrial development. Moreover, when an integral German state did come into being, it was achieved under the leadership of Prussia, whose semi-feudal autocracy, founded upon the power of the Junker landowner, the civil service bureaucracy and the officer corps, contrasted considerably with the more liberalized constitutions and traditions of some of the southern German states. The full impact of industrial development, experienced during the closing decades of the nineteenth century, thus took place within the framework of a social and political order which was in important ways quite different from that characterizing the emergence of capitalism in its 'classical' form: that is to say, in the case of Britain in the earlier part of the century. The Industrial Revolution in Britain took place in a society where prior developments had created a 'compromise' social order in which, as Marx once expressed it, the aristocratic landowners 'rule officially', while the bourgeoisie 'in fact *dominate* all the various spheres of civil society'.[4] But in Germany, the liberal bourgeoisie did not engineer a 'successful' revolution. Germany achieved political unification as a consequence of Bismarck's promotion of an aggressively expansionist policy; and industrialization was effected within a social structure in which power still devolved upon traditionally established elite groups.

When Weber began to take an active interest in politics, he found the liberal wing of the German bourgeoisie in decline, a phenomenon which could be directly traced to the results of Bismarck's domination.[5] In the face of the 'social question' or the 'red spectre' – the growth of the Social Democratic Party – the liberals opted for the security and economic prosperity seemingly offered by a continuing affiliation to conservative interests. Weber's *Antrittsrede* of 1895 contained his first systematic analysis of this situation. In the *Antrittsrede*, he set himself firmly both against the proponents of an 'ethical' approach to politics, and against those who looked to economic development to lead inevitably to the furtherance of political liberties:

> There can be no *peace* in the economic *struggle* for existence; only he who confuses appearance with reality can believe that the peaceful enjoyment of life is what the future holds for our descendants. . . . It is not for us to show our successors the way to peace and human contentment, but rather to show them the *eternal struggle* for the maintenance and cultivation of our national integrity.[6]

The lecture expressed a fervent advocacy of the interests of the 'power-state' as the necessary foundation of German politics. Germany had secured its unity through the assertion of its power in the face of international rivalry; the future of Germany thus lay with the preservation of the capacity of the nation to exert its will in international affairs. But the political leadership necessary to accomplish this, Weber asserted, was lacking. The creation of such a leadership was not merely a matter which depended upon the economic power of the various classes in German society: 'We ask whether they are *politically mature*: that is to say, whether they possess respectively the understanding and the capacity to place the political *power*-interests of the nation above all other considerations.'[7]

The Junkers, Weber continued, were a declining class, who could not continue to monopolize the political life of the society. But while it was 'dangerous' for an economically fading class to maintain political power, it was even more so if the classes which were acquiring an increasingly secure economic position aspired to national leadership without possessing the political maturity necessary to guide the fortunes of a modern state. Neither the working class nor the bourgeoisie as yet possessed such a maturity. The working class was led by a collection of 'journalistic dilettantes', at the head of the Social Democratic Party: they had no organic connection with the class they claimed to represent, and their revolutionary posture in fact acted against the further advancement of the working class towards political responsibility. The bourgeoisie remained timid and unpolitical; they longed for the emergence of another 'Caesar' who would shelter them from the need to assume a leadership role. This was a consequence of their 'unpolitical past', which no amount of economic power in itself could replace. Weber concluded:

> The *threatening thing* in our situation . . . is that the bourgeois classes, as the bearers of the *power*-interests of the nation, seem to wilt away, while there are no signs that the workers are beginning to show the maturity to replace them. The danger does *not* . . . lie with the masses. It is not a question of the *economic* position of the *ruled*, but rather the *political* qualification of the *ruling* and *ascending* classes which is the ultimate issue in the *social*-political problem.[8]

Thus, in 1895, Weber saw as the principal question affecting the future of Germany that of whether the economically prosperous bourgeoisie could develop a political consciousness adequate to undertaking the leadership of the nation. The bulk of his subsequent political writings and actions can be interpreted as an attempt to stimulate the emergence of this liberal political consciousness in Germany. For Weber, this could not be achieved on 'ethical' grounds: there could be no question of refounding German liberalism upon a 'natural law' theory of democracy. He rejected, moreover, the classical conception of 'direct' democracy, in which the mass of the population participated in decision making; this might be possible in small communities, but was quite irrelevant to the contemporary age. In the modern state, leadership had to be the prerogative of a minority: this was an inescapable characteristic of modern times. Any idea 'that some form of "democracy" can destroy the "domination of men over other men"' was utopian.[9] The development of democratic government necessarily depended upon the further advance of bureaucratic organization.

According to Weber, the relationship between democracy and bureaucracy created one of the most profound sources of tension in the modern social order. There was a basic antinomy between democracy and bureaucracy, because the growth of the abstract legal provisions which were necessary to implement democratic procedures themselves entailed the creation of a new form of entrenched monopoly (the expansion of the control of bureaucratic officialdom). While the extension of democratic rights demanded the growth of bureaucratic centralization, however, the reverse did not follow. The historical example of ancient Egypt gave an illustration of this, involving as it did the total subordination of the population to a bureaucratized state apparatus. The existence of large-scale parties, then, which themselves were bureaucratic 'machines', was an unavoidable feature of a modern democratic order; but if these parties were headed by leaders who had political expertise and initiative, the wholesale domination of bureaucratic officialdom could be avoided. Weber saw the likelihood of 'uncontrolled bureaucratic domination' as the greatest threat of the hiatus in political leadership left by Bismarck's fall from power. The development of representative democracy became for him the principal means whereby this could be avoided: 'there is only the choice: leadership-democracy [Führerdemokratie] with the "machine", or leaderless democracy – that is, the domination of "professional politicians" without a vocation, without the inner charismatic qualities that alone make a leader.'[10]

But for most of his life Weber found himself unable to identify wholly with any one of the organized political parties in Germany. At the turn of the century, several of the leading parties offered elements of what he sought, but none combined these elements in an acceptable way. He shared the nationalistic aspirations of the Conservative Party, but rejected both the 'mystic fervour' with which these were expressed, and the policy of giving economic support to the semi-feudal agrarian structure in the east. Neither of the two main liberal parties seemed to him to give any indication that it could overcome the lack of political inspiration analysed in the Antrittsrede. He accepted, with the National-Liberals (the right wing), the need for the expansion of industrial capitalism as necessary to the foundation of a modern economy; but the National-Liberals, through promoting protective tariffs, maintained close ties with Conservative interests, and continued to support the Prussian 'three-tier' system of suffrage in the face of Social Democratic demands for a democratic franchise. The Left-Liberals Weber regarded as having little appreciation of the 'power' characteristics of politics: their position was primarily based upon an 'ethical' support of democratic ideals of constitutional government, and consequently they posed no threat to the existing order.[11]

In this situation, it was inevitable that Weber should have felt drawn towards the Social Democratic Party (SPD): this was the only party of considerable political strength which was openly committed to a 'progressive' platform. Marianne Weber wrote that Weber often considered joining the SPD; but he was effectively deterred from doing so by several basic factors in his assessment of the role of the party in German politics. He regarded what he saw as a dogmatic insistence upon Marxism on the part of the SPD leadership as one of the main elements producing the stagnation of German political development. The interests of bourgeoisie and working class, Weber held, were compatible for the foreseeable future: both stood to gain from the emergence of a fully industrialized German state. Moreover, if it were the case that the Social Democrats were to come to power by revolutionary means, the result would certainly be a vast expansion of bureaucratization, since the economy would become centrally administered – Weber commented on several occasions that such an eventuality would produce a society which would be comparable to the bureaucratic state of ancient Egypt. But he was clear at an early date that the revolutionary ideology of the Social Democrats was markedly different from the actual interests of the party in German politics. This in itself provided ample evidence of the political naïveté of the party's leaders: the leadership of the party, according to Weber, was distinguished by its 'complacent innkeeper face, the visage of the petty bourgeois'.[12] His assessment of the SPD in 1907 is well conveyed in the following statement: 'What has most to fear in the long run, bourgeois society or Social Democracy? As concerns those elements within it which advance a *revolutionary ideology*, I believe it is the latter. It is now quite plain that there are definite conflicts with the Social Democratic bureaucracy.' The more, he went on to say, the Social Democrats succeeded in becoming a recognized party, the more they would come to find that their 'revolutionary ardour' would be 'in great danger': 'We should see then that Social Democracy would never permanently conquer the towns or the state, but that, on the contrary, the state would conquer the Social Democratic Party.'[13] Thus he wrote to Michels in 1907 that he felt, at least for the immediate future, that there was little chance of his working together with the Social Democrats; while he was not officially affiliated to any party, he stood nearer to the bourgeois parties.

In the effects of World War I upon German society, Weber saw both a vindication of his earlier analysis of the German social structure and the possibility of transforming the political order. For some time prior to 1914, he had foreseen the increasing likelihood of the outbreak of a major European conflict. Moreover, he made no secret of the positive sentiments which the 'great and wonderful' war inspired in him: the passivity, and the lack of a national political sense, which he had criticized in the past were replaced by a collective assertion of the integrity of the nation in the face of the other world powers. But even in the midst of the early military successes, he was also pessimistic about the chances of a German victory. The most that could come out of the war, concerning Germany's position among the other European nations, would be the successful establishment of Germany as a recognized 'great power' in Central Europe – thus in effect finally bringing about what Bismarck had originally sought to attain. Most of Weber's attention, even from early on in the war, was in fact directed towards what could be achieved in changing the *internal* political structure of the country. Of the various political writings which he published towards the end of the war, the most important consisted in a number of articles first published in the *Frankfurter Zeitung* of 1917, later collected together as *Parlament und Regierung im neugeordneten Deutschland* ('Parliament and government in a reconstructed Germany'). Here he again deals with the 'Bismarckian legacy' – but in the context of the changes wrought by the war upon the character of German politics.

In *Parlament und Regierung*, on the basis of a sociological interpretation of German political institutions, Weber set out an analysis of the conditions necessary to implement a parliamentary system in Germany which would be something more than what he had previously referred to as the 'sham constitutionalism' of the Wilhelmine era. The earlier forms of liberal and Social Democratic critique of government in Germany, for the most part, had been 'arrogant and extravagant', and had failed 'to understand the preconditions of effective parliaments'. But Weber still insisted that the formation of a genuine parliamentary system was a necessity which was imposed by the position of the German national state, and was a means, not an end: 'For a rational politician the form of government appropriate at any given time is a technical question which depends upon the political tasks of the nation. . . . In themselves, technical changes in the form of government do not make a nation vigorous or happy or valuable. They can only remove technical obstacles and thus are merely means for a given end.' In every modern state, he reiterated, but especially in Germany, the main problem facing the formation of political leadership was that of controlling 'bureaucratic despotism'. The trend towards bureaucratization, moreover, was characteristic of other institutions besides the state: decision making increasingly became an 'administrative' matter, carried out according to the regularized precepts of 'experts'. Thus the modern military commander directed the conduct of battles from his desk. In industry, the private officialdom of white-collar employees increased in numbers relative to the proportion of manual workers. The bureaucratization of the division of labour was founded in 'the "separation" of the worker from the material means of production, destruction, administration, academic research, and finance in general [which] is the common basis of the modern state, in its political, cultural and military sphere, and of the private capitalist economy'.[14] The significance of parliamentary government, according to Weber, was that it offered both the possibility of effective control of officialdom and a source for the education of political leaders. In holding that political leaders should be elected from within parliament, he looked, of course, to the British model. But parliament as a whole could not 'rule' any more than the rank-and-file members of a modern political party could do so. As with the latter – and, indeed, with the mass of the population, who remained a 'passive' force in politics except at periods when they exercised their voting rights – members of parliament had to accept the leadership of a minority. A 'Caesarist' element was inseparable from the modern state; a party leader had to possess the charismatic qualities necessary to acquire and maintain the mass popularity which brought electoral success. The 'plebiscitary' leader could use his charismatic appeal to initiate new policies and to depart from established bureaucratic procedure. It was a primary objective of parliament, however, to act as a safeguard against the excessive acquisition of personal power by a plebiscitary leader.

The existence of a functioning parliament was basic to the political training of leaders, through the skills developed in committee work and the framing of policy and legislation which were demanded of 'middle-level' professional politicians. But it was vital, Weber concluded, for parliamentary government to be grounded in a universal franchise. An enfranchised democratic order which lacked a firm parliamentary foundation would lead to an unchecked Caesarism – such as had tended to characterize French politics, in which the relative lack of organized party 'machines' had weakened parliamentary control. On the other hand, a parliamentary system which was not constituted through universal suffrage, so that leaders could emerge who commanded mass support, was likely to be subverted by the rule of officialdom. In Germany, a schism had been enforced between the electorate and party machinery on the one side, and the filling of high executive positions on the other. Those parliamentary leaders who had become ministers had had to resign their party affiliations: hence the talented political leaders had been drawn off, and had become executive officials outside of parliament itself. In *Deutschlands künftige Staatsform* ('The future form of the German state'), published towards the end of 1918, Weber argued that the president of the future German republic should be plebiscitary, elected by the mass of the population and not through parliament – a clause which eventually, partly under his influence, became written into the Weimar Constitution.[15]

Towards the latter years of the war, Weber witnessed the progressive disintegration of the national unity which the opening of hostilities had fostered. The political divisions between right and left, which were temporarily bridged in the collective enthusiasm of 1914, began to open up again. Weber attributed this less to the activities of the revolutionary Spartakus group than to the intransigent position of Prussian-based conservatism. The deteriorating military and economic fortunes of Germany, culminating in 1918, led to a situation in which Weber's demands for the constitutional reorganization of the German political system were achieved almost at one stroke – not within a state which had achieved the goal of enforcing its 'power-equality' with the other European countries, but as a nation in defeat. Weber's attitude towards the possibilities of setting up a socialist government as a result of the German Revolution is of considerable interest, since this serves to underline the leading themes of his political analysis. Democratic government had come to Germany, he pointed out, not from the sort of 'successful struggle' which the bourgeoisie fought in Britain, but as a consequence of defeat. But the exigencies stated in the earlier political writings still stood: the political representatives of the bourgeois classes had to assume responsibility for the future of Germany. The protection offered by the landed elite had finally been stripped away. In these circumstances, Weber believed, it would be possible and desirable to subject certain enterprises, such as insurance and mining, to state control. But a socialization of the rest of the economy was definitely to be avoided. However great the default of the bourgeoisie in the past, especially the big industrialists, there was no other possible option open to Germany:

> We have truly no reason to love the lords of heavy industry. Indeed, it is one of the main tasks of democracy to break their destructive *political* influence. However, *economically* their leadership is not only indispensable, but becomes *more so* than ever *now*, when our whole economy and all its industrial enterprises will have to be organized anew. The *Communist Manifesto* quite correctly emphasized the *economically* (not the politically) *revolutionary* character of the work of the bourgeois-capitalist entrepreneur. No trade union, least of all a state-socialist official, can carry out these functions for us. We must simply make use of them, in their right place: hold out to them their necessary premium – profits – without, however, allowing this to go to their heads. *Only* in this way – today! – is the advance of socialism possible.[16]

Weber scathingly denounced the activities of the extreme left in 1918 and 1919. While prepared to admit the feasibility of a restricted socialization of the economy, he dismissed as an 'intoxication' or a 'narcotic' the hopes for a radical transformation of society. Of the attempts to establish breakaway revolutionary states in Germany, he wrote to Lukács: 'I am absolutely convinced that these experiments can and will only bring discredit upon socialism for a hundred years.' In another context he remarked: 'Liebknecht belongs in the madhouse and Rosa Luxemburg in the zoological gardens.' The labour movement in Germany, he reiterated, could only have a future *within* a capitalist state. Underlying this assessment, of course, were the more general implications of the formation of a socialist society which Weber had previously elaborated – in particular, his anticipation of the bureaucratized state to which this would lead. But to this, in the context of a nation in military defeat and economic penury, he added other, more specific factors which would attend any attempt to establish a revolutionary regime. Only a bourgeois government could obtain the foreign credits necessary to economic recovery; and, in any case, a revolutionary government would soon be overthrown by the military intervention of the victorious Western countries: this could lead subsequently to 'a reaction such as we have never yet experienced – and then the proletariat will have to count the cost'.[17]

The fact that Weber 'moved to the left' over the course of his political career has often been noted. In terms of the substantive policies which he advocated, this is undoubtedly true; but while shifting his specific political alignments, in fact he remained committed to a definite set of premises which guided the whole of his political views. Although he later came to modify aspects of the views stated in the *Antrittsrede*, his inaugural lecture gave a preliminary statement of principles (some specific, others more general) which reappeared in most of his subsequent political writings. These became more precisely formulated in the period following his recovery from his nervous breakdown: the same time at which he produced his first important methodological writings and *The Protestant Ethic and the Spirit of Capitalism*. Briefly stated, they consisted of the following suppositions:

1 The most significant problems facing the German polity derived from the 'legacy of Bismarck': Germany had secured its political unification under the domination of a 'Caesar' whose downfall had left the new state with a dearth of capable political leadership.

2 The future of the German state depended upon its becoming a developed industrial power. The Junker 'aristocracy' was inevitably a declining class; but neither of the major classes created by capitalist development, the bourgeoisie and the working class, had generated the leadership capable of successfully promoting the interests of the German state. It was the bourgeoisie which had to assume this task in the immediate future.

3 The threat of 'uncontrolled bureaucratic domination' was in no way to be resolved through the programmes of the revolution-

ary socialists, who presumed that the bureaucratic state apparatus could be 'destroyed'; nor through the partial nationalization schemes advocated by certain of the 'academic socialists'. All such programmes could only succeed in furthering the advance of bureaucracy.

4 The establishment of democratic government, any more than the projected future society of the revolutionary socialists, would neither abolish nor reduce the 'domination of man by man'. Democratic government, in a modern society, depended upon the existence of strictly bureaucratized 'mass' parties: however, in conjunction with the operation of parliament, these could create a leadership capable of independent initiative, which could thus guide the fortunes of the state.

5 The furtherance of the nation-state had to take primacy over all other objectives. The interests of the German nation-state were the ultimate criteria according to which political policies were to be judged.

6 All politics, in the last analysis, involved struggles for power; there could be no final conclusion to such struggles. Hence any sort of approach to politics which was based purely upon universalistic ethical appeals (such as those for 'freedom' or 'goodness') was futile.

The political context of Weber's sociology

It is often said that Weber's work represents a response to 'late' capitalism. Thus expressed, this is a misleading statement. What is specifically important as the political and economic background to Weber's sociological writings is, in fact, the *retardation* of German development. Judged in terms of the British model, the concluding decades of the nineteenth century were indeed a period of 'mature' capitalist evolution: by 1900, Britain could be adjudged to have been 'industrialized' for more than half a century. Most sociologists in fact, when they speak generically of 'nineteenth-century capitalism', have in mind the case of Britain, which is treated as the exemplar of capitalist development. But the point is that the transition to capitalist industrialism took place in Germany only towards the latter part of the nineteenth century; it proceeded without the occurrence of a 'successful' bourgeois revolution, and in the framework of a process of political centralization secured by Prussian military imperialism.

Weber's concern with 'capitalism', its presuppositions and consequences, in his sociological writings, thus has to be understood as an outcome, in large degree, of a preoccupation with the characteristics of the specific problems facing German society in the early phases of its industrial development. Such a concern underlay his study of the estates to the east of the Elbe. On its initial publication, the work received some considerable praise from conservative circles, because of its stance on the 'Polish question'. But his more general observations in the study actually contained an appraisal of the declining economic position of the large landowners; and this formed one main strand of his later political thinking. The 'feudal' agrarian structure in the east, which was the economic foundation of Prussia, would necessarily have to cede place to commercial capitalism.

Weber's analysis led him to the conclusion, however, that neither the pre-existing hegemony of the Junkers, nor their declining position, could be explained in strictly economic terms. The Junker estates were not simply founded upon the economic 'exploitation' of the peasantry, but were spheres of political domination, rooted in strongly defined and traditional relationships of superordination and subordination. The military successes of Prussia, and its political accomplishments in Germany, Weber asserted, were attained on the basis of this traditionalistic power of the Junkers. But precisely because of their accomplishments in securing the unity of the German state, the Junkers had 'dug their own grave': the political unification of the country which made Germany for the first time a major power-state in Central Europe could henceforth be maintained only by the promotion of industrialization. Only an industrialized state could hope to match the strength of the other Western countries – and would have the resources to meet what Weber, throughout his life, saw as the major threat in the east: Russia. In fact, Weber said, while they maintained 'aristocratic' pretensions, the Junkers had already effectively become commercialized land proprietors. Capitalism had

> gnawed at the social character of the Junker and his labourers. In the first half of the last century [i.e. the nineteenth century]

the Junker was a rural patriarch. His farm hands, the farmers whose land he had appropriated, were by no means proletarians . . . they were, on a small scale, agriculturalists with a direct interest in their lord's husbandry. But they were expropriated by the rising valuation of the land; their lord withheld pasture and land, kept his grain, and paid them wages instead. Thus, the old community of interest was dissolved, and the farm hands became proletarians.

The result of the increasing undermining of the position of the *Instleute*, the bonded labourers, produced an emigration of workers from the east to the expanding industries of the western part of Germany. 'For Germany, all fateful questions of economic and social policy and of national interest are closely connected with this contrast between the rural society of the east and that of the west, and with its further development.'[18]

Weber's analysis of these issues differed considerably from that advanced in orthodox SPD circles at the turn of the century. Whereas Marxist authors sought to interpret the changing character of the agrarian east almost wholly in economic terms, Weber distinguished a complicated interplay of economic, political and ideological relationships. Thus, in explaining the emigration of labourers from the landed estates, Weber rejected the notion that this could be explained by reference to purely economic considerations: rather, the immediate driving force was a generalized notion of attaining 'freedom', from the restrictive ties of bonded labour. The ' "bread and butter question" ', Weber asserted, 'is of secondary importance'.[19]

The Protestant Ethic combined together, and projected on to a general level, several of the implications which Weber drew from his interpretation of the agrarian question and its relationship to German politics. It is misleading to regard the work, as many have, as a frontal attack upon historical materialism. Rather, the emergent line of Weber's reasoning, both in relation to the social structure of Germany, and on the more general intellectual plane, led him towards a standpoint which cut across the typical conceptions embodied in Marxism. His rejection of affiliations with the Social Democrats in the political sphere, while based upon his interpretation of the trends of development in German society, received an intellectual underpinning from acceptance of certain elements of the neo-Kantianism of the Heidelberg school.

Weber's methodological position, as elaborated during the course of 1904–5, leaned heavily upon Rickert, and upon the dichotomy between fact and value which was basic to the latter's philosophy. Weber used this to formulate a methodological critique of both idealism and Marxism, as overall schemes applied to history; on the level of political action, this underlay his rejection of Social Democracy, as representing an illegitimate fusion of ethical and political claims. As he once remarked of socialism, 'I *shall not* join such Churches.'[20]

To these methodological objections to Marxism, Weber conjoined his appraisal of the specific characteristics of the economic and political development of Germany. He agreed with certain elements of the conventional Marxist analysis of religious ideology, but none the less rejected that 'one-sided' historical materialism which allowed no positive influence to the symbolic content of specific forms of religious belief-system. Thus he accepted that 'The Church belongs to the conservative forces in European countries: first, the Roman Catholic Church . . . but also the Lutheran Church.' In Calvinism, however, he found a religious impulse which was not conservative, but revolutionary. While, as is shown in *The Protestant Ethic*, Lutheranism marked an important 'advance' over Catholicism in promoting the penetration of religious ethics into the sanctioning of rational labour in a 'calling', the Reformation did not, in itself, mark a radical break with traditionalism. On the whole, Lutheranism, like Catholicism, had acted to 'support the peasant, with his conservative way of life, against the domination of urban rationalist culture'. Both churches considered that the personal ties pertaining between lord and serf could be more easily ethically controlled than the commercial relations of the market. 'Deep, historically conditioned contrasts, which have always separated Catholicism and Lutheranism from Calvinism, strengthen this anti-capitalistic attitude of the European Churches.'[21]

Thus, in seeking to identify the historical linkage between Calvinism and modern rational capitalism, Weber at the same time cast light upon the specific circumstances of the German case. Calvinism, by sanctioning 'this-worldly asceticism', served to cut through the traditionalism which had characterized previous economic formations. Germany experienced the first 'religious revolution' of modern times, but Lutheranism was not the break

with traditionalism which generated the ethical impulse that underlay modern capitalism. Instead, the Lutheran church became
the bulwark of a system of political domination which lasted into
the twentieth century. In his political writings, Weber made this
point explicitly, pointing out a direct connection between Lutheranism and the growth of the Prussian state: 'Protestantism legitimated the state as a means of violence, as an absolute divine
institution, and as the legitimate power-state in particular. Luther
took from the individual the ethical responsibility for war and
transferred it to the state authority; to obey this authority in all
matters other than religious belief could never entail guilt.'[22]

Since it brought Weber into a confrontation with Marxist analyses of 'ideology' and 'superstructure', it was inevitable that much
of the controversy about *The Protestant Ethic* should centre upon
the 'role of ideas' in historical development. Weber himself scathingly dismissed the claims of historical materialism in this respect:
the notion that systems of ideas could be in any sense 'ultimately'
reduced to economic factors was 'utterly finished'; the truth was
that there was no unilateral line of relationship between 'material'
and 'ideal' factors. But standing behind the work was a more
deeply rooted divergence from Marxism, concerning the essential
structure of capitalism and bourgeois rationality; and in working
out the implications of this standpoint, as elaborated in his studies
of the non-European civilizations, Weber again took his point of
departure from his interpretation of the German situation and
'Bismarck's legacy'.

A key theme in Weber's writings is his emphasis upon the
independent influence of the 'political' as opposed to the 'economic'. Now it is important to recognize that both of the most
significant forms of social-political theory originating in the earlier
part of the nineteenth century – liberalism and Marxism – were in
accord in minimizing the influence of the state. The 'political' was
seen as secondary and derived. Marxism did admit the importance
of the state in capitalism, but regarded it as expressing the asymmetry of class interests, and therefore as a social form which
would 'disappear' when class society was transcended by socialism. Weber readily perceived the disjunction between this conception, as advanced by the spokesmen for the Social Democrats, and
the realities of the social circumstances in which the Marxist party
found itself. The SPD was certainly – especially during the period

of the anti-socialist laws – 'outside' the state; but the only chance, as Weber saw it, which the party had of acquiring power was through the electoral system. However, the more it became successful in this way, according to his analysis, the more it was forced to become a bureaucratized, 'mass' party, which would become integrated with the existing state mechanism, and would no longer offer any 'alternative' to it. He rejected the standpoint of the Left-Liberals for similar reasons. The 1848 style of liberalism, in Weber's eyes, was obsolete in the context of the post-unification period in Germany. The assumptions underlying the Left-Liberals' standpoint – of the 'minimizing' of political power through the full extension of rights of political franchise – were to Weber irreconcilable with the trend of development of German politics. Inside Germany, the main residue of Bismarck's domination was the existence of a bureaucratic state officialdom: a 'leaderless democracy' would be no advance over the present situation of the political hegemony of a doomed and declining class. Externally, Germany found itself surrounded by powerful states: the unification of Germany had been achieved through the assertion of Prussian military power in the face of the other major European nations. Thus, in becoming a 'bourgeois' society, Germany could not follow the same pattern as was shown by the political development of either Britain or the United States. On more than one occasion, Weber drew an explicit contrast between the historical circumstances of Germany and those of the United States. Germany had been placed in circumstances which 'have forced us to maintain the splendour of our old culture, so to speak, in an armed camp within a world bristling with arms'. The United States, on the other hand, 'does not yet know such problems', and 'will probably never encounter some of them'. The territorial isolation of the subcontinent which the United States occupied was 'the real historical seal imprinted upon its democratic institutions; without this acquisition, with powerful and warlike neighbours at its side, it would be forced to wear the coat of mail like ourselves, who constantly keep in the drawer of our desks the march order in case of war'.[23]

This assessment guided Weber in his general conceptualization of the state and political power, as formulated in *Economy and Society*. In contrast to those contemporary thinkers (such as Durkheim) who regarded the modern nation-state primarily as a

moral institution, Weber emphasized above all the capacity of the
state to claim, through the use of force, a defined territorial area.
The modern state was 'a compulsory association with a territorial
basis', and monopolized, within its borders, legitimate control of
the use of force. It was impossible, he held, to define a 'political'
group (*Verband*) in terms of any definite category of ends which it
served: 'there is no conceivable end which *some* political association has not at some time pursued. And from the protection of
personal security to the administration of justice, there is none
which *all* have recognized.'[24] Thus the 'political' character of a
group could only be defined in terms of its monopoly of the
disposal of a force – which was a 'means' rather than an 'end'.

The organization of the legal-rational state, in Weber's sociology, was applied to derive a general paradigm of the progression
of the division of labour in modern capitalism. His application
of this scheme, which was mediated by the conception of
bureaucratization, again expressed, in a definite sense, the independent character of the 'political' as compared to the 'economic'.
For Marx, and for most nineteenth-century social thought generally, the problem of bureaucracy was given little prominence – a
fact which is to be traced directly to the treatment of political
organization as heavily dependent upon economic power (class
domination). Weber did not deny, of course, that modern capitalism involved the emergence of a class system based upon capital
and wage-labour. But this was not for him, as it was for Marx, the
main structural axis of the increasing differentiation of the division of labour which accompanied the advance of capitalism.
Rather than generalizing from the economic to the political,
Weber generalized from the political to the economic: bureaucratic specialization of tasks (which was, first and foremost, the
characteristic of the legal-rational state) was treated as the most
integral feature of capitalism. Thus Weber rejected the conception
that the expropriation of the worker from the means of production had been confined to the economic sphere alone; any form of
organization having a hierarchy of authority could become subject
to a process of 'expropriation'. In the modern state, 'expert officialdom, based on the division of labour' was wholly expropriated
from possession of its means of administration. 'In the contemporary "state" – and this is essential for the concept of state – the
"separation" of the administrative staff, of the administrative of-

ficials, and of the workers from the material means of administrative organisation is completed.'[25]

At this point, Weber's analysis of the political development of Germany rejoined his general conception of the growth of Western capitalism and the likely consequences of the emergence of socialist societies in Europe. The specific 'problem' of German political development was that of the 'legacy' of Bismarck, which had left Germany with a strongly centralized bureaucracy that was not complemented by an institutional order which could generate an independent political leadership, as was demanded by the 'tasks of the nation'. Such a political leadership, provided in the past by the Prussian aristocracy, could no longer be derived from this source in a capitalist society. This left the working class and the bourgeoisie. Both Weber's analysis of the specific characteristics of the SPD, and his generalized formulation of the growth of the bureaucratized division of labour in capitalism, reinforced his conviction that a bourgeois constitution was the only feasible option for Germany. The ideological impetus of the Social Democrats, fostering the notion that the bureaucratic apparatus of the state could be overthrown and destroyed by revolutionary means, he considered simply as fantasy. Not only was it the case that a capitalist economy necessitated bureaucratic organization, but the socialization of the economy would inevitably entail the further spread of bureaucracy, in order to co-ordinate production according to central 'planning'. On the more general level, this conclusion was reached via the analysis of the process of 'expropriation' in the division of labour. The Marxist anticipation of socialism was grounded in the belief that capitalist society could be transcended by a new social order; but in Weber's conception, the possibility of the transcendence of capitalism was completely eliminated. The essential character of capitalism was given not in the class relationship between wage-labour and capital, but in the rational orientation of productive activity. The process of the 'separation' of the worker from the means of production was only one instance of a process of the rationalization of conduct which advanced in all spheres of modern society. This process, giving rise to bureaucratic specialization, was irreversible. Since socialism was predicated upon the further imposition of rational control of economic conduct (the centralization of the economy), and upon the 'disappearance' of the 'political' through its merging with the 'economic' (state control of economic enterprises), the result could only be an enormous expansion in bureaucratization. This would be not the 'dictatorship of the proletariat', but the 'dictatorship of the official'.[26]

Weber's analysis of the political structure of Germany was concerned with the interplay of three main elements: the position of the traditionally established 'feudal' Junker landowners; the tendency towards 'uncontrolled bureaucratic domination' by the state officialdom; and the dearth of political leadership bound up with each of these factors. These three components reappeared on the more general level in Weber's political sociology, in his typology of domination: traditional, legal and charismatic. The domination of the Junkers undoubtedly served him as the proximate model (together with the case of Rome, which he used as offering certain comparisons with Germany in his early writings) in drawing out the general implications of the contrast between the 'pure types' of traditional and legal domination, and the relationship between both and economic activity. 'The domination of a feudal stratum tends,' Weber made clear, 'because the structure of feudalized powers of government is normally predominantly patrimonial, to set rigid limits to the freedom of acquisitive activity and the development of markets.'[27] But in common with his general emphasis, he stressed that it was the administrative practices of traditional domination, rather than their purely economic policy, which inhibited the growth of rational capitalistic activity. Of particular significance here was the 'arbitrary' character of traditional administration, which militated against the emergence of formal rationality or 'calculability' in social action. The historical circumstances of Western Europe, according to Weber, were unique in having fostered the development of the rational state, with its expert officialdom. This had been one major condition (among others) which had facilitated the rise of modern capitalism in the West.

The case of Germany, however, showed that the growth of the rational state was in no sense a sufficient condition for the emergence of modern capitalism. In the countries in which capitalism came into being at an early date, England and Holland, the bureaucratic state had been less developed than in Germany. It was the existence of a bureaucratic state in Germany, and the specific direction in which it was channelled under Bismarck, which had left the country in the hands of politicians 'without a calling'. 'Professional politicians', as Weber demonstrated in his studies of the Eastern civilizations, had emerged in all developed patrimonial states. These were individuals who had come to prominence in the service of a king: 'men who, unlike the charismatic leader, have not wished to be lords themselves, but who have entered the *service* of political lords'. But only in the West had there been professional politicians whose lives had been devoted to 'the service of powers other than the princes'; who lived 'off' politics, and who recognized only the legitimacy of impersonal legal principles. The development of this process occurred in Europe in different ways in different places, but had always involved the eventual development of a struggle for power between the king and the administrative staff which had grown up around him. In Germany, this took a particular form:

> Wherever the dynasties retained actual power in their hands – as was especially the case in Germany – the interests of the prince were joined with those of officialdom *against* parliament and its claims for power. The officials were also interested in having leading positions, that is, ministerial positions, occupied by their own ranks, thus making these positions an object of the official career. The monarch, on his part, was interested in being able to appoint the ministers from the ranks of devoted officials according to his own discretion. Both parties, however, were interested in seeing the political leadership confront parliament in a unified and solidary fashion.[28]

All modern states, of course, involved these two forms of official: 'administrative' and 'political' officials. Weber's discussion of the relationship between these two forms of modern officialdom in Germany was based upon analysis of the qualities of political leadership which was directly connected with his formulation of charismatic domination in general. The bureaucratic official had to carry out his duties in an impartial fashion: as Weber frequently said, *sine ira et studio*. The political leader, by contrast, had to 'take a stand' and 'be passionate'. The 'routinization' of politics – that is to say, the transformation of political decisions into decisions of administrative routine, through domination by bureaucratic officialdom – was specifically foreign to the demands which

were most basic to political action. This phenomenon, which occupied much of Weber's attention in his analysis of the lack of
political leadership in Germany, formed a major component of his
generalized comparison of charisma with both traditional and
rational-legal domination. Charisma was, as a 'pure type', wholly
opposed to the routine, the *alltäglich*. Traditional and legal domination, on the other hand, were both forms of everyday administration, the one being tied to precedents transmitted from
previous generations, the other being bound by abstractly formulated universal principles. The charismatic leader, 'like . . . every
true leader in this sense, preaches, creates, or demands *new* obligations'.[29] It was for this reason that the 'charismatic element' was
of vital significance in a modern democratic order; without it, no
consistent policymaking was possible, and the state relapsed into
leaderless democracy, the rule of professional politicians without
a calling.

The sociological framework of Weber's political thought

In the preceding discussion I have sought to identify some of the
connections between Weber's political writings and his general
sociological works, placing the emphasis upon those aspects of his
sociology which were most directly influenced by his analysis of
the political development of Wilhelmine Germany. The influence
of 'the German model' on Weber's thinking was profound: virtually all of his major intellectual interests were shaped by it. But
his evaluation of the political development of Germany was also
brought into sharper focus, and more systematically formulated,
within the abstract framework of thought which he worked out
from the turn of the century onwards. The methodological position which he established at the outset of this period is particularly important in this connection. As with other parts of his
works, the tendency has been – again, particularly in the English-
speaking world – to stress the existence of a disjunction between
his methodological essays on the one hand, and his more empirical
writings on the other. However, as Löwith has emphasized, Weber's methodological standpoint is inseparable from his other
works, and more particularly from his general interpretation of
the rise of modern capitalism. The main elements of Weber's

methodological views were elaborated at the same time as he was working on *The Protestant Ethic*; and these views were a major intellectual 'input', helping to mould his analysis of the trend of development of Western capitalism in general, and of the German social and political structure in particular.

Weber's methodological essays are heavily polemical in character, and have to be seen against the background of the various schools of social and economic thought in nineteenth-century Germany. In his lengthy essay on Roscher and Knies, he dealt with two sets of overlapping problems: the confusion, in the works of these writers, of commitment to rigorous empirical method with the use of 'mystical' concepts adopted from classical idealist philosophy; and the question of the supposed 'irrational subjectivity' of human behaviour compared to the 'predictability' of the natural world. Human conduct, Weber asserted, was as 'predictable' as were events in the natural world: 'The "predictability" [*Berechnenbarkeit*] of "processes of nature", such as in the sphere of "weather forecasts"., is not nearly so "certain" as the "calculation" of the actions of someone known to us.'[30] Thus 'irrationality' (in the sense of 'free will' = 'incalculability') was by no means a specific component of human conduct: on the contrary, such irrationality, Weber concluded, was 'abnormal', since it was a property of the behaviour of those individuals who were designated as 'insane'. It was thus fallacious to suppose that human actions were not amenable to generalization; indeed, social life depended upon regularities in human conduct, such that one individual could calculate the probable responses of another to his or her own actions. But, equally, this did not imply that human actions could be treated wholly on a par with events in the natural world – that is, as 'objective' phenomena, in the way assumed by positivism. Action had a 'subjective' content not shared by the world of nature, and the interpretative grasp of the meaning of actions to the actor was essential to the explanation of the regularities discernible in human conduct. For this reason, Weber insisted that the individual was the 'atom' of sociology: any proposition involving reference to a collectivity, such as a party or a nation, had ultimately to be resolvable into concepts which referred to the actions of individuals.

The position which Weber adopted in these respects, then, refused to identify 'free will' with the irrational. Human actions

which were propelled by such forces were governed by the very
opposite of freedom of choice: the latter was given to the degree
to which conduct approximated to 'rationality', which signified
here the correspondence of means to ends in motivated action.
Hence he identified the two pure types of rational action, each of
which was 'intelligible' to the social scientist in terms of means–
ends relationships: 'purposeful rationality' (*Zweckrationalität*), in
which the actor rationally assessed the full range of consequences
entailed by the selection of a given means to achieve a particular
end, and 'value-rationality', in which an individual consciously
pursued one overriding end with single-minded devotion, without
'counting the cost'. Both of these Weber contrasted with irrational
action, and set up as a basic methodological tenet the prescription
that 'all irrational, affectually determined elements of behaviour'
should be treated 'as factors of deviation from a conceptually pure
type of rational action'.[31]

It is important to emphasize that, according to this methodological scheme, the 'moral' was logically quite separate from the
'rational'. The assessment of rationality took moral objectives or
'ends' as *givens*; Weber wholly rejected the conception that the
sphere of the 'rational' could extend to the evaluation of competing ethical standards. What he often referred to as the 'ethical
irrationality of the world' was fundamental to his epistemology.
Statements of fact, and judgements of value, were separated by an
absolute logical gulf: there was no way in which scientific rationalism could provide a validation of one ethical ideal compared to
another. The unending conflict of divergent ethical systems could
never be resolved by the growth of rational knowledge. It followed that what was 'worth' knowing could not itself be determined rationally, but had to rest upon values which specified why
certain phenomena were 'of interest': the objective investigation
of human action was possible, but only on the prior basis of the
selection of problems which had value-relevance.

Weber's methodological standpoint thus hinged upon the establishment of certain polarities between 'subjectivity' and 'objectivity', and between 'rationality' and 'irrationality':

The *objective* validity of all empirical knowledge rests exclusively
upon the ordering of the given reality according to categories which
are *subjective* in a specific sense, namely, in that they present the

presuppositions of our knowledge and are based on the presupposition of the *value* of those *truths* which empirical knowledge alone is able to give us. . . . But these data can never become the foundation for the empirically impossible proof of the validity of the evaluative ideas. The belief which we all have in some form or other, in the meta-empirical validity of ultimate and final values, in which the meaning of our existence is rooted, is not incompatible with the incessant changefulness of the concrete viewpoints, from which empirical reality gets its significance. Both these views are, on the contrary, in harmony with each other. Life with its irrational reality and its store of possible meanings is inexhaustible.[32]

Hence for Weber, there could be no sense in which history could be 'rational', as postulated by either Hegelian 'objective idealism', or by Marxism, whereby human social development unfolded a progression towards the attainment of rationally determined ideals. Marx's statement that 'Mankind always sets itself only such tasks as it can solve' was as antithetical to Weber's position as was Hegel's famous proposition that 'what is rational is actual, and what is actual is rational.' As Weber sometimes expressed it, truth and goodness stood in no definite historical relationship to each other.

This epistemological position had consequences in Weber's sociological and political thought which extended far beyond the immediate sphere of the methodology of the social sciences. The 'ethical irrationality' of the world was a major element in the conceptions underlying his studies of the 'world religions', and in his analysis of the specific path of development taken by rationalization in the West. According to Weber's standpoint, there could never be a rational solution to the competing ethical standards which existed: all civilizations thus faced the problem of 'making sense' of the 'irrationality' of the world. Religious theodicy provided a 'solution' to this problem, and the need to 'make sense of the senseless' was a main psychological impetus towards the rationalization of systems of religious beliefs. The growth of rationalization depended upon forces which were not themselves rational; hence the importance of charisma in Weber's thought. Charisma was 'specifically irrational' force, in that it was 'foreign to all rules'.[33] It was this which made charismatic movements the major revolutionary element in history, the most potent source of new forms of rationalization.

Weber's concept of 'rationalization' was a complex one, and he used the term to cover three sets of related phenomena: (1) what he variously referred to (from its positive aspect) as the 'intellectualization' or (from its negative aspect) as the 'disenchantment' (*Entzauberung*) of the world; (2) the growth of rationality in the sense of 'the methodical attainment of a definitely given and practical end by the use of an increasingly precise calculation of adequate means';[34] (3) the growth of rationality in the sense of the formation of 'ethics that are systematically and unambiguously oriented to fixed goals'. As he showed in his studies of India and China, the rationalization of systems of ultimate beliefs could take numerous different forms, involving various combinations of these three elements. The specific form of social and economic development of Western Europe embodied a combination which was, in certain definite ways, quite distinct from the directions which rationalization had taken elsewhere.

Weber detailed several major spheres of social and economic life in which rationalization had proceeded in a specific way, or to an advanced degree, in the West, even prior to the advent of modern capitalism. These prior developments – such as the formation of rational jurisprudence inherited from Roman law – played a definite role in facilitating the rise of contemporary capitalism. The importance of Calvinism and other branches of ascetic Protestantism, as Weber made clear in *The Protestant Ethic*, is not that they were a 'cause' of the rise of modern capitalism, but that they provided an *irrational* impetus to the disciplined pursuit of monetary gain in a specified 'calling' – and thereby laid the way open to the further spread of the distinctive types of rationalization of activity stimulated by the voracious expansion of capitalism. Ascetic Protestantism sanctioned the division of labour which was integral to modern capitalism, and which inevitably conjoined the spread of capitalism to the advance of bureaucracy. The bureaucratized division of labour, which, with the further development of capitalism, became characteristic of all major social institutions, henceforth functioned 'mechanically', and had no need of the religious ethic in which it was originally grounded. The further expansion of capitalism thus completed the disenchantment of the world (through a commitment to scientific 'progress'); transmuted most forms of social relationship into conduct which approximated to the *Zweckrational* type (through the rational coordination of tasks in bureaucratic organizations); and advanced the spread of norms of an abstract, legal type which, principally as embodied in the state, constituted the main form of modern 'legitimate order'.

Each of these three aspects of the rationalization promoted by capitalism had consequences to which Weber attributed an essential significance in analysing the modern political order.

(1) Since Weber established as a logical principle that scientific propositions or empirical knowledge could not validate judgements of value, it followed that the growth of scientific intellectualization which was characteristic of capitalism could not, in and of itself, confer meaning. Thus the very progress of science, he concluded, had dispelled the view which once promoted scientific endeavour:

> To artistic experimenters of the type of Leonardo and the musical innovators, science meant the path to *true* art, and that meant for them the path to true *nature*. . . . And today? Who – aside from certain big children who are indeed found in the natural sciences – still believes that the findings of astronomy, biology, physics, or chemistry could teach us anything about the *meaning* of the world? . . . If these natural sciences lead to anything in this way, they are apt to make the belief that there is such a thing as the 'meaning' of the universe die out at its very roots.[35]

A stress upon the necessity of facing up 'without illusions' to the realities of the modern world was a constant theme of Weber's political writings. 'Whosoever . . . wishes to carry on politics on this earth must above all things be free of illusions.'[36] This theme was itself closely integrated with his conception of the 'ethical irrationality' of the world. The creation of a sphere of rational political activity, freed from the penetration of gods, spirits or the trappings of traditional symbols, made plain the irremediable power conflicts which were the essence of politics. The consequence of the disenchantment of the world was that the transcendental values which conferred meaning otherwise existed only in 'the brotherliness of direct and personal human relations', or became projected into forms of mystic withdrawal. Those individuals who could not 'face the fate of the times' could take refuge in such withdrawal, either into the traditional churches, or into one of the newer cults. But they thereby forfeited the capacity to participate directly in politics. Those who looked to the transcendence of human conflict through the medium of politics, who sought to attain an end to the 'domination of man by man', were in flight from reality as much as those who abandoned public life in favour of mystic retreat: hence Weber's scathing critique of the 'radical illusionists' in politics – the revolutionary socialists – 'who would like to strike down every independent man who tells them uncomfortable truths'.[37] The person 'who wishes to live as modern man', even if this be 'only in the sense that he has his daily paper, railways, electricity, etc.', had to resign himself or herself to the loss of ideals of radical revolutionary change: indeed he or she had to abandon 'the *conceivability* of such a goal'.[38]

The active politician, therefore, according to Weber, needed 'passion in the sense of *matter-of-factness*', the 'everyday wisdom' which balanced devotion to a 'cause' with an awareness of the ever-present tension between means and ends, and of the 'paradox of consequences'. It was this awareness which was lacking among the revolutionaries, who failed to see that the *means* which had to be used to reach their goal must bring about a state of affairs which was quite discrepant from their stated end. Thus the Bolshevik government in Russia, Weber wrote in 1918, was simply a military dictatorship of the left, no different in content from dictatorship of the right, except that it was a 'dictatorship of *corporals*' rather than of generals.[39] The problem of the 'paradox of consequences', of course, was at the root of Weber's differentiation between the 'ethic of responsibility' and the 'ethic of conviction' (*Gesinnungsethik*), which corresponded, on the level of ethics, to the distinction between purposeful and value-rationality. It followed from Weber's own logical standpoint that the adherent of an ethic of ultimate ends in politics could not be *shown*, by rational demonstration, that he or she was mistaken in pursuing the course of action which he or she did; but such a person was one who 'cannot stand up under the ethical irrationality of the world', who had no awareness of the 'daemonic' character of political power.

(2) The intellectualization characteristic of modern capitalism, according to Weber, was intimately bound up with the rationalism of human conduct in the second sense, especially as this manifested itself in the bureaucratized division of labour. In both his sociological and political writings, he identified the advance of

bureaucratic rationality as an inevitable component of the growth of capitalism: the 'alienative' effects of the modern social order, which Marx traced to the character of the class system in capitalist production, were in fact derivative of bureaucratization. Weber often used the imagery of the machine in analysing the nature of bureaucratic organization. Like a machine, bureaucracy was the most rational system of harnessing energies to the fulfilment of specified tasks. The member of a bureaucracy 'is only a single cog in an ever-moving mechanism which prescribes to him an essentially fixed route of march'. A bureaucracy, in common with a machine, could be placed in the service of many different masters. Moreover, a bureaucratic organization functioned efficiently to the degree that its members were 'dehumanized': bureaucracy 'develops the more perfectly . . . the more completely it succeeds in eliminating from official business love, hatred, and all purely personal, irrational, and emotional elements which escape calculation'.[40]

But, according to Weber, there could be no possibility of transcending the subordination of individuals to the specialization of tasks entailed in bureaucratization. The advance of bureaucracy imprisoned people in the *Gehäuse der Hörigkeit*, the 'iron cage' of the specialized division of labour upon which the administration of the modern social and economic order depended. *The Protestant Ethic* ends with a striking exposition of this:

> Limitation to specialised work, with a renunciation of the Faustian universality of man which it involves, is a condition of any valuable work in the modern world; hence deeds and renunciation inevitably condition each other today. . . . The Puritan wanted to work in a calling; we are forced to do so. For when asceticism was carried our of monastic cells into everyday life, and began to dominate worldly morality, it did its part in building the tremendous cosmos of the modern economic order. This order is now bound to the technical and economic conditions of machine production which today determine the lives of all the individuals who are born into this mechanism, not only those directly concerned with economic acquisition, with irresistible force.[41]

In Weber's view, both conservatives and socialists shared the misconceived belief that it was possible for modern people to 'escape from the cage': the former looked to a reversion to a previous age, the latter to the formation of a new form of society which would radically change the existing conditions of capitalist production. Both had in mind the 'universal man' of humanist culture, and anticipated the disappearance of the 'fragmented specialization' of the capitalist division of labour. But this culture was irretrievably destroyed by bureaucratization. The ideal of the 'universal man' provided a substantive goal of education in systems of patrimonialism in which administrative tasks manifested only a low level of rationalization. Qualification for office in those circumstances could be based upon the conception of the 'cultivated personality': someone of all-round competence, whose educational attainments were primarily demonstrated in demeanour and bearing, rather than in the possession of specialized skills. Today, however, in education as in social life generally, specialization was unavoidable, and professional education replaced humanism.

It is these considerations which underlay his famous discussion of 'ethical neutrality'. The professors of the 'old school', such as Schmoller, belonged to the time when Germany stood on the threshold of its capitalist development, a time when it was usual to 'assign to the universities and thereby to themselves the universal role of moulding human beings, of inculcating political, ethical, aesthetic, cultural or other attitudes'. According to Weber – and this, of course, following his standpoint, cannot be rationally proved, since it entails a judgement of value – this conception ought to be abandoned in favour of one which regarded the university as having 'a really valuable influence only through specialized training by specially qualified persons'. It followed from the latter viewpoint, Weber held, that 'intellectual integrity' should be the only general objective which was promoted in the lecture-hall. Thus discipline and self-limitation, the characteristic properties of a modern 'calling', had to apply to the position of professor (and of student) as much as any other modern occupation. The professor, therefore, ought to confine himself within the university setting, to the rigorous exposition of the subject which he or she was specially qualified to teach. The charismatic properties of professorial personalities ought to be excluded as far as possible from influencing their teaching: 'Every professional task has its own "inherent norms" and should be fulfilled accordingly. . . . We deprive the word 'vocation' [*Beruf*] of the only meaning which still retains ethical significance if we fail to carry out that specific kind of self-restraint which it requires'. The 'dilettante', a term Weber used so frequently as a derogatory epithet, was precisely one who failed to perform his or her 'calling' in a disciplined fashion, and who instead laid claim to a universal competence which he or she could not possess.

Weber favoured the completion of the process of the internal rationalization of university education only in order to emphasize more fully the need to recognize politics as the all-important area in modern social life in which the 'war of the competing gods' should be legitimately carried on. The maintenance of the assumption that the university provided a proper platform for the dissemination of value-judgements was to Weber a manifestation of the continuing power of conservative circles over university education. He himself witnessed the retardation of the careers of some of his friends, notably Michels and Simmel, as a result of strictly non-intellectual considerations – Michels because he was a Social Democrat, and Simmel because he was a Jew. The conception which allowed that the university chair might be used to advance value-positions was only tenable if all points of view were represented; this was patently not the case where 'the university is a state institution for the training of "loyal" administrators'.[42]

(3) The growth of what Weber sometimes termed 'technical rationality' in the West, as evinced in social relationships in the form of bureaucratization, was, of course, necessarily closely tied to the development of rationalized norms of the 'legal' type (i.e. to rationalization in the third sense). It is difficult to overstress the significance which Weber placed upon the development of rational law in his analysis of modern capitalism. The importance of the heritage of Roman law in Western Europe was not that it was directly incorporated into the institutions which gave rise to rational capitalism, but was to be traced to the fact that it was a main element in the creation of formally rational juristic thought. In every type of absolutist or hierocratic administration the enforcement of juridical process was based upon substantive criteria of procedure which were not applied as formal 'principles'. Law was administered either arbitrarily from case to case, or according to tradition. The rise of rational law thus signalled the diminishing power of such traditional systems of domination. The affinity

between capitalist production and rational law derived from the factor of 'calculability' which was intrinsic to both. In the West, and nowhere else, this relationship, in significant degree, had been mediated by the state. The creation of the corpus of rational law in the West 'was achieved through the alliance between the modern state and the jurists for the purpose of making good its claims to power'.[43]

The abstract categorization of the pure type of 'legal domination' which forms part of *Economy and Society* is directly integrated with Weber's analysis of the rise of the rational state. He did not live to complete the systematic treatment of the modern state which he planned to write, and while his writings refer at many points to the distinctive features of the Western form of the state, these are nowhere treated at length. Thus some of the general propositions underlying his conception of rational legal domination, as manifest in the modern state, have to be reconstructed from a diverse range of materials. One such proposition concerns the *limits* of legal domination. It was of basic importance to Weber's analysis of the modern state that, as he expressed it, 'no domination is *only* bureaucratic, that is, is only led by a contractually employed and appointed officialdom'. Bureaucracy, however, was not the only type of legal domination: 'Parliamentary administration' and 'all sorts of collegial authority and administrative bodies fall into this type'.[44] Collegial bodies, according to Weber, played an essential role in fostering the legitimate order of the rational state: the concept of constituted 'authorities' had its origin in the power of these agencies. The characteristic problem facing the modern political order was that of reconciling the prevalent demands for 'democratization', which had been partially developed in former times through the agency of collegial bodies, with the necessarily declining significance of these bodies – because the era during which real power was vested in such agencies was one in which traditionally established 'notables' (who lived 'for', rather than 'off', politics) were dominant. Modern political forms, which 'are the children of democracy, of mass franchise, of the necessity to woo and organize the masses', entailed the formation of bureaucratized parties, whose leaders (who live 'off' politics) held the real power; thus the power of parliament declines.

Since bureaucracy could not itself 'lead', but depended upon the setting of objectives from 'outside', political leadership had to devolve upon the charismatic properties of the individuals at the head of the party organizations. In thus juxtaposing the rational (bureaucracy) and the irrational (charisma) in the modern political system, Weber's writings expressed a major line of connection between his general sociology and his specific analysis of German politics. As he insisted in his methodological writings, rational analysis could not validate, or 'disprove', judgements of value. The correlate of this epistemological proposition, in Weber's sociological writings, was that rationalized systems of social organization did not create values, but instead only functioned as *means* to the furtherance of existing values. 'This limitation', he made clear, 'is inherent in the legal type at its highest level of development [that is to say, in bureaucratic organizations] because administrative action is limited to what is in conformity with rules.'[45] It was this consideration which underlined Weber's discussion of plebiscitary democracy. While leadership within systems of legal domination could be provided, in the early stages of modern political development, by circles of 'notables', the declining power of such groups with the advance of bureaucracy brought into the sharpest focus the fact that the rationalization (whether 'intellectual' or 'practical') of conduct could provide only 'means', not 'ends'. Hence the charismatic component previously embodied in the 'hereditary charisma' associated with collegial systems of administration had now to be built upon the emotional loyalty between modern political leaders *as personalities* and the mass of their followers. Thus while recognizing the potential dangers of Caesarism, Weber was led by the postulates of his own theoretical system to recognize the necessity of the charismatic properties of leadership generated by the mass franchise.

Conclusion

In terms of the discussion developed in the preceding sections, it becomes possible to unravel some of the principal dilemmas in Weber's political thought. The overriding problem which occupied Weber's political energies was that of the 'leadership question', resulting from Bismarck's domination. Germany was a 'power-state', which had forged its unity in a struggle with the other European nations. In the political conflicts of the nation-states, the unending war of the 'gods', now manifested in the form of 'impersonal powers', continued to hold sway. 'Here . . . ultimate *Weltanschauungen* clash, world-views among which in the end one has to make a choice.'[46] From the earliest phase of his political career, Weber determined his 'choice': that the values embodied in the German cultural heritage could be defended and furthered only by the acceptance and advancement of the power of the German nation-state. Since those who had been the previous bearers of this culture in the political sphere (the Junker 'aristocracy') were a declining group, responsibility for political leadership had to be derived from other sources. The same processes which had undermined the position of the Junkers had furthered the rationalization of the political order. Weber's general sociological formulation of the relationship between rationalization and social change involved a polar contrast between the rule-bound character of bureaucracy and the value-creative properties of charisma. Thus the bureaucratization of political life, while elevating the conduct of human affairs to a peak of technical efficiency, could not itself generate the capacities involved in 'genuine' leadership. In the democratic order, he saw both the need and the possibility to create the charismatic element necessary to the modern political leader.

It thus followed from Weber's whole analysis that democratic government could not be founded upon any conception of natural law, such as that embodied in the classical democratic theory of the eighteenth and early nineteenth centuries. Democracy was a technique, a means to an end.[47] In stressing the significance of this point, in his analysis of Weber's political writings, Mommsen is surely correct. But the brutal clarity of Weber's statements on this issue has led to substantial misinterpretation of his political views, in three respects: firstly, in regard to his supposed 'Machiavellianism'; secondly, in relation to his sanctioning of German 'imperialism'; and thirdly, as concerns his 'rejection' of liberalism in favour of a Nietzschean 'aristocratic ethic'. Whatever affinities his writings may have with those of Machiavelli, Weber resolutely avoided any implication that power should be attributed with either the ethical or the aesthetic qualities which it had in the latter's conception. As Weber wrote: 'The mere "power politician" may get strong effects, but actually his work leads nowhere and is senseless.'[48] In his view, this was exactly the form of *Realpolitik* which characterized the vacillating policies followed by Germany from the time of Bismarck's downfall. The strength of Weber's commitment to 'imperialism' has been particularly stressed by Marcuse and by Lukács. According to Lukács, democracy is to Weber only a 'technical measure to facilitate a more adequately functioning imperialism'.[49] But as an expression of Weber's views, this is as misleading as that which sees in his political writings nothing more than a new Machiavellianism, and for the same reason: Weber nowhere gave *normative* significance to German expansionism. In Weber's political thought, 'imperialism' (in the same way as 'power' itself) was a means, not an end.

Much of the literature on Weber's political writings and involvements (including Mommsen's work) has neglected the strong personal affiliation which he himself felt for the yearnings and the aspirations of the underprivileged. If Weber refused to adopt the ethical premises of democratic theory, his writings were none the less steeped in the traditions of European liberalism. He constantly reaffirmed his advocacy of the values of 'man's personal autonomy' and 'the spiritual and moral values of mankind'.[50] But, within the context of Weber's political sociology, both the rising aspiration of the lower classes, and the tenets of liberal individualism to which he adhered, could only be furthered through the power-interests of the state: 'All culture today is, and will remain, completely tied to the nation.'[51] Moreover, there was a tragic antinomy between the historically closely related values of equality and levelling on the one hand, and individual freedom and spontaneity on the other. The growth of mass politics necessarily limited the degree to which the latter values could be realized in the contemporary social order. Thus Weber saw plebiscitary democracy as the only mode of partially releasing modern humanity from the 'iron cage' of the bureaucratized division of labour.

If these views were rooted in Weber's assessment of the political structure of Wilhelmine Germany, they were also logically and empirically related to, and were partly shaped by, his methodological conceptions and his studies of the 'world civilizations'. Weber spoke in the language of his contemporaries when he talked of the 'power-interests' of the nation and of the *Herrenvolk*. But his usage of these notions, especially in his later writings, was in very definite respects quite different from that of the sources from which he adopted his terminology. In the first place, he rejected the emphasis upon the state *itself* as the ultimate value in his personal political objectives. While there was still an ambiguity in Weber's position on this matter in the *Antrittsrede*, in his subsequent writings this was quite clear. In the 'nation-state', it was the first half of the conjunction which was significant in Weber's personal scale of values. Secondly, Weber did not utilize the term *Herrenvolk* in a way which carried the connotation that German culture could claim a 'legitimate' domination over that of other nations. On the contrary, in Weber's view such a claim was both factually invalid and (which was a logically separate question) normatively rejected. The political struggle of nation-states was a sphere of power relations; and the values comprised in the national culture of these states could not be adjudged as 'ethically' superior to German culture.

Weber's epistemological conception of the 'ethical irrationality' of the world, and the methodological apparatus which he constructed upon this basis, involved an attempt to integrate various diverse tendencies in German social thought. Rejecting both 'intuitionism' and 'scientism', he borrowed elements from each in elaborating a framework which hinged upon certain antinomies between the 'rational' and the 'irrational', and between the 'subjective' and 'objective'. As has been indicated earlier in this chapter, these underlay the sociological conceptions which Weber both developed as a set of 'pure categories' and applied empirically in his studies of history and society. These conceptions involved the notion that all human actions which approximated to rationality (in either of Weber's two principal senses) *had* necessarily to be grounded in irrationality ('ultimate values'); but that there was a fundamental dichotomy between reason and value. Hence sociology and history had to entail recourse to the interpretation of 'meaning', but sociological or historical analysis could not 'prove' any given set of values to be normatively 'valid'.

In Weber's typology of domination, these two emphases were built into the conception of charisma. Charisma was irrational in the sense of being foreign to rule-bound action, and was therefore the value-creative force in history; and the concept, as he formulated it, completely cross-cut all differences in the *content* of charismatic attachments, such that Hitler was as 'genuine' a charismatic leader as was Gandhi. Hence, in Weber's thought, the notion of 'value' became synonymous with (irrational) conviction;

his conceptual categories, in this respect, bore no direct relation to 'egoism' and 'altruism' as these are traditionally conceived in ethical theory. In Weber's analysis of German politics, what in the *Antrittsrede* was seen as the 'leadership problem' came to be analysed in the later political writings as turning upon the opposition between bureaucratic rationality and charisma. Thus Weber was inevitably led towards the conclusion that the *content* of the charismatic element was irrelevant to what he consciously took as his own ultimate value (the autonomous furtherance of German culture). This, conjoined with his analysis of the bureaucratization entailed in the modern capitalist state, brought him into a position in which the liberal democratic values which he was drawn to could at most be conceived as a 'means', and therefore as denuded of intrinsic significance.

Weber's political thought thus concealed an inherent tension, which gave his writings their strongly defined character of pathos. On the one hand, he expressed sympathies with certain of the tenets of classical liberalism and even socialism; but both his starting point in politics (as set out in the *Antrittsrede*), and the intellectual standpoint which he elaborated in his academic writings, directed his views towards a position in which, as he himself put it, 'such concepts as the "will of the people", the true will of the people . . . are *fictions*'.[52] A short while before he died, he remarked that Marx and Nietzsche represented the two dominant influences in modern culture. The whole corpus of Weber's works could be said to constitute a grandiose attempt to integrate the most profound insights of these two seemingly incompatible streams of thought. His political views both helped to form, and were formed by, this massive, but brittle, intellectual synthesis, and they shared the dualities which it embodied.

A satisfactory critique of Weber's political sociology must itself be both political and intellectual. That is to say, it must examine, in detail, as related questions, the dependence of his ideas upon a specific historical context, and the logical weaknesses of his theoretical formulations. Such a critique has not, thus far, emerged from the continuing debate over his political writings. Marxist critics of Weber, on the one side, have tended to treat his sociological writings as little more than ideological expressions of his political interests. Weber's sociology is, absurdly, reduced largely to a particular manifestation of 'bourgeois culture' in

Wilhelmine Germany. On the other side, the 'orthodox' interpreters of Weber defend the view that his academic contributions to social science are to be treated as quite separable from his political attachments. But these positions, at least in the extreme form in which they have sometimes been stated, simply obstruct an adequate evaluation of Weber's work. For each of these states something which is little more than a truism; it must be true of any major social thinker that his work is expressive of the particular social and political context in which he lived, but also embodies conceptions which are capable of generalized application.

2 Marx, Weber and the Development of Capitalism

There are few intellectual relationships in the literature of sociology as difficult to interpret as that between the writings of Karl Marx and those of Max Weber. It has been the view of many that Weber's writings – particularly *The Protestant Ethic and the Spirit of Capitalism* – provide a 'refutation' of Marx's materialism; others have taken an opposite view, considering that much of Weber's sociology 'fits without difficulty into the Marxian scheme'.[1]

One main problem which helped to obscure the nature of the relationship between the views of the two thinkers was that it was only years after Weber's death that it became possible to evaluate Marx's output in the light of his previously unpublished early writings.[2] These works made two things clear. First, that Marx's conception of 'historical materialism'[3] is considerably more subtle, and much less dogmatic, than would appear from certain of his oft-quoted statements in such sources as the Preface to *A Contribution to the Critique of Political Economy*.[4] Second, that Engels's contributions to Marxism[5] have to be carefully distinguished from the underlying threads of Marx's own thought.[6] In order, therefore, to assess the main points of similarity and divergence between Marx and Weber, it is necessary to reconsider the nature of historical materialism in general, and Marx's conception of the genesis and trend of movement of capitalism in particular. While one must, of course, respect Weber's own statements on the subject of his relationship to Marx, these are not always a sufficient index.

The confusion in subsequent literature over the nature of Weber's critique of Marx stems also from a failure to distinguish a number of different, although interrelated, themes in Weber's writings. Weber's insistence upon the absolute logical separation between factual knowledge and value-directed action should not be allowed to obscure his equally emphatic stress upon the relevance of historical and sociological analysis to practical participation in politics.[7] Some of Weber's most important sociological ideas are, indeed, more clearly revealed in his directly political writings than in his academic publications.[8] Weber wrote, therefore, not simply as an intellectual critic of Marx, but also in response to the writings and political involvements of the prominent Marxist politicians and authors of his day. Three partially separable aspects of Weber's views may thus be isolated: (1) his attitude towards 'Marxism' in the shape of the main Marxist political agency in Germany, the Social Democratic Party; (2) his views upon the academic contributions of Marxist authors to history and sociology; (3) his views upon what he considered to be Marx's own original ideas. These three aspects of Weber's thought may in turn be distinguished from the analytic problem of how far Weber's understanding of Marx's theory of historical materialism was in fact valid.

In analysing these four dimensions of the relationship between Marx and Weber I shall concentrate mainly on that issue which was of primary importance to both: the interpretation of the development of modern capitalism in Europe. The sequence of changes which took place in the social and political structure of Germany from the middle up until the concluding years of the nineteenth century constitutes an essential background to the whole of the chapter: Weber's attitudes towards Marx and Marxism cannot be adequately understood and analysed outside of this context. Weber's work was not written merely as a rejoinder to a wraith-like 'ghost of Marx', but also formed part of a debate involving a force – Marxism – which played a major political and intellectual role in Imperial Germany. The analysis thus falls into three parts: the historical background of the development of German society over the latter half of the nineteenth century; Weber's attitudes towards, and views upon, Marx and Marxism; and the analytic problem which faces an observer today who attempts to assess the logical and empirical similarities and divergences between the writings of Marx and Weber. These three parts are, however, linked together by a single underlying theme. This is that the series of changes described in the first category – the social and political development of Germany in the second part of the nine-teenth century – help to elucidate key features both in the evol-ution of Marxism in that country[9] and also in Weber's response to it as a political influence and an academic doctrine.

The historical background

At the turn of the nineteenth century, Germany consisted of thirty-nine competing principalities. The two leading German states, Prussia and Austria, were both major powers: their very rivalry was one factor hindering German unification. The hopes of German nationalism were, however, also obstructed by the ethnic composition of Austria and Prussia themselves. Austria, after 1815, had more non-Germans in its population than Germans; Prussia incorporated large numbers of Poles within its territories to the east. The nationalist doctrine could foreseeably entail, for Prussia, the return of these lands to a Polish state. Thus the Aus-trian government was flatly opposed to any movement towards an integral German state; and, in spite of a strong current of nationalism, the case with Prussia was not very different.

But of greater importance than these factors in retarding the political unification of Germany were more basic characteristics of the social and economic structure of the country. Germany was, compared to the most advanced capitalist country, Britain, still almost in the Middle Ages, both in terms of the level of its econ-omic development, and in terms of the low degree of political liberalization within the various German states. In Prussia, the landed aristocracy, the Junkers, whose power sprang from their ownership of the large ex-Slavic estates to the east of the Elbe, maintained a dominant position within the economy and govern-ment. The emergent German bourgeoisie, then, had virtually no access to the reins of government in the early part of the nine-teenth century.

But Germany could hardly remain completely isolated from the sweeping currents of political change which had been set in mo-tion in France by the events of 1789. Marx's early works were written in the anticipation of a German revolution. Indeed, it might be said that Marx's awareness of the very backwardness of Germany in its social and economic structure was at the root of his original conception of the role of the proletariat in history. In France, Marx wrote in 1844, 'partial emancipation is the basis of complete emancipation'; but in Germany, so much less developed, a 'progressive emancipation' was impossible: the only possibility of advancement was through a radical revolution. In Germany, 'complete emancipation is the *conditio sine qua non* of any partial emancipation'. This can be accomplished, Marx wrote, only by the formation of the proletariat, 'a class which has *radical chains* . . . a class which is the dissolution of all classes, a sphere of society which has a universal character because its sufferings are universal'.[10] The proletariat at this time barely existed in Germany; a fact which, if Marx was not fully aware of it in 1844, he certainly recognized by 1847. By the latter date Marx was clear in his mind that the imminent revolution in Germany would be a bourgeois one;[11] but the peculiar characteristics of the social structure of Germany, so it still seemed to Marx, might make it possible for a bourgeois revolution to be followed closely by a proletarian one.[12] Marx was, however, conscious of the weakness of the German bourgeoisie, and noted that, even before having made any direct claim to power, the bourgeoisie were prone to waste whatever strength they possessed in premature and unnecessary conflicts with the nascent working class.[13] The failure of the 1848 revolutions in Germany bore witness to this fact, and dispelled Marx's optimism about an immediate 'leap into the future' in Germany – or indeed in Britain or France.

The 1848 uprisings were nevertheless a salutary experience for the ruling circles in the German states, and especially in Prussia. Following this date, a number of social and political reforms were instituted which moved the country away from the traditional semi-feudal autocracy. The failure of 1848 to produce any more radical reforms, however, served as something of a death-knell to the hopes, not merely of the small groups of socialists, but also of the liberals. The maintenance of Junker economic power, of their dominance of the officer corps in the army and in the civil service bureaucracy, led the German liberals perforce to acceptance of a series of compromise measures introducing nothing more than a semblance of parliamentary democracy.[14] The events of 1848 mark a line of direct linkage between Marx and Weber. For Marx, the result was physical exile in England, and an intellectual recognition of the importance of showing in detail the 'laws of movement' of capitalism as an economic system. Within Germany, the failures of 1848 paved the way for the ineptness of liberalism, which, as compared to the bold successes of Bismarck's hegemony, formed such an important background to the whole of Weber's thinking in his political sociology. Perhaps most important of all, the persistence of the traditional social and economic structure in Germany after 1848 drastically affected the role of the labour movement, placing it in quite a different position to that of either Britain or France.[15]

There is no space here to discuss in any detail the complicated issue of Marx's relationship to Lassalle and to the movement which Lassalle founded. Certain aspects of this relationship are, however, relevant. There was from the beginning of the Social Democratic movement a built-in ambivalence towards Marx's doctrines which formed a permanent source of schism within the party. While on the one hand Lassalle was deeply indebted in his theoretical views to Marx's theory of capitalism, in his practical leadership of the new movement he constantly acted in a way opposed to Marx's own views on specific issues, and advocated policies contrary to the very theory which he professed to accept. Thus, in contrast to Marx, who held that the German working class should throw in its weight with the bourgeoisie, in order to secure the bourgeois revolution which would subsequently provide the conditions for the assumption of power by the proletariat, Lassalle led the working-class movement away from any sort of collaboration with the liberals. In doing so, he fostered the sort of separation between theory and practice which was heinous to Marx, and Lassalle also thereby sowed the first seeds of the debate between 'evolution' and 'revolution' which later was really the *caput mortuum* of the Social Democratic Party as an agent of radical social change.

Lassalle died the same year that Weber was born. By this time the future of Germany had already been set. The detachment of the labour movement from the liberals, in conjunction with other factors, set the scene for Bismarck's unification of Germany in which, as Bismarck said, 'Germany did not look to Prussia's liberalism, but to her power.' In 1875, when Marx's leading advocates in Germany – Liebknecht and Bebel – accepted union with the Lassallean wing of the labour movement, Germany was in both political and economic terms a very different nation from that which Marx originally wrote about in the 1840s. Political integration had been achieved, not through the rise of a revolutionary bourgeoisie, but as a result, largely, of a policy of *Realpolitik* founded essentially upon the bold use of *political* power 'from the top', and occurring within a social system which retained, in large degree, its traditional structure.

The difficult phases of initial political integration and the 'take-off' into industrialization were accomplished in quite a different fashion in Germany from the typical process of development in Britain – and, in *Capital*, Marx accepted the latter country as providing the basic framework for his theory of capitalist development. In Germany, political centralization and rapid economic advancement took place without the formation of a fully liberalized bourgeois society. Thus neither the Marxists of the Social Democratic Party – even before Marx's death in 1883 – nor the German liberals possessed an adequate historical model within which they could comprehend the peculiarities of their own position within the German social structure. The Social Democrats clung tenaciously to a revolutionary catechism which became increasingly irrelevant to the real social and economic structure of an industrialized German state. Eventually, therefore, the inherent tension within the Social Democratic Party, between Marxian views of the revolutionary transcendence of capitalism and the Lassallean emphasis upon the appropriation of the capitalist state *from within* through the achievement of a fully universal franchise, became forced out into the open. Bernstein's *Evolutionary Socialism* (1899),[16] although itself based partly upon a British model, provided a coherent theoretical interpretation of the social forces which were driving the Social Democratic Party towards acceptance of the putative acquisition of power from within the existing order. *Evolutionary Socialism* made manifest the realization that the relationship between the political and economic development of capitalism could not be adequately comprehended in terms of the main theses of *Capital*: the progressive formation of a two-class society, the 'pauperization' of the vast majority, and the imminent collapse of capitalism in a 'final' catastrophic crisis. These latter conceptions survived as Social Democratic orthodoxy in the face of Bernstein's challenge; but they assumed an increasingly deterministic form. What were for Marx tendential properties of capitalism thus became regarded by his followers as mechanically given inevitabilities. This perspective allowed the preservation of revolutionary phraseology without demanding a concomitant revolutionary activism; if capitalism was necessarily doomed, all that needed to be done, so it appeared, was to wait in the wings until the final disintegration of the capitalist economy occurred.

Weber's attitude towards Marx and Marxism

The German liberals faced comparable dilemmas. Liberalism also had its roots in an earlier period, and in forms of society considerably different from that of Imperial Germany. While maintaining an adherence to the liberal values of individual freedom and political participation, the liberals were heavily compromised by their enforced adaptation – and subordination   to the dominant autocratic order. Weber's own political writings and involvements constantly manifest his consciousness of this fact.

Weber's appreciation of the significance of political power, particularly as wielded by Bismarck in successfully promoting the rapid internal consolidation and economic development of Germany (and, more specifically, his use of the bureaucracy to do so), is one key dimension of his approach to politics, and of his sociology more generally.[17] Weber's commitment to nationalism, and his lifelong emphasis upon the primacy of the German state, also have to be understood in these terms.[18] This determination to recognize the realities of the use of political power, however, was counterpointed in Weber's writing by an equally resolute adherence to the values of classical European liberalism. The pathos of Weber's thought, whereby he found himself compelled to recognize an increasing divergence between the main lines of development in modern societies and the values which he himself recognized as representing the distinctive ethos of Western culture, was an expression – albeit in a highly subtle and ratiocinated form – of the peculiar dilemmas of German liberalism as a whole.

Weber's attitude towards the Social Democratic Party

Weber's famous inaugural address at Freiburg in 1895 outlined his interpretation of the hopes of German liberalism in the face of Romantic conservatism on the one side, and the Marxist party on the other.[19] Weber specifically dissociated himself from the 'mystical' advocacy of the German state,[20] but he also expressed the conviction that the working class was politically incapable of leading the nation. While expressing agreement with some elements which constituted part of the programme of the Social Democrats, including that the working class should enjoy full rights of political representation, Weber argued that the working class 'is politically immature'. According to him much of the revolutionary fervour of the leaders of the working-class movement was quite divergent from the real trend of development of the Social Democratic Party – which, as he perceived at an early date, would move towards accommodation to the prevailing German state rather than providing a realistic revolutionary alternative to it. As Weber expressed it, the German state would conquer the Social Democratic Party, and not vice versa.[21]

Weber was scornful of the continuing claims of the Junkers to power, although he was forced to recognize that, in practice, their influence in the officer corps and, to a lesser degree, in the government bureaucracy was still considerable. The Junkers were, nevertheless, in Weber's eyes, obviously a declining class. The main source of hope, therefore, for a German state which would maintain its national integrity, but which would reach a level of political democracy compatible with an industrialized society, was through the strengthening of the liberal bourgeoisie as a group capable of providing national leadership. This meant, Weber increasingly came to emphasize, developing a governmental system which would vest real political power in parliament. The result of Bismarck's domination, he believed, had left Germany without effective political leadership which could take control of the bureaucratic machine of government, and threatened Germany with 'uncontrolled bureaucratic domination'.[22] His attitude towards the possibility of socialism in Germany was by and large simply a logical extension of this position. Should a socialist government, and a planned economy,[23] be set up, the result would be an even greater bureaucratic repression. Not only would there be no counterweight to the spread of bureaucracy in the political sphere, but this would inevitably be true of the economic sphere also. 'This would be socialism', Weber wrote, 'in about the same manner in which the ancient Egyptian "New Kingdom" was socialist.'[24]

Weber's views on the Social Democratic Party remained fairly consistent over the course of his life; his evaluation of his own political position with regard to the policies of the party did, however, change, together with the changing nature of the German social and political structure. Thus, towards the end of his life, having witnessed the occurrence of what he had previously foreseen – the increasing integration of the Social Democratic Party into the existing parliamentary order – he declared in 1918 that he was so close to the Social Democratic Party as to find it difficult to separate himself from it.[25] But his consistent view of 'Marxism' in the shape of the Social Democratic Party in Germany was that its professed objectives – the revolutionary overthrow of the state, and the institution of a classless society – were entirely divergent from the real role which it was destined to play in German politics.

Weber's views on the academic contributions of Marxist authors

Weber's position with respect to the theoretical notions which the main advocates and 'interpreters' of Marxism expounded cannot simply be deduced from his relationship to the Social Democratic Party, since the latter was determined in some degree by his appreciation of the political realities of the German situation. Weber recognized that certain of the leading Marxist theoreticians of his time had made distinct and even brilliant contributions to history, economics and jurisprudence; and he maintained close academic contact with some scholars who were heavily influenced by Marx.[26] It is important to recognize that the bulk of Weber's writing on capitalism and religion was written within the context of the appearance of a spate of scholarly works which claimed Marxian ancestry, but many of which either employed what Weber regarded as a vulgarization of Marx's ideas, or departed considerably from what he considered to be the main tenets of Marx's historical materialism.[27]

Although Weber once spoke of *The Protestant Ethic and the Spirit of Capitalism* as offering 'an empirical refutation of historical materialism', the essay had, in fact, a complicated genealogy. Weber was interested in religion as a social phenomenon from his early youth.[28] While his studies of law and economic history diverted him for some period from following this interest in his academic writings, the *Protestant Ethic* is clearly an expression of concerns which had always been in the forefront of Weber's mind. He undoubtedly wrote the essay in some part as a conscious polemic against the 'one-sided' conception of religion as portrayed by historical materialism. But 'historical materialism' here referred partly to the writings of Kautsky and others.[29] Moreover, it was probably Weber's association with Sombart which provided the most direct source of stimulus to his attempt to analyse the role of ascetic Protestantism in the rise of capitalism.[30]

Weber was sympathetic to the ideas of some of the prominent Marxist 'revisionists', although he regarded them as still being caught up, whatever their departures from Marx, within a metaphysical theory of history which was simply a handicap to their accurate perception of socio-economic reality. In general, he accepted, in common with Bernstein and others, that modern capitalism was not marked by a progressive differentiation between an increasingly wealthy minority and a 'pauperized' mass; that the white-collar middle class did not develop a consciousness of class identity with the manual working class; and that there was no sign of an imminent cataclysmic break-up of capitalism.[31] It can hardly be said, however, that Weber derived these views from any of the Marxist 'revisionists': Weber was clear in his own mind that the capitalist mode of production was not leading towards an open and irresistible class struggle between labour and capital. His own references to stratification in modern society show that he recognized the existence of multiple divisions of interest and of status which tended to obscure the Marxist class divisions. Thus he pointed out, for example, that the manual working class, far from having become a homogeneous unskilled group, was cut across by differences of skill-level which created divisions of class interest within the working class as a whole.[32]

Weber's relationship to the leading Marxist thinkers of his time was, therefore, a complex one; necessarily so, by virtue of the variety of differing positions assumed by those who claimed to be following Marx.

Weber's views on Marx

Weber, of course, considered that Marx had made fundamental contributions to historical and sociological analysis. But, to Weber, Marx's theories could not be regarded as anything more than sources of insight, or at most as ideal-typical concepts, which could be applied to illuminate particular, specific sequences of historical development. The radical neo-Kantian position which Weber adopted from Rickert and Windelband[33] effectively excluded any other possibility: in Weber's conception, Marx's attribution of overall 'direction' to the movement of history was as illegitimate as the Hegelian philosophy of history which helped to give it birth.[34] While Weber admitted, with strong reservations, the use of 'developmental stages' as a 'heuristic means' which could facilitate the explanatory interpretation of historical materials, he rejected totally the construction of 'deterministic schemes' based upon any sort of general theory of historical development.[35]

The necessary corollary of this was the rejection of Marx's materialism as a key to the explanation of historical change. The thesis that economic factors in any sense 'finally' explained the course of history, Weber asserted, as a scientific theorem was simply false.[36] He recognized that Marx's writings varied in the degree of sophistication with which the materialist conception of history was presented – the *Communist Manifesto*, for example, set out Marx's views 'with the crude elements of genius of the early form'.[37] But even in its more thorough formulation in *Capital*, he pointed out, Marx nowhere defined precisely how the 'economic' is delimited from other spheres of society. Weber's distinction between 'economic', 'economically relevant' and 'economically conditioned' phenomena was aimed at clarifying this problem. Economic action he defined as action which sought by peaceful means to acquire control of desired utilities.[38] There were, however, many forms of human action – such as religious practices – which, while they were not 'economic' according to this definition, had relevance to economic phenomena in that they influenced the needs or propensities which individuals had to acquire or make use of utilities. These were economically relevant forms of action. Phenomena which were economically relevant could in turn be separated from those which were economically conditioned: these were actions, which although again not 'economic' according to Weber's definition, were causally influenced by economic factors. As he pointed out: 'After what has been said, it is self-evident that: firstly, the boundary lines of "economic" phenomena are vague and not easily defined; secondly, the "economic" aspect of a phenomenon is by no means *only* "economically conditioned" or *only* "economically relevant".'[39] Calvinism was in these terms both economically conditioned and economically relevant with regard to the early formation of rational capitalism in Western Europe.

He also pointed to another source of conceptual ambiguity in Marx's 'economic' interpretation of history: that Marx failed to distinguish in a clearly formulated way between the 'economic' and the 'technological'. Where Marx slipped into a more or less direct technological determinism, Weber claimed, his argument was inadequate. Marx's famous assertion that 'the hand-mill gives us feudalism, the steam-mill, capitalism'[40] was, according to Weber, 'a technological proposition, not an economic one, and it can be clearly proven that it is simply a false assertion. For the era of the hand-mill, which lasted up to the threshold of the modern period, showed the most varied kinds of cultural "superstructures" in all places.'[41] A given form of technology might be associated with varying types of social organization, and vice versa; this could be seen in the very fact that socialism, as Marx expected it to develop – although being a different social and economic system from capitalism – was to involve essentially the same technological base as capitalism.

The positive influence of Marx's writings over Weber is most evident in Weber's insistence that values and ideas, while most definitely not being merely 'derivations' of material interests, nevertheless had always to be analysed in relation to such interests. Weber, of course, recognized the importance of class conflicts in history, while denying that their prevalence or significance was anything like as great as that postulated by Marx. For Weber, conflicts between status groups of various kinds, and between political associations – including nation-states – were at least equally important in the historical development of the major civilizations. The conception of sectional 'interest', therefore, could not be limited to economic interests, but had to be extended to other spheres of social life; political parties, for example, had interests which derived from their situation as aspirants to or as wielders of power, and which did not necessarily in any direct sense rest upon shared economic interests.[42]

There has been some considerable debate over the degree to which Weber's methodological works,[43] written relatively early on in his career, accord with the substantive content of his later writings, particularly *Economy and Society*. What is certain, however, is that Weber never abandoned his basic stand upon the complete logical separation of fact and value, nor his correlate assumption of the irreducibility of competing values. It was this epistemological position, Weber recognized, which separated him most decisively from Marx. Marx's work involved an 'ethic of ultimate ends', and therefore committed the person who accepted it to a 'total' conception of history. For Weber, science could not answer the question: ' "Which of the warring gods should we serve"?'[44]

Weber and Marx: the analytic problem

Weber's critique of Marx was sophisticated, and was not simply an abstract analysis of the 'logic' of Marx's theories, but embodied the very substance of Weber's studies of history and society. This very fact, however, means that Weber's own explicit evaluations of Marx's views cannot be regarded as the sole source of evidence on the matter. That Weber's own remarks on *The Protestant Ethic*, for instance, were not completely unambiguous is indicated by the confusion over the objectives of the work in the large literature which has surrounded the subject since the first publication of Weber's essay.[45] Obviously, moreover, the evaluation of the differences between Marx and Weber must depend upon an accurate evaluation of the characteristic views of the former. In order to make clear the substance of Marx's basic theoretical position, it is necessary to touch briefly upon some themes in Marx's writings which, thanks to the enormous body of secondary works written on Marx since World War II, have by now become very familiar.

Much of the post-war literature on Marx centred upon the writings of the 'young Marx': that is, prior to the completion of *The German Ideology* (1846). The debate over the relevance of these early writings to Marx's mature works was inconclusive; but it cannot be doubted that, firstly, there are, at the very least, certain definite threads of continuity which run through the whole of Marx's work, and that, secondly, some of the early writings allow us to clarify what these continuities are.[46] Marx did not ever write a systematic exposition of his 'materialism'. Yet his early writings make it clear that his conception of his materialistic approach to history is quite different from what he called 'perceptual materialism'.[47] Marx, in common with the other 'Young Hegelians', began his intellectual development from the standpoint of the critique of religion, derived from a radicalization of Hegel, and based largely upon the thought of David Strauss and Feuerbach. Feuerbach's philosophy was founded upon a reversal of the major premise of Hegel's system. In place of Hegel's idealism, Feuerbach substituted his own version of materialism, stating bluntly that the starting point of the study of 'man' must be 'real man' living in the 'real material world'.[48] Feuerbach's writing remained mainly confined to the examination of religion: by 'standing Hegel on his feet',[49] he tried to show that the divine was an illusory product of the real. God was an idealized projection of humanity itself; God was the mythical projection of humanity's most cherished values, humanity alienated from its own (potential) self-perfection.

The consequence of Feuerbach's view was that religion was a symbolic 'representation' of human aspirations, and that to eliminate human self-alienation all that needed to be done was for religion to be demystified, and placed on a rational level. Marx rapidly perceived what appeared to him as fundamental defects in this notion. Feuerbach's errors were, first, to speak of 'man' in the abstract, and thus to fail to perceive that people only exist within the context of particular societies which change their structure in the course of historical development; and, second, to treat ideas or 'consciousness' as simply the 'consequence' of human activities in the 'material' world. In Marx's words: 'The chief defect of all previous materialism (including Feuerbach's) is that the object, actuality, sensuousness, is conceived only in the form of the *object of perception*, but not as *sensuous human activity, practice*, not subjectively.'[50]

Marx referred to his materialism only as 'the guiding thread' in his studies: ideologies were 'rooted in the material conditions of life', but this did not entail that there was a universal or unilateral relationship between the 'real foundation' of society (the relations of production) and 'legal and political superstructures'.[51] On the contrary, the specific conclusion which Marx reached in criticizing Feuerbach was that ideas were social products, which could be explained not by the philosopher who stood outside of history, but only by the analysis of particular forms of society.[52] We had to reject, Marx insisted, any kind of 'recipe or scheme . . . for neatly trimming the epochs of history', and had to 'set about the observation and arrangement – the real depiction – of our historical material'.[53]

Where Marx did generalize about the relationship between ideology and material 'substructure', this was in terms of analysing class relations as the main mediating link between the two. The class structure of society exerted a determinate effect upon which ideas *assumed prominence* in that society. This was the sense of Marx's proposition that the ruling ideas in any epoch were the ideas of the ruling class.[54] It should be pointed out that, even in Feuerbach's theory, religion was something more than merely a complete reflection of material reality: it also provided values and ideals towards which people should strive. God was humanity as it ought to be, and therefore the image of the deity held out the hope of what humanity could *become*. Marx took over this notion from Feuerbach, but mated it with the dialectical conception that it was the reciprocal interaction of such religious ideas with the social actions of 'earthly men' which had to be examined. This reciprocity could be understood in terms of analysing the historical development of societies; we cannot understand the relationship between ideology and society if we 'abstract from the historical process'.[55] There is no question, then, but that Marx recognized both that ideologies might have a partially 'internal' autonomous development, and that the degree to which this was so depended upon factors particular to specific societies, which in every case had to be studied in empirical detail. This was both consistent with his general conception of materialism, and evidenced in his more detailed studies.[56] Marx's position, in other words, is not incompatible with recognition of the unique characteristics and influence of ascetic Protestantism in Europe.

All this is quite well known; what has not been so generally appreciated is that even in matters of detail, Marx's discussion of the course of historical development in Europe is in several ways

strikingly close to Weber's analysis: this is a fact which only became fully apparent with the publication of the draft notes
(*Grundrisse*) which Marx wrote for *Capital* in 1857–8. Marx acknowledged the importance of the early forms of capitalism which
developed in Rome, and his explanation of why these led to a
'dead end' is quite similar to that subsequently set out by Weber.[57]
Marx pointed out that certain of the conditions – including the
existence of a nascent capitalist class – which played an essential
part in the development of capitalism in Western Europe at a later
period were already present in Rome. Among the factors he isolated as significant in inhibiting the emergence of full-scale capitalism in Rome was that there was strong ideological pressure
against the accumulation of wealth for its own sake: 'Wealth does
not appear as the aim of production ... The inquiry is always
about what kind of property creates the best citizens. Wealth as an
end in itself appears only among a few trading peoples.'[58] Wealth
was valued, not intrinsically, but for the 'private enjoyment' it
could bring; moreover, labour in general was regarded with contempt, and as not worthy of free men.

Marx recognized that there existed numerous prior forms of
capitalism before the emergence of bourgeois society in post-
medieval Europe. Thus mercantile capital had often been found –
as in Rome – in societies in which the dominant mode of
production was not capitalist. Mercantile operations had usually
been carried on by marginal groups, such as Jews. Mercantile
capital had existed 'in the most diverse forms of society, at the
most diverse stages of the development of the productive forces'.[59]
There were cases of societies, other than Rome, where certain
segments of the social structure had been quite highly evolved, but
where the lack of development of other sectors had limited the
ultimate level of economic advancement. Marx quoted the instance of ancient Peru, which in certain respects had a developed
economy, but which was kept to a low level of development by
the geographical isolation of the society, and by the lack of a
monetary system.[60]

Marx's views on the emergence and significance of Christianity
in the development of the European societies have to be inferred
from various oblique statements in his critiques of Hegel and the
'Young Hegelians'. As a close student of Hegel, Marx was obviously aware of the overriding importance which historians and
philosophers attributed to Christianity in the West. Marx did not

question the validity of this. What he did attack was the idealistic standpoint within which the influence of Christianity was analysed. Thus he objected to Stirner's treatment of the rise of early Christianity in that it was conducted wholly upon the level of ideas.[61] Christianity arose, Marx stated, as a religion of wandering, uprooted vagrants, and the causes of its expansion had to be related to the internal decay of the Roman Empire: 'the Hellenic and Roman world perished, spiritually in Christianity and materially in the migration of the peoples.'[62] The Christian ethical outlook formed a vital new moral current, contrasting with the moral decadence of Rome. Christianity substituted for Roman pantheism the conception of a single universal God, whose authority was founded upon uniquely Christian notions of sin and salvation. In the later evolution of Christianity in Europe, the Reformation provided a similar moral regeneration in relation to an internally disintegrating feudal society. 'Luther . . . overcame bondage out of devotion by replacing it by bondage out of conviction. He shattered faith in authority because he restored the authority of faith . . . He freed man from outer religiosity because he made religiosity the inner man.'[63]

To suppose that Marx was unaware of the 'ascetic' and 'rational' character of modern European capitalism is to miss some of the most basic premises upon which his analysis and critique of bourgeois society was founded. The 'rationalizing' character of capitalism was manifest most directly, for Marx, in the utter dominance of money in human social relationships, and in the pursuit of money as an end in itself. Money was the epitome of human self-alienation under capitalism, since it reduced all human qualities to quantitative values of exchange.[64] Capitalism thus had a 'universalizing' character, which broke down the particularities of traditional cultures: 'capital develops irresistibly beyond national barriers and prejudices . . . it destroys the self-satisfaction confined within narrow limits and based upon a traditional mode of life and reproduction.'[65] Capitalism was 'ascetic' in that the actions of capitalists were based upon self-renunciation and the continual reinvestment of profits. This was manifest, Marx pointed out, in the theory of political economy: 'Political economy, the science of wealth, is, therefore, at the same time, the science of renunciation, of privation and saving . . . Its true ideal is the ascetic usurious miser and the ascetic but productive slave.'[66] The pursuit of wealth for its own sake was a phenomenon which was, as a general moral ethos, found only within modern capitalism. Marx was as specific on this matter as Weber: 'The passion for wealth as such is a distinctive development; that is to say, it is something other than the instinctive thirst for particular goods such as clothes, arms, jewellery, women, wine ... The taste for possessions can exist without money; the thirst for self-enrichment is the product of a definite social development, it is not natural, but historical.'[67]

The point to be stressed, however, is that in broad terms Marx's conception of, and empirical treatment of, the role of ideology in society is quite compatible with the more detailed studies undertaken by Weber of the sociology of religion. Marx did not study religion in any detail because, in breaking with the 'Young Hegelians' and with Feuerbach, and in perceiving the need to begin to analyse sociologically the relationships between economy, politics and ideology, Marx effectively overcame – in terms of his own objectives – the need to subject religion to detailed analysis. The 'Young Hegelians', as Marx made clear in *The Holy Family*, continued to devote most of their efforts to the critique of religion, and thus always remained imprisoned within a worldview which was, even if only negatively, a religious one.[68]

To emphasize the general theoretical congruity of much of what Marx and Weber wrote on the history and origins of capitalism is obviously not to argue that their views were wholly identical, either in relation to particular problems or in respect of more general issues of social and political theory. It is evident that Marx, while disavowing 'the *passe-partout* of a general historical–philosophical theory whose main quality is that of being super-historical',[69] sought to impose a pattern on historical development which Weber treated as quite impermissible. The concept of charisma, and the basic role which it plays in Weber's sociology, express Weber's conviction that human history was not (as Marx believed it to be) rational. The attribution of a discoverable rationality to history was an essential element in the whole of Marx's thought, and was the main tie by which he always remained bound to Hegel. But charisma was specifically irrational; thus the revolutionary dynamic in history, which for Weber was constituted by the periodic emergence of charismatic movements, could not be connected to any overall rational pattern in the historical development of humanity. Moreover, by stressing the importance of class, and thus of economic interests, in social development, Marx tended to assimilate economic and political power much more than Weber.[70] This is very definitely a difference of fundamental significance between the two authors. Nevertheless, the divergence here must not be over-exaggerated.[71] Marx anticipated Weber, for example, in recognizing a parallel between the organization of professional armies and the separation of labourers from their product under modern capitalism. Thus Marx noted: 'In Rome there existed in the army a mass already quite distinct from the people, disciplined to labour . . . it sold to the State the whole of its labour-time for wages . . . as the worker does with the capitalist.'[72]

Conclusion

My objective here has been to separate several basic strands in the relationship between the writings of Marx and Weber. I have tried to make it clear that the tendency to assimilate these together as forming a blanket 'critique of Marx' has led many commentators to oversimplify Weber's assessment of 'historical materialism'. It has become something of a truism to say that the 'founders' of modern sociology – Weber, Pareto and Mosca in particular – developed their theories, at least in part, as 'refutations' of Marx. Each of these authors has at some time been called 'the bourgeois Marx'. This label, however, is inapt in the sense that it implies that their work represents nothing more than a bourgeois response to Marxism. It was this, but it was also much more. Thus Weber's relationship to Marx and to Marxist thought cannot be assessed along a single dimension of 'confirmation' or 'refutation'. Weber's historical studies both destroy some of the cruder Marxist interpretations of historical development, and at the same time, as I have tried to show in this chapter, *partly* vindicate Marx against his own professed disciples.

Weber wrote at a period when the character of the leading Western European countries generally, and that of Germany more specifically, had changed considerably from the time at which Marx formed his main views. All of the economically advanced societies of the West, by the turn of the twentieth century, had reached a high degree of economic maturity without experiencing the revolutionary reorganization which Marx expected. In Weber's time Marx's thought was carried, in Germany, by the Social Democratic Party. 'Historical materialism' came to be largely identified, in the eyes of Weber and other liberal critics of Marxism, as well as by Marxists themselves, with the systematic exposition of Engels in *Anti-Dühring* and, later, *The Dialectics of Nature*.[73] While some commentators have exaggerated the difference between the thought of Marx and Engels, the implications of the position which Engels took in these works are quite definitely at variance with the conception central to most of Marx's writing. By transferring the dialectic to nature, Engels obscured the most essential element of Marx's work, which was 'the dialectical relationship of subject and object in the historical process'.[74] In doing so, Engels helped to stimulate the notion that ideas simply 'reflect' material reality.[75] The political quietism of the Social Democratic Party – which Weber accurately perceived behind its revolutionary phraseology – was bound up with the general adoption of such an outlook, which made possible the preservation of a revolutionary posture in a set of social circumstances which had diverged substantially from the pattern of development anticipated by Marx. The wheel thus in a way came almost full circle. At the risk of oversimplifying what is actually a complicated question, it could be said that Weber's critique of Marxism, as regards the role of ideas in history, in fact came close to restating, in vast detail, certain elements of the original Marxian conception.

This went hand in hand, ironically, with a rejection of certain key aspects of Marx's analysis of contemporary capitalism, and of the latter's hopes for a future form of radically new society. Marx, writing a generation before Weber, believed that capitalism could, and would, be transcended by a new form of society. Weber wrote with the hindsight of having witnessed the formation of industrial capitalism in Germany in quite different circumstances from those in Britain or France. Weber's appreciation of this fact was one element in his thought allowing him, while drawing heavily from Marx, to escape from the strait-jacket which the followers of Marx in the Social Democratic Party sought to impose upon history in the name of historical materialism.

Yet it might be held that, in his analysis of the imminent trend of development of capitalism, Weber himself fell prey to a sort of materialistic determinism of his own. Weber perceived a major irrationality within capitalism: the 'formal' rationality of bureau-cracy, while it made possible the technical implementation of large-scale administrative tasks, was 'substantively' irrational in that it contravened some of the most distinctive values of Western civilization. But he foresaw no way of breaking through this irra-tionality: the future held out only the likelihood of the increasing submergence of human autonomy and individuality within an ever-expanding bureaucratization of modern life.

3 Durkheim's Political Sociology

Durkheim's theory of politics and the state is undoubtedly the most neglected of his contributions to social theory. There are perhaps two reasons why Durkheim's political sociology has not received the attention which it demands. One is that some standard expositions of his work (especially Parsons's *The Structure of Social Action*)[1] were written before the publication of the series of lectures in which he most directly confronted the problems of political analysis.[2] A second, although related, factor in this neglect derives from the phases through which the secondary interpretation of Durkheim's work has passed.[3] During his own lifetime, and for some little while after his death, Durkheim was generally seen as the originator of a radical form of 'sociological realism', which subordinated the individual to a hypostatized 'group mind'; and his political thought was widely regarded as a form of mystical nationalism.[4] Later accounts provided much more sophisticated, and accurate, evaluations of Durkheim's general sociology, but these tended to direct attention away from the political content of Durkheim's writings, emphasizing other aspects of his works.

Parsons's interpretation of Durkheim even today remains among the most influential.[5] According to this standpoint, Durkheim's thought underwent a series of profound changes over the course of his career: beginning from an initially 'positivistic'[6] position (as manifest primarily in *The Division of Labour in Society* and *The Rules of Sociological Method*), he eventually moved to one which was 'idealistic' in character. The effect of this interpretation is definitely to underplay the importance of *The Division of Labour* in Durkheim's writings. Since any examination of Durkheim's political ideas must be grounded in the theory established in that work, it follows that this tends to obscure the degree to which Durkheim's general sociology is concerned with political problems and with the nature of the modern state. Such a tendency was accentuated even more forcibly by Nisbet, who argued that, in his subsequent writings, Durkheim relinquished all of the most important theses which he had established in *The Division of Labour*:

> Durkheim never went back, in later studies, to any utilization of the distinction between the two types ('mechanical' and 'organic') of solidarity, nor to the division of labour as a form of cohesion, much less to any rationalization of conflict and anomie in society as mere 'pathological forms of division of labour'. The kinds of society, constraint, and solidarity dealt with in all his later works – either in theoretical or practical terms – have nothing whatsoever to do with the attributes that he had laid down for an organic and (presumably) irreversibly modern society in *The Division of Labour*.[7]

It is undoubtedly correct to say that Durkheim's thought was modified and elaborated upon over the course of his intellectual career. But the view which sees a pronounced discrepancy between Durkheim's earlier and later works is misleading. The substance of my discussion, indeed, is founded upon the premise that the truth of the matter is almost completely the reverse of the view suggested by Nisbet: that Durkheim continued in his later thinking to base his works upon the distinction between 'mechanical' and 'organic' solidarity; that the existence of solidarity deriving from the division of labour was always conceived by Durkheim to be the most distinctive feature of contemporary as opposed to traditional societies; that Durkheim's treatment of 'conflict and anomie' in his later writings cannot be understood apart from his analysis of the 'pathological' forms of the division of labour; and that 'the kinds of society, constraint, and solidarity dealt with in all his later works' have everything to do with the attributes of contemporary society as formulated in *The Division of Labour*. The overall continuity between Durkheim's early and later works does not become fully apparent, however, unless considerable attention is given to his political theory. Far from being of peripheral significance to his sociology, Durkheim's political thought has an important role in his ideas; and, as I shall seek to demonstrate in a subsequent section of this chapter, an appreciation of this fact allows the correction of a prevalent, but mistaken, interpretation of the main sociological problem with which Durkheim was concerned in all of his major works: the theory of moral authority.

The social and political background of Durkheim's thought

It has often been remarked that Durkheim's sociology has to be understood as a response to the shattering effects upon French society of the German victory of 1870–1. But this says too much and too little. Too much, because Durkheim's writing also has to be seen as rooted in the traditions of French positivist philosophy which stretch back to Comte, Saint-Simon and beyond; too little because – by this very token – the social and political background to Durkheim's thought embodies important elements which were the legacy of the Revolution in the eighteenth century, and of which the events of 1870–1 were in part a direct outcome.[8] If the Revolution successfully disposed of the *ancien régime*, it also prepared the ground for certain generic social and political problems which were to haunt France for more than a century afterwards. Rather than introducing the liberal, bourgeois society which was proclaimed in its slogans, the Revolution opened up social cleavages of a chronic nature. If it was a 'successful' revolution, it was not successful enough, and produced that cycle of revolution and restoration which has dominated French history to the present day. The 1789 Revolution did not create a 'bourgeois society', if this be taken to mean one which conjoined political democracy and the hegemony of a capitalist class; throughout the nineteenth century, heavily conservative elements, centred particularly in the church, rentiers and peasantry, retained a deep-seated influence in government and society. The writings of Saint-Simon and Comte, in their somewhat variant ways, embodied and gave expression to this precarious balance of liberal and conservative influences. Both writers perceived this as a transitory situation, and both looked forward to a new and more 'stable' order in the future.

Their divergent conceptions of this future order are among the major problematic issues which Durkheim sought to resolve in his sociology. Is the emergent form of society to be one in which there is a single 'class' of *industriels*, where equality of opportunity will prevail, and in which government is reduced to the 'administration of things', not of persons; or is it to be the hierocratic, corporate state of Comte's *Positive Polity*?

As in the writings of Max Weber, the problem, not of 'order' in a generic sense,[9] but of the form of *authority* appropriate to a modern industrial state, is the leading theme in Durkheim's work. But whereas in Germany a different combination of political and economic circumstances helped to establish a tradition of *Nationalökonomie* which led liberal scholars of Weber's generation to an overwhelming concern with 'capitalism', in France the problem was posed within the context of the long-standing confrontation between the 'individualism' embodied in the ideals of the Revolution, and the moral claims of the Catholic hierocracy. Thus the Third Republic certainly came into being amid an atmosphere of crisis – and of class conflict as manifest in the Paris Commune and its repression – but, so it seemed to Durkheim and his liberal contemporaries, the disasters of 1870–1 also provided both the possibility and the necessity of at last completing the process of social and political change which had been initiated in the Revolution almost a century earlier. In his sociological works, Durkheim was not, as is often stated, concerned above all with the nature of 'anomie', but rather with exploring the complex interrelationships between the *three* dimensions of 'anomie', 'egoism' and 'individualism'. *The Division of Labour* stated Durkheim's thinking on this matter, and he did not afterwards deviate from the position set out therein, although he did not fully elaborate certain of its implications until later. The most important substantive conclusion which Durkheim reached in *The Division of Labour* was that organic solidarity presupposed *moral* individualism: in other words, that 'it is wrong to contrast a society which comes from a community of beliefs (mechanical solidarity) to one which has a cooperative basis (organic solidarity), according only to the first a moral character, and seeing in the latter simply an economic grouping.'[10] The immediate source of this moral individualism, as Durkheim made clear in his contribution to the public discussion of the Dreyfus affair,[11] was in the ideals generated by the 1789

Revolution. Moral individualism was by no means the same as egoism (that is, the pursuit of self-interest), as was posited in classical economic theory and utilitarian philosophy. The growth of individualism, deriving from the expansion of organic solidarity, was not to be necessarily equated with anomie (the anomic condition of the division of labour was a *transitory* phenomenon, which stemmed precisely from the fact that the formation of contracts was insufficiently governed by moral regulation). Thus the social order which was coming into being demanded the realization or *concrete implementation* of the ideals of the French Revolution.

This theory, therefore, provided a resolution of the issues separating Saint-Simon's and Comte's otherwise closely comparable views.[12] The emergent social order was certainly to be one founded in the complex division of labour entailed by modern industry – as specified by Saint-Simon; Comte was mistaken in supposing that the condition of unity in traditional societies, the existence of a strongly formed *conscience collective*, was necessary to the modern type of society. But it was not to be a society in which authority would be confined to the 'administration of things', as Saint-Simon envisaged: on the contrary, the division of labour in industry had to be infused with *moral* controls, and these had to be under the general moral guidance of the state.

Durkheim's assessment of the underlying factors in the Dreyfus affair, as well as his own active participation in it, focused these issues with great clarity. The immediate stimulus to Durkheim's discussion of the questions raised by the Dreyfus controversy was the publication of an article by Brunetière, the Catholic apologist, who accused the *dreyfusards* of fostering moral anarchy by rejecting traditional values in favour of an egoistic rationalism. Durkheim replied by asserting the existence of a radical distinction between 'egoism' and 'rationalist individualism'. It was true that no society could be built upon the pursuit of self-interest; but the latter was not at all the same thing as 'individualism'. Individualism was not to be identified with 'the utilitarian egoism of Spencer and of the economists'.[13] Indeed, Durkheim continued, there would be no need to attack individualism if it possessed no other representatives, for utilitarian theory was in the process of dying a natural death. Individualism was in fact quite distinct from this: it was not merely a 'philosophical construction', but was a living part of the social organization of contemporary society. It was 'that which the Declaration of the Rights of Man sought, more or less successfully, to give a formula to; that which is currently taught in our schools, and which has become the basis of our moral catechism'.[14] This was, in an important respect, the very opposite of egoism. It involved, not the glorification of self-interest but that of the welfare of others: it was the morality of co-operation. Individualism, or the 'cult of the individual', was founded upon sentiments of sympathy for human suffering, a desire for equality and for justice. It in no sense derived from egoism, but was social in origin. The growth of individualism did not, therefore, intrinsically promote anomie, the decay of moral authority.

There could be no retreat to the traditional deism of the church, or to the patterns of hierocratic control associated with it. Individualism none the less preserved a 'religious' character, as did all moral rules. This 'cult of the individual' was the only moral form possible in an industrial society, having a highly differentiated division of labour:

> To the degree that societies become larger, and embody broader territorial areas, traditions and practices must necessarily exist in a state of plasticity and ambiguity which no longer offers as much resistance to individual differences; thus traditions and practices are able to adapt themselves to a diversity of situations and to changed circumstances. Individual differences, being much less confined, develop more freely, and multiply; that is to say, everyone pursues, to a greater degree, his own bent [*son propre sens*]. At the same time, because of the more advanced developments of the division of labour, each person finds himself turned towards a different point on the horizon, reflects a different aspect of the world and, consequently, the content of individual minds differs from one man to another. Thus we move little by little towards a situation, which has now almost been reached, where the members of the same social group will share nothing in common save their quality of humanness [*leur qualité d'homme*], the constitutive characteristics of the human person in general. This idea of the human person, somewhat modified according to differences in national temperament, is thus the only one which is maintained, immovable and impersonal, above the flux of particular opinions . . . nothing remains which men can love and worship in common, except man himself . . . Let us therefore use our liberties in order to seek what must be done, and in order to do it; to soften

the functioning of the social machine, which is still so harsh on men, to make available to them all possible means for the development of their faculties without obstacle, to work to finally make a reality of the famous precept: to each according to his works![15]

As Richter pointed out,[16] Durkheim's political liberalism and his sociological defence of republicanism played a major role in the promotion of his own academic career, and in facilitating the rise of sociology as a recognized discipline in the French academic system. The opprobrium which was directed at sociology – especially from Thomist critics[17] – bears witness to the degree to which the new discipline (especially in its Durkheimian form) came to be regarded as the hand-maiden of an ascendant republicanism. The struggle for the secularization of education, of course, was an element of primary significance as a background to this: Durkheim was first appointed to the Sorbonne in 1902 as a professor of education, and in his courses on pedagogy he set out a systematic theoretical exposition of the factors which necessitated the transformation of the educational system.[18] But while it was true that the ideological complementarity between Durkheim's sociology and victorious republicanism accounted for much of the considerable influence which he and the *Année sociologique* school exerted in French intellectual circles, it would be quite misleading to imply that his assessment of concrete political issues or personalities played a significant part in shaping his sociological views. Durkheim, in Davy's phrase, always kept aloof from the *cuisine politique*;[19] he had little feeling for, or interest in, the practical problems of politics. Consequently, he never affiliated himself directly to any political party, although he maintained a close contact with his fellow *normalien* Jaurès, and both influenced and was influenced by some of the leading trends in Radical Socialism.

To trace Durkheim's intellectual indebtedness to socialism is to reveal some of the most profound sources of his thought. Mauss has stated that Durkheim originally conceived the subject matter of *The Division of Labour* in terms of an analysis of the relationship between individualism and socialism.[20] 'Socialism' here does not refer, however, to the traditions of revolutionary thought which are so richly represented in French political life from the concluding decades of the eighteenth century onwards. If

Durkheim's attitudes towards other branches of socialism were less than wholly unambiguous, his views on revolutionary socialism were clear-cut and unchanging. Major social change was not brought about by political revolution. According to Durkheim, the history of France in the first two-thirds of the nineteenth century bore witness to this. 'It is among the most revolutionary peoples', he wrote, 'that bureaucratic routine is often most powerful'; in such societies, 'superficial change disguises the most monotonous uniformity'.[21] Thus the class struggles which manifested themselves in 1848 and 1870–1, rather than being the harbingers of an entirely new social order,[22] bore witness to the fact that the underlying social changes (of which even the 1789 Revolution was more of a symptom than a cause) had not yet been accommodated within the general framework of modern French society. *The Division of Labour* established the theoretical grounding of this position, showing that the existence of class conflict derived from the fact that the transitional phase between mechanical and organic solidarity had not been completed. In reviewing Labriola's *Essais sur la conception matérialiste de l'histoire* in 1879, Durkheim made this position fully explicit. The 'sad class conflict of which we are the witnesses today' was not the cause of the *malaise* which the contemporary European societies were experiencing; on the contrary, it was secondary and derived. The transition from the traditional to the newly emergent type of social order was a protracted process, which did not begin at any definite date, and which was evolutionary rather than revolutionary in character. The elimination of class conflict, therefore, did not necessitate an 'upheaval and radical reorganization of the social order', but instead demanded the consolidation and absorption of the basic social and economic transformations which had already taken place.[23]

Although Durkheim seems to have been acquainted with Marx's writings at a very early stage in his intellectual career, according to his own testimony[24] he was in no way directly influenced by Marx, either in formulating his general conception of sociology and sociological method, or in arriving at the theory of social development set out in *The Division of Labour*. In France prior to the turn of the twentieth century, Marxism was not, of course, the major political and intellectual force which it was in the last two decades of the nineteenth century in Germany. The thought of Max and Alfred Weber, Sombart, Tönnies, and the other younger members of the Verein für Sozialpolitik was in substantial part shaped through a confrontation with Marxism. Whatever the naïvetés and oversimplifications of Marx's ideas which became current in Germany, both Marx's self-professed followers and the leading critics of Marxism there possessed an understanding of Marx which was vastly more advanced than that which became diffused into French intellectual circles from the 1880s onwards. The Guesdist variety of Marxism, which held sway up until the middle of the 1890s, when translations of more sophisticated Marxist writings (such as those by Labriola) became available, was raucous and shallow. Hence, by the time Marxism made a substantial penetration into French intellectual consciousness, Durkheim had already worked out most of the essential components of his sociology.

His lectures on socialism, given at Bordeaux in 1895–6 were, however, partly stimulated by the spread of Marxism at this period;[25] some of his own students, indeed, became converted to Marxism at this time. But Durkheim was, by this stage, equipped to meet with and to assimilate the challenge of Marxism in his own terms. His *Socialism* lecture-course set out, in the face of the revolutionary left, the same basic position which, at the height of the Dreyfus affair, was to be made against the reactionaries of the right, and at the same time affirmed the key role of sociology in the analysis and resolution of the 'contemporary crisis'. Moreover, in these lectures, Durkheim made explicit the continuity between the intellectual problems tackled by Saint-Simon and those which faced the modern age. The writings of Saint-Simon, and of his followers, comprised – in a confused form – three sets of ideas: first, the conception of a scientific sociology; second, the notion of a religious revival; and third, a body of socialist doctrine. It was not by chance, Durkheim asserted, that these three sets of ideas had again come to the fore, since 'there are striking analogies between the period we have just been studying and the one in which we now live.'[26] These sets of ideas appeared at first sight to be quite distinct, and even opposed to each other: in fact, each derived from the same circumstance – the 'condition of moral disorder' which prevailed before 1848, and which had been reactivated after 1870.[27] Each expressed, in a partial fashion, aspects of this 'disorder'. The religious movement arose from a felt need to control egoism, and hence to recreate a strong moral authority; it was inadequate, because it sought to re-establish forms of ecclesiastical domination which were only appropriate to an earlier type of society. Socialism recognized that the old order had been superseded, and that consequently traditional institutions had to cede place to new forms of social organization; but it looked to purely economic transformations in order to remedy a situation of crisis which was primarily moral in character. The impetus towards sociology stemmed from the desire to understand and to explain the origins of the changes which were taking place. It, too, was limited because, as a scientific study, it necessarily proceeded only cautiously and slowly, while the demands of the day stimulated a desire for instant and all-embracing solutions. Nevertheless, it is clear that, in Durkheim's thinking, sociology claimed a definite primacy over the other two. For while each of the others gave only a distorted picture of the modern crisis,[28] sociology was able to reveal its true nature. Sociological analysis could not in and of itself be a substitute for the other two sets of ideas. Each had something to offer which no science could provide. But only sociology could show what those necessary elements are:

> Our conclusion therefore is that if you wish to allow these practical theories (which have not advanced much since the beginning of the century) to go forward a step, you must force yourself habitually to take account of their different tendencies and discover their unity. That is what Saint-Simon attempted. His undertaking must be renewed and in the same direction. His history can serve to show us the way.[29]

But Saint-Simon's thought contained an essential weakness: that he looked to 'industry' – that is, economic change – to supply the main remedy for the modern crisis. This emphasis was in turn transferred to subsequent branches of socialism, including that created by Marx. Marxist socialism, in common with all other forms, was a product of the social and economic changes set into motion in the late eighteenth and early nineteenth centuries in Western Europe. It was certainly a more 'scientific' type of socialism than other more idealistic strains in socialist thought – 'it has thus rendered social science more services perhaps than it received from it'[30] – but, however valid certain of its propositions and insights, its programme still rested upon a combination of purely economic measures. The principal thesis of *Capital* was that the 'anarchy of the market', characteristic of capitalism, would, under socialism, be replaced by a system in which production would be centrally regulated: 'In short, in Marxist socialism, capital does not disappear: it is merely administered by society and not by individuals.'[31] Marx's works thus conformed to what Durkheim took to be a central principle of socialism: namely that the productive capacity of society was to be regulated centrally. But while this might allow the overcoming of the 'forced' division of labour (*la division du travail contrainte*), it would do nothing to reduce the moral hiatus which derived from the anomic condition of modern industry. On the contrary, it would deepen it, since it would further elevate the importance of the 'economic' at the expense of the 'moral'.

Although this was not made explicit in *Socialism*, there can be no doubt that the theory of the division of labour was basic to the differentiation between 'communism' and 'socialism', as this was formulated by Durkheim.[32] Communist ideas, which had sprung up at many diverse periods of history, advanced the notion that private property was the essential source of all social evils and that therefore the accumulation of material wealth had to be subject to severe restrictions. According to communist theory, the political sphere had to be strictly separated from the potentially corrupting influence of economic production. Socialism, on the other hand, which had only come into being with the social and economic transformations of the late eighteenth century, was founded upon the view that the progress of human welfare depended upon the expansion of industry. The main principle involved in socialism was exactly contrary to that proposed in communist theory: socialism advocated the fusion of the political and the economic. Socialism claimed, not simply that production should be *controlled* by the state, but that the role of the state should be defined in economic terms: that is, that the 'administration of things' should replace the 'administration of men'. Whereas, therefore, the aim of communism was the regulation of consumption, that of socialism was the regulation of production.[33] Thus communism, in Durkheim's understanding of the term, was a form of political protest and theory which corresponded to societies having a low division of labour. Everyone worked in a like fashion, as a separate producer, and there was not a large measure of economic interdependence; consequently, the conception of the regulation of *production* could not emerge. In the ideal society envisaged by communism, 'There is no common rule which determines relationships among the different workers, or the manner in which all these diverse activities should cooperate for collective goals. As each one does the same thing – or almost the same – there is no cooperation to regulate.'[34] The appearance of socialism, on the other hand, was only possible with the development of a differentiated division of labour, since it presupposed the idea of a (co-ordinated) economy of interdependent producers.

Durkheim's proposals for the revival of occupational associations (*corporations*), within the general framework of the state, had definite affinities with the solidarism of the Radical Socialists, and more broadly with the traditions of corporatism which intertwined with socialism in the history of French political theory. But it would be mistaken to suppose that Durkheim developed these ideas in close and direct relation to the political interests of the solidarists, although his views did exert some considerable degree of influence over a number of major contemporary figures associated with the movement. The solidarists advocated a programme of state intervention in economic affairs which was roughly comparable to that proposed by the *Kathedersozialisten* in Germany. Durkheim made the acquaintance of the writings of the 'older generation' of the *Kathedersozialisten* at an early stage in his career, while studying in Germany in 1885–6. He was especially impressed with what he perceived in the writings of Schmoller, Wagner and others as an attempt to break away from utilitarianism in political and social theory. They showed that, in utilitarian theory, 'the collective interest is only a form of personal interest', and 'altruism is merely a concealed egoism.'[35] Neither society nor the state could be understood except as moral agencies: no society existed where economic relationships were not controlled by the regulative force of custom and law. Thus measures involving state intervention in economic life had to be clothed in a moral and legal framework. The emphasis upon the moral role of the modern state, which was the ultimate guarantor of just contractual relations, found a place in *The Division of Labour*: 'There is, above all, an agency upon which we are tending to become increasingly dependent: this is the state. The points at which we are in contact with it multiply as do the occasions when it is entrusted with the duty of reminding us of the sentiment of common solidarity.'[36] The first edition of *The Division of Labour* already contained a fragmentary analysis of the role of the occupational associations.[37] But a much fuller exposition was given in the preface to the second edition of the book in 1902. The connections are clear between Durkheim's call for an expansion of the functions of the occupational associations, and the analysis of the anomic division of labour contained in the work. The occupational system was in an anomic condition in so far as moral regulation was absent at the 'nodal' points of the divisions of labour – the points of 'intermesh' between the different occupational strata. The main function of the occupational associations was to provide the appropriate moral co-ordination at these points, and thus to promote the operation of organic solidarity.

Durkheim's ideas on the role of the occupational associations, which he worked out in detail in the latter part of the 1890s, were formulated in close relationship to the development of his thinking on the state. While *The Division of Labour* allowed Durkheim to elucidate some of the major problems, as he perceived them, in the legacy of Saint-Simon and Comte, it left aside the problem of the state as a system of political power. The work simply assumed an inverse correlation between the advance of the division of labour and the diminishing of state absolutism: 'the place of the individual becomes greater and the governmental power becomes *less absolute*.'[38] But Durkheim later came to see this position as an oversimplified one, which failed to come to terms with some of the central issues which the social philosophy of the late eighteenth and early nineteenth centuries had left unresolved. The tradition of French thought on the matter, which Durkheim saw as coming primarily from Rousseau,[39] failed to examine the institutions which mediated between the state and the individual. If the state directly represented the 'will of the people', then it tended to become 'merely a carbon-copy of the life underlying it. It does no more than translate what individuals think and feel, in a different notation.' It was precisely this situation which had characterized French political history throughout the nineteenth century, and it explained the alternating phases of revolution and absolutist dictatorship through which the French polity had passed. 'The state does not move of its own power, it has to follow in the wake of the obscure sentiments of the multitude. At the same time, however, the powerful means of action it possesses makes it capable of exerting a heavy repression over the same individuals whose servant, otherwise, it still remains.'[40] In these conditions it seemed as though all was change. But this was only superficial: the bewildering flux of events on the political level masked a deep stagnation in the rest of society. A democratic order, therefore, which was capable of implementing the ideals comprised in the 'cult of the individual', had to depart from the contemporary form of the French political system. The 'paradox', which Rousseau 'wrestled with in vain', of the fact that the state had to rest upon common moral sentiments and yet play an active part in promoting genuine social change, could be resolved if the occupational associations were given an intermediary role in the electoral system. Durkheim thus proposed that the regionally based electoral system should be abandoned, arguing that regional differences in culture and interests were becoming increasingly eradicated by the advance of industrialization. The main contemporary differences stemmed from the diversification of the division of labour, and these were not bound to regional variations:

> nowadays, the links that bind each one of us to a particular spot in an area where we live are extremely weak and can be broken with the greatest ease . . . Professional life, on the other hand, takes on increasing importance, as labour goes on splitting up into divisions. There is therefore reason to believe that it is this professional life that is destined to form the basis of our political structure. The idea is already gaining ground that the professional association is the true electoral unit, and because the links attaching us to one another derive from our calling rather than from any regional bonds of loyalty, it is natural that the political structure should reflect the way in which we ourselves form into groups of our own accord.[41]

Durkheim's portrayal of the moral character of the state, and his version of democratic republicanism, gave minimal importance to the external relationships of the modern nation-state. Although Durkheim rejected Spencer's contention that industrial society necessarily tended to be pacific in character, he none the less emphasized that there was no intrinsic incompatibility between the republican state and the progress of international harmony. The ideals of moral individualism, at their most abstract level, referred not to the citizens of any particular nation, but to humanity in general. Consequently, it was probable that the future would see an evolution towards the decline of national differences, and that the expansion of the division of labour in the international context would eventually lead to the formation of a supra-national community. At the time of the writing of *The Division of Labour*, Durkheim thought he discerned a definite movement towards the creation of a European community, quoting Sorel in order to substantiate this judgement.[42] This optimistic perspective, of course, contrasted sharply with the subsequent deterioration of the relationships between the major powers which culminated in World War I. Although Durkheim, together with most other intellectuals of his generation, experienced the outbreak of the war with a profound sense of tragedy and shock, he did not abandon the notion that it 'is the tendency of patriotism to become, as it were, a fragment of world patriotism'.[43] This was made clear in the various patriotic pamphlets which Durkheim wrote during the war.[44] These have often been dismissed as mere exercises in propaganda, but in fact they stand in close relationship to his theory of the state. The main point in the most important of Durkheim's wartime publications, *L'Allemagne au-dessus de tout*, was that German militarism rested upon a 'pathological' form of mentality which was a kind of 'collective anomie'. This phenomenon resulted from 'a certain manner of conceiving the state, its nature and its role',[45] which Durkheim found to be expressed in a clearly defined way in the thought of Treitschke. Treitschke, according to Durkheim, was not an original thinker, but a writer whose works represented the ideas and sentiments of the collectivity, and thus contained 'all the principles which German diplomacy and the German state has daily put into practice'.[46]

For Treitschke the state was the highest value, could accept no limits to its power, and had ultimately to pursue its aims by warfare: constant struggle between nation-states was an inevitable characteristic of the modern world. According to his conception, the power of the state was the criterion in terms of which all other values were to be judged; but the state itself was not a moral entity. This was a 'pathological' form of national patriotism, in Durkheim's analysis, because it treated the state purely as a system of power, which recognized no intrinsic limits to its hegemony. But, as in the case of the individual, the state could not exist as an amoral being which acknowledged no constraints upon the expansion of its ambitions. Treitschke's conception of the state was based upon a fallacious view of the relationship between state and society. According to him, 'there is a difference in nature . . . between the individual and the state.'[47] This was a standpoint which perpetuated the Hegelian notion of the state as existing on an utterly different plane from that of life in civil society, and which readily served to legitimize an autocratic tyranny. To admit the sovereignty of the state, internally and in external relations, Durkheim concluded, did not at all entail acceptance of such a view: the sovereignty of the state was 'relative', both to the internal moral structure of civil society – 'a multitude of moral forces which, although not possessing a rigorous juridical form and organization, are none the less real and efficacious' – and to the morals of international relations, 'the attitudes of foreign peoples'.[48] Although German imperialism had to be defeated militarily, it was by its very nature an unstable phenomenon, and was incompatible with the moralization of international relations which characterized the modern world: 'There is no state which is not incorporated into the broader *milieu* formed by the totality of other states, that is to say, which is not part of the great human community.'[49]

Examination of Durkheim's writings on the growth of moral individualism, socialism and the state, in the context of the social and political issues which he saw as confronting the Third Republic, shows how mistaken it is to regard him as being primarily conservative in his intellectual standpoint. The advocates of this view[50] have recognized Durkheim's liberalism in politics, but have sought to show that the most important intellectual themes of his sociology were derived from those traditions of French social philosophy (especially the so called 'counter-reaction' to the French Revolution) which emphasized cohesion rather than conflict, order rather than change, and authority rather than freedom. 'Conservatism' here means, in Coser's words, 'an inclination to maintain the existing order of things or to re-enforce an order which seems threatened'.[51] As a description of Durkheim's concerns, however, this is quite one-sided. Not the defence of the 'order' against change, but the objective of *achieving* change was what Durkheim sought to promote. The point is that France in the first two-thirds of the nineteenth century, while manifesting various periods of apparently rapid political 'change', in fact remained basically stable: the socio-economic transformations necessary to further the transition to a modern industrial order had not been realized.

The structure and substance of Durkheim's political sociology

The formula which identifies Durkheim with a conservative intellectual standpoint has been reinforced by the view which holds that his thought was radically modified in the course of his career: for the interpretation which minimizes the importance of *The Division of Labour* in his writings also serves to underplay the significance which he attributed to the historical element in sociology.[52] Durkheim always stressed that 'history is not only the natural framework of human life; man is a product of history.'[53] This emphasis gives a clear continuity to his life's work, within the evolutionary scheme set out in *The Division of Labour*. But the 'orthodox' viewpoint of the development of Durkheim's thought places most weight upon Durkheim's functionalism, conceived in terms of an abstract and ahistorical relationship between the individual and society. In these terms the leading theorem in Durkheim's sociology appears to be the need for a *consensus omnium* in society, to counter the Hobbesian 'war of all against all' which constantly threatens to destroy social order. If, however, the whole of Durkheim's writings is seen in terms of the historical framework of the movement from mechanical to organic solidarity, the resultant picture is quite different: a guiding theme of Durkheim's work is the depth of the *contrast* between traditional forms of society and the modern social order. This contrast, according to Durkheim, had not been adequately understood by those forms of social theory which, in the earlier part of the nineteenth century, had grasped the significance of the fact that the traditional order had gone forever. Both utilitarians and socialists had mistakenly proceeded by separating the 'moral' character of traditional society from the 'economic' basis of the modern type. The crucial problem facing sociology was that of defining what were the social forms capable of realizing the ideals of freedom and equality generated by the transition from the traditional order. The dilemma which Durkheim faced, and which was clarified – but not fully resolved – in *The Division of Labour*, stemmed, therefore, from his conviction that, while 'the defenders of the old economic theories are mistaken in thinking that regulation is not necessary today', 'the apologists of the institution of religion are wrong in believing that yesterday's regulation can be useful today.'[54] The work which Durkheim undertook on primitive religion, culminating in *The Elementary Forms of the Religious Life*, allowed the solution of this dilemma in terms of a more elaborate theory of authority. The functional theory of religion advanced in *The Elementary Forms* has to be understood in relation to Durkheim's explicit statement that,

> the importance we thus attribute to the sociology of religion does not in the least imply that religion must play the same role in present-day societies that it has played at other times. In a sense, the contrary conclusion would be more sound. Precisely because religion is a primordial phenomenon, it must yield more and more to the new social forms it has engendered.[55]

What *The Elementary Forms* demonstrated was not that 'religion creates society',[56] but that the collective representations embodied in religion were the expression of the *self-creation* of human society. The force of religiosity was thus a symbolic consciousness of the capabilities of human society to dominate and to change the world. Read as a *genetic*, and not simply as a functional theory, *The Elementary Forms* provided the foundation for an understanding of the processes which had led to the emergence of moral individualism. As Max Weber demonstrated in a different context, the advance of rationalistic individualism was grounded in the 'irrationalism' of sacred symbols: all forms of thought, including science, had their origins in religious representations. In an important but neglected work,[57] Durkheim detailed some of the elements of this process in the history of the European societies. Christianity in general, and Protestantism in particular, were the proximate source of the ideals which later became transferred to the political sphere in the French Revolution. The Christian ethic, Durkheim sought to show, broke in a radical way with the pagan religions of Rome, by focusing its emphasis upon the 'internal' state of the soul, rather than upon the 'external' world of nature. For the Christian, 'virtue and piety do not consist in material procedures, but in interior states of the soul'; of the 'two possible poles of all thought, nature on the one hand, and man on the other', it is 'around the second that the thought of the Christian societies has come to gravitate.'[58]

Clarification of the origins and nature of moral individualism made possible for Durkheim a clear elucidation of the differences between 'individualism' and 'egoism' – differences which, although already fundamental in *The Division of Labour* and *Suicide*, remained in some degree ambiguous until after 1895. The theory which was subsequently set out in *The Elementary Forms* was organized in terms of a duality between the 'sacred' and the 'profane' which cross-cut the more conventional distinction between the 'sacred' and the 'secular'. Any ideal which was a collective product had, *ipso facto*, a sacred character in these terms, and hence possessed the twin aspects of all morality: it was 'as if surrounded by a mysterious barrier which keeps violators at arm's length'[59] – that is, imbued people with positive sentiments of respect and commitment – and it carried a sense of duty or obligation. It followed that the process of 'secularization' (meaning by this the decline of traditional deism), although a progressive trend within modern societies, did not mean the disappearance of the 'sacred': on the contrary, human freedom from the repressive moral controls of former times was dependent upon the continuing 'sacred' quality of the ideals which comprised moral individualism. Freedom could not, however, be identified with the liberation from all moral controls (as utilitarians and socialists asserted); acceptance of the moral regulation of the 'cult of the personality' was the *condition* of freedom:

> rights and liberties are not things inherent in man as such. . . Society has consecrated the individual and made him pre-eminently worthy of respect. His progressive emancipation does not imply   a weakening but a transformation of the social bonds . . . For man freedom consists in the deliverance from blind, unthinking physical forces; this he achieves by opposing against them the great and intelligent force which is society, under whose protection he shelters.[60]

There is in Durkheim's writings no yearning for a former age, no wistful search for the revitalization of the stability of the past. There can be no reversion to the social forms of earlier types of society, and neither, in Durkheim's eyes, would this be a desirable prospect if it were possible. In traditional society people were subject to the tyranny of the group: individuality was subordinated to the pressure of the *conscience collective*. The expansion of the division of labour, and the weakening of the *conscience collective*, were the agencies of the escape from this tyranny; but the dissolution of the old moral order threatened the individual with another tyranny, that of his or her own inexhaustible desires. An individual could only be free if he or she were an autonomous actor, capable of mastering and of realizing his or her impulses.[61] The distinctions between 'anomie', and 'egoism' and 'individualism', were thus of key importance. The sort of modern social order represented by the utilitarians and socialists was one built upon the supposed mutuality of individual egoisms. But no form of society, traditional or modern, could exist on this basis. The common error of these authors, therefore, was to assimilate 'egoism' and 'individualism': these derived from essentially different sources. Moral individualism was a product of human society, the outcome of a very long period of social evolution. Egoism, on the other hand, was anchored in the needs and desires of the pre-social individual. This opposition between the egoistic inclinations of the individual and the moral products of society, according to Durkheim, was expressed in religious thought in the distinction between the body and the soul. The body was the source of sensation, and of appetites which were 'necessarily egoistic';[62] the soul, by contrast, was a primitive representation of the concepts and moral rules which were created by society. The child began life as an egoistic being, whose needs were defined purely in terms of personal sensory wants. These became overlaid with modes of thought and moral ideals which were taken from society: the developed individual always had an egoistic side to his or her personality, at the same time as he or she was a social being.

If 'individualism' was to be separated from 'egoism', it was also to be carefully distinguished from 'anomie'. While a (hypothetical) society formed out of the conjunction of individual egoisms would be one of moral anarchy or anomie, such was not at all the case in a society founded upon moral individualism within a differentiated division of labour. On the contrary, the condition of anomie which prevailed within certain sectors of contemporary societies derived from the *lack* of institutionalization of individualism – as Durkheim made clear in his reply to Brunetière during

the course of the Dreyfus affair. This institutionalization, according to the premises established in *The Division of Labour*, had to
involve the formation of integrating links between the political
and economic orders: the progression towards a more just distribution of functions (that is, the elimination of the forced division
of labour) under the general guidance of the state and the moralization of economic relationships through the occupational
associations. There were, therefore, the closest of ties between
Durkheim's theory of moral authority and his analysis of the
modern political system.

The conception of the 'political', Durkheim pointed out, was
one which had only come into being with the development of the
modern form of society, since it presupposed a differentiation
between government and the governed which did not exist in
more primitive societal types. A 'political society' for Durkheim,
however, was not to be defined purely in terms of the existence of
constituted authority in a grouping: a family, for example, was not
a political society, even though it might possess an individual or
group in authority, such as a patriarch or a council of elders. An
additional criterion was necessary. This was not to be found in
the characteristic of the fixed territorial area; unlike Weber,
Durkheim rejected this as of critical importance. Rather it was to
be discerned in the degree of complexity in social organization: a
political society was one which manifested a clear-cut authority
division, but which was composed of a plurality of kinship groups,
or of larger secondary groups. A political society did not necessarily possess a state: a 'state', in Durkheim's terminology, referred
to an administrative staff or officialdom which was formally entrusted with the function of government.[63]

According to the thesis of *The Division of Labour*, the development of society towards increasing internal differentiation produced the progressive emancipation of individual thought and
action from subordination to the *conscience collective*. *Prima facie*
this would appear to lead to a paradox: for if the growth in the
division of labour was associated with the expansion of the self-
determination of the individual, it also went hand in hand with a
widening of the powers of the state to subject the individual to its
authority. In fact this was no paradox, because it was the state
which, in the modern type of society, was the institution which was
concerned with the implementation and the furtherance of indi-

vidual rights. In *The Division of Labour*, just as he saw a direct correlation between the advance of social differentiation and the development of the state, Durkheim also conceived of a direct relationship between the growth of the division of labour and the decline of coercive sanctions.

> Similarity between individuals gives rise to juridical rules which, with the threat of repressive measures, impose uniform beliefs and practices upon all ... The division of labour produces juridical rules which determine the nature and the relations of divided functions, but whose violation calls forth only restrictive measures without any expiatory character.[64]

Later Durkheim came to see that 'kinds of society should not be confused with different types of states',[65] and that the coercive powers possessed by the state apparatus could vary in some degree independently of the level of the development of the division of labour. In *Deux lois de l'évolution pénale*,[66] written at the turn of the century, Durkheim presented a systematic and cogent analysis of the implications of this position. The coercive sanctions which had existed in different types of society could be classified along two partially independent dimensions: the 'quantitative' and the 'qualitative'. The first referred to the intensity of punishment for deviation from a norm or a law, the second to the modality of punishment (that is, death versus imprisonment, for example). The intensity of sanctions varied in relation not only to the level of development of the division of labour, but also to the centralization of political power. We could thus establish a 'law of quantitative variation', which held that, 'The intensity of punishment is greater to the degree that a society belongs to a less advanced type, and that the central power is of a more absolute character.'[67]

There was, according to Durkheim, an intrinsic connection between how far 'all of the directive functions of society [are] in the same hands', and the degree of absolute power wielded by government. What determined the existence, or otherwise, of absolutism was not, as Spencer held, the number of functions exercised by the state, but how far there were other sources of institutional power which could act as a counterweight to that possessed by the state.[68] It followed from this – and Durkheim made this one of the cornerstones of his exposition of the nature of democratic government –

that the extension of the directive influence of the state, which was
a 'normal' characteristic of contemporary societies, did not in
itself lead to a growth in state absolutism. Conversely, it did not
follow that, where the state only had a relatively limited range of
operations, it could not be absolute in character: indeed, this was
often the case. It was not the degree of absolutism of state power,
but the range of activities engaged in by the state, which varied
directly with the division of labour:

> for the degree of development of the regulative organ simply
> reflects the development of collective life in general in the same
> way as the dimensions of the nervous system of the individual
> differ according to the importance of organic connections. The
> directive functions of society are thus only rudimentary when
> other social functions are of the same nature; and the relation
> between the two hence remains the same ... Nothing is simpler
> than the government of certain primitive kingdoms; nothing is
> more absolute.[69]

Thus as society moved towards increasing complexity, there
was not necessarily a decline in the repressive character of punishment: if this was accomplished, as it might be, by a heightening of
state absolutism, it would cancel out the effects of the expansion
of the division of labour. The relationship between societal and
political development was a complex one.

The 'law of quantitative variation' referred only to the intensity
of punitive sanctions. This was complemented by a 'law of qualitative variation', concerning modalities of punishment: this law
stated that there was a direct relationship between the level of
societal development and the use of deprivation of liberty as a
mode of punishment. Imprisonment for criminal activity was almost unknown in primitive societies; and it was only among the
peoples of Western Europe (since the latter part of the eighteenth
century) that it had become the primary type of sanction. Such a
development happened in the following way. Imprisonment was
absent from the penal system of the less developed societies because responsibility was collective: when a crime was committed,
the demand for reparation fell not upon the culpable individual,
but upon the whole clan group. But with the development of more
complex forms of society, and the increasing emergence of organic
solidarity founded upon co-operative interdependence in the div-

ision of labour, responsibility became individualized, and the concept of punishment of the individual through imprisonment made its appearance.

The most important point of this analysis was that, while maintaining the basic standpoint of *The Division of Labour*, it faced squarely the previously neglected problem of political power, and more specifically the problem of coercive power, in society. The theme, so strongly developed in *The Division of Labour*, that the tyranny of the *conscience collective*, through the growth of organic solidarity, was gradually dissolved in favour of a co-operative order, was affirmed: the 'normal' tendency of the advancing complexity of society was both to produce a decline in the intensity of coercive sanctions, and to 'individualize' punishment through imprisonment. But the nature of political power in a given form of society could not simply be treated as a 'consequence' of changes on the level of 'infrastructure'. The discussion in *Deux lois de l'évolution pénale* makes abundantly clear how far Durkheim was, in his insistence upon the continuing relevance of the 'sacred' in contemporary society, from minimizing the contrast between traditional religion and the moral character of the modern order. For what gave rise to the heavy dominance, in the less developed forms of society, of repressive sanctions was the fact that crime was interpreted as an offence against the collectivity, and therefore as a *religious* transgression. It was crime against strongly held collective values, against 'transcendent beings', and 'the same act which, when it concerns an equal, is simply disapproved of, becomes blasphemous when it relates to someone who is superior to us; the horror which it stimulates can only be assuaged by violent repression.' This 'religious' quality was appropriated by the absolutist state, and was what enabled it to legitimate the use of coercive power: offences against the state were treated as 'sacrilege, and hence, to be violently repressed'.[11]

If the political structure of society was not, at least in any simple manner, 'determined' by the level of complexity of the division of labour, then the status of democratic republicanism in the modern social order was, in an important sense, problematic. What were the conditions which provided for the implementation of a democratic political order? Durkheim's answer to this question effected a neat tie with his treatment of the role of the occupational associations in the division of labour. The state became absolutist to

the degree to which secondary groupings, which intervened between the state and the individual, were not strongly developed: in
modern society, these groupings were the occupational associations. The family, Durkheim argued, was of declining significance
in this respect, and had to cede place to the *corps intermédiaires*,
the occupational associations. He rejected the traditional theory
of democracy, according to which the mass of the population
'participated' in the exercise of government. For Durkheim, this
was a situation which was only possible in a society which, according to his own definition, was not a 'political' society. Such a
conception of democracy could not be sustained:

> We must therefore not say that democracy is the political form of
> a society governing itself, in which the government is spread
> throughout the *milieu* of the nation. Such a definition is a contradic-
> tion in terms. It would be almost as if we said that democracy is a
> political society without a state. In fact, the state is nothing if it is
> not an organ distinct from the rest of society. If the state is every-
> where, it is nowhere. The state comes into existence by a process of
> concentration that detaches a certain group of individuals from the
> collective mass . . . If everyone is to govern, it means in fact that
> there is no government . . . If we agree to reserve the name democ-
> racy for political societies, it must not be applied to tribes without
> definite form, which thus far have no claim to being a state and are
> not political societies.[71]

Government, by definition, had to be exercised by a minority of
individuals. 'Democracy', therefore, had to concern the relationship between the differentiated political agency, or the state, and
the other institutional structures of society: more specifically, according to Durkheim, how far there was an interplay of communication between state and society. Where the citizens were
regularly informed of the activities of the state, and the latter in
turn was aware of the sentiments and wishes of all sectors of the
population, then a democratic order existed. A democratic system
thus presupposed a balance between two opposed tendencies: on
the one hand, that in which the state directly reflected the 'general
will', and on the other that in which the absolutist state, 'closed in
upon itself', was cut off from the people. Each of these conditions
tended to inhibit the effective occurrence of social change. As has
been indicated previously, the first, in Durkheim's view, produced

a situation in which only superficial change could take place. In the second case, although it might appear as though the political power wielded by the state would allow the possibility of bringing about radical social transformation, this was not in fact the case: such states 'are indeed all-powerful against the individual and this is what the term "absolute" means, as applied to them . . . But against the social condition itself, against the structure of society, they are relatively powerless.'[72] In a democratic order, however, the pace of change could be advanced, because the conduct of social life assumed a more 'conscious' and 'controllable' character. Democratic government made it possible for many aspects of social organization previously dominated by unthinking custom or habit to become open to effective intervention on the part of the state. In a democratic order, the state did not simply express the sentiments held in a diffuse fashion among the population, but was often the origin of new ideas: it led society as well as being led by it. The extension of the activities of the state, whereby it penetrated into many spheres of society formerly controlled by custom or tradition – in the administration of justice, in economic life, in science and the arts – was therefore certainly not to be identified as necessarily leading to the autocratic domination of state over society. On the contrary, it was just this phenomenon which permitted the active interplay between the 'government consciousness' and the views and feelings of the mass. A democracy, therefore, had two major characteristics: the existence of close, and two-way, communication between government and governed; and the increasing extension of the contacts and ties of the state with other sectors of the society. But these characteristics did not imply that the state 'merged' with society. Rather, they presupposed the existence of a differentiated political agency: this was what saved a society from being the 'victim of traditional routine'.[73]

The occupational associations played a vital role in both of these respects. Since they were the intermediaries between the state and the individual, they were a principal medium whereby the expanding range of activities of the state were channelled to the rest of society, and they also thereby facilitated communication between the state and the less organized levels of the society. It was thus the occupational associations which were most important for checking two different ways in which democracy

could be undermined: the emergence of an autocratic state, separated from the people, and the 'absorption' of the state by the
society. This was why it was desirable that the occupational associations should intervene in the electoral process between electorate and government: 'These secondary groups are essential if the
state is not to oppress the individual: they are also necessary if the
state is to be sufficiently free of the individual . . . They liberate
the two confronting forces, whilst linking them at the same time.'[74]
In this analysis, even if it was partly latent, there was a theory of
bureaucracy. A bureaucratic state, in which officialdom possessed
the real power – and thereby, through adherence to bureaucratic
routine, effectively promoted the maintenance of the *status quo* –
was more likely to arise where the state was weak than where it
was strong. In an absolutist state, although the officialdom might
be used as the instrument of the domination of a ruler or an
oligarchy, it was not the officials who dominated. But, as in
France, where the state tended to become 'absorbed', this situation of apparent 'democracy' actually concealed a bureaucratic
domination. In modern societies, where the hold of traditional
customs and beliefs had been largely dissolved, there were many
avenues for the display of critical spirit, and changes of opinion
and mood among the mass of the population were frequent.
Where government simply 'reflected' this, the outcome was a
constant vacillation in the political sphere, and because of this
dearth of active leadership, power devolved upon the officialdom:
'Only the administrative machine has kept its stability and goes on
operating with the same automatic regularity.'[75]

A democratic society therefore, according to Durkheim, was a
society which was 'conscious of itself'. On analogy with an organism, one could say, as Durkheim frequently did, that the state was
the 'brain' – the conscious, directive centre – which operated, via
the intermediary organs, within the complex nervous system of a
differentiated society. Thus a democratic order enjoyed the same
relative superiority over other societies as the self-conscious being
did over an animal whose behaviour was unreflective or instinctive. Durkheim placed considerable emphasis upon the 'cognitive'
as opposed to the 'active' significance of the state. In particular,
the state made articulate and furthered the moral aims and sentiments embodied in the diffuse *conscience collective*.[76] This is important to the understanding of Durkheim's conception of moral

authority as it existed in modern societies. The state within a democratic polity was the main agency which actively implemented the values of moral individualism; it was the institutional form which replaced that of the church in traditional types of society. But only when it tended towards absolutism did the moral authority of the state approach that characteristic of earlier societal types, in which the individual, 'absorbed, as he was, into the mass of society . . . meekly gave way to its pressures and subordinated his own lot to the destinies of collective existence without any sense of sacrifice'.[77] The specific role of the democratic state was not to subordinate the individual to itself, but in fact to provide for his or her self-realization. This was not something which could occur (as was held in the theories of the utilitarians and socialists) when the operations of the state were kept to a *minimum*. The self-realization of the individual could only take place in and through his or her membership of a society in which the state guaranteed and advanced the rights embodied in moral individualism.

Of course, for Durkheim, discipline, in the sense of the control of egoism, was an essential characteristic of all moral authority. But, according to his analysis, the view which equated discipline *inherently* with the limitation of human self-realization was fallacious. All forms of life-organization, both biological and social, were controlled by defined, regular principles; by this very fact the mere existence of any type of society presupposed the regulation of behaviour according to moral rules. Certainly the moral authority characteristic of traditional forms of society, or of autocratic states, was inherently repressive, denying any great range of possibilities of self-development to the individual; but the moral regulation of the modern society and state was the very condition of the individual's self-realization, and his or her freedom. Durkheim's theory of moral authority is thus far from being the rationale for authoritarianism which it is often portrayed as. The misinterpretation which presents Durkheim's conception of moral authority in this way again originates in the failure to inject an historical element into his analysis, and from the supposition that there are close parallels between Durkheim's position and that of Hobbes on the relationship between the individual and society in the modern order. According to this view, Durkheim's theory of moral authority rests upon the premise that the individual is 'naturally' a refractory being, and so must be rigidly restrained by society. In fact, however, Durkheim criticized Hobbes on precisely this point. Hobbes's error was to stand outside of history, by positing a 'state of nature', and thereby to assume that there was a 'break in continuity between the individual and society': this resulted in the notion that 'man is thus naturally refractory to the common life; he can only resign himself to it when forced.'[78]

In Durkheim's theory, even the category of 'egoism' was historical in nature. Egoism was certainly anchored in the biological or 'pre-social' needs and sensations of the individual organism; but these organic needs of the infant became overlaid with other motivations. Egoism and moral individualism, Durkheim constantly stressed, derived from inherently opposed sources: the one from the appetites of the organism, the other from the collective activity of the group. But, while opposed in origin, and thus always potentially in tension with each other, the growth of moral individualism nevertheless acted to expand the range of egoistic inclinations. This was why, in modern society, egoism and anomie were intimately linked; this reflected the very advance in the variety of motives and sensibilities of individuals which was the outcome of a long process of social development. Egoism and anomie were not closely tied in a biologically 'given' fashion: the hypothetical savage in a pre-societal 'state of nature' would be an egoistic being, but not an anomic one, since his or her needs would be bound to biologically given limits – just as was the case with the infant.

'Our very egoism' was thus, according to Durkheim, 'in large part a product of society.' Moral individualism involved values which stressed the dignity and worth of the human individual *in abstracto*; and individuals applied these to themselves as well as to others, and hence became more sensitive both to the feelings and needs of others and to their own. 'Their griefs, like our own, are more readily intolerable to us. Our sympathy for them is not, accordingly, a mere extension of what we feel for ourselves. But both are effects of one cause and constituted by the same moral state.'[79] The characteristic problems facing the constitution of moral authority in the modern age derived from this confrontation of egoism and moral individualism, from the fact that 'it is wholly improbable that there will ever be an era in which man is required to resist himself to a lesser degree, an era in which he can live a life that is easier and less full of tension', and that 'all evidence compels us to expect our effort in the struggle between the two beings within us to increase with the growth of civilization.'[80] These were problems of a pluralistic society, in which the despotism of the moral authority of traditional types of social order had been broken. The moral authority characteristic of traditional societies, founded upon a poverty of individuality and repressive discipline, was wholly inappropriate in modern, highly differentiated society.

The critical evaluation of Durkheim's political thought

In this analysis I have stressed the central rôle of Durkheim's political thought in his sociology as a whole. Any attempt at a critical assessment of his political ideas must be placed within a broader evaluation of his writings in sociology and social philosophy. The 'orthodox' interpretation of Durkheim readily delivers him up to a number of apparently conclusive criticisms, such as that he emphasized the importance of cohesion or *consensus* in society to the almost total exclusion of conflict; that he failed to develop a theory of institutions, because he concentrated above all upon the relationship between society and the individual, neglecting intermediate structures; that he displayed a lack of concern with the role of political power, since he was overwhelmingly interested in the nature of moral ideals; and that 'he did not duly appreciate the import of social innovation and social change because he was preoccupied with social order and equilibrium.'[81] While each of these accusations contains an element of truth, none of them can be sustained in the sweeping fashion in which they are frequently made. Those who interpret Durkheim's work as being essentially concerned with a conservative 'inclination to maintain the existing order of things'[82] have inevitably tended to present a misleading picture of Durkheim's position on each of these dimensions.

Both in political temper and in sociological conviction, Durkheim was an opponent of revolutionary thought. Evolution, not revolution, provided the framework for his conception of social change: he frequently emphasized that significant change only took place through the cumulation of long-term processes of social development. His refusal to see in class conflict the mechanism which would generate a radical social transformation separated him conclusively from Marxism and from any other type of revolutionary activism. But to say this is not to say that he neglected the phenomenon of social conflict, or of class conflict, or that he sought to accommodate them to his theoretical position by denying the reality of the aspirations of the poor. His constantly echoed assertion that 'the social problem' (that is, the problem of class conflict) could not be solved through purely economic measures, because of the 'instability' of human appetites, has to be read against his equally emphatic stress upon the basic changes in the economic order which had to be made to complete the institutionalization of moral individualism. The reality behind the occurrence of class conflict was the new desire for self-realization and equality of opportunity of those in the lower socio-economic strata: this could not be denied, and demanded ultimately the abolition of all economic and social barriers to 'external equality', to 'everything that can even indirectly shackle the free unfolding of the social force that each carries in himself'.[83] Like Marx, Durkheim anticipated the emergence of a society in which class conflict would disappear, and where the element of coercion in the division of labour would evaporate. But this scheme did not at all absolve Durkheim from a concern with conflict. Indeed, the reverse is nearer to the truth: that the starting point of his sociology was an attempt to analyse the sources of the conflicts which have characterized the expansion of industrialism.

A profound transformation of the institutional organization of traditional forms of society was a necessary complement to the transition from mechanical to organic solidarity; the relationship between the state and the *corporations* was seen to be fundamental to the modern social order. It was in these terms that Durkheim sought to tackle the question of political power. Although it can hardly be said that he dealt satisfactorily with the nature and sources of political power, it is quite clearly not the case that he merely ignored the issues posed by it. Finally, as I have emphasized throughout, not only is it wrong to hold that 'he did not duly appreciate the import of social innovation and social change', but it is not possible to understand the main themes in his work without locating it within the scheme of social development, set out in *The Division of Labour*, which underlay all of his major writings. In one of his earliest works, a dissertation on Montesquieu, Durkheim established his position on this point. Montesquieu, he showed, 'fails to see that every society embodies conflicting factors, simply because it has gradually emerged from a past form and is tending towards a future one'.[84]

Durkheim frequently asserted that sociology should, at some point, find its justification in practice: that a sociology which had no relevance to practical problems would be a worthless endeavour. It was one of the major tasks of sociology to determine the nascent directions of change which a society at any given time was experiencing, and to show which trends 'should' be fostered as the coming pattern of the future. This closure between the 'is' and the 'ought' Durkheim sought to achieve in terms of his distinction between the 'normal' and 'pathological', conceived on analogy with health and disease in the organism. The theory set out in *The Division of Labour* was founded upon this conception: the work was conceived by Durkheim to show that the ideals of moral individualism corresponded to the 'social needs' engendered by the growth of mechanical solidarity – that these ideals were 'normal' to the modern type of society, and hence were to be protected and promoted. No aspect of Durkheim's writings has been more universally rejected than his notion of normality and pathology, and rightly so: even if it were possible to determine 'scientifically' whether or not a given moral norm were a 'necessary' element in the functioning of a particular society, it is altogether another thing to hold this *ipso facto* to be 'desirable'. The questions at issue here are not to be resolved by any sort of appeal to the criteria of health and disease in biology: medicine, in this respect, is a technology to be applied in pursuit of given values. In spite of – or perhaps because of – the fact that the conception of normality was integral to Durkheim's work, he never fully clarified his position in this respect. In his most systematic formulation of the principle, in *The Rules of Sociological Method*, he did attempt to establish scientific criteria for the verification of ethical ideals, rejecting the view that 'science can teach us nothing about what we ought to desire.'[85] But in replying later to critics of these views, he appeared to retract his earlier formulation, indicating that ethics and sociology were concerned with two 'different spheres', and claiming that 'we ask simply that ethical constructions should be preceded by a science of morality which is more methodical than the ordinary speculations of so-called theoretical ethics.'[86]

Durkheim's ambiguity on this matter is reflected in his failure to deal in an explicit manner with the relationship between sociological analysis and political intervention in the interests of securing practical social change. As Marx realized, this demands a dialectical conception of the character of knowledge as a means of knowing the world and at the same time as a mode of changing it. When pursued to its logical consequence, this leads to a stress upon the directly *political* role of sociology. But, although Durkheim wished to relate sociology to practical concerns, he also sought to advance a conception of the 'neutral' character of sociological analysis as a 'natural science of society'. Although this was no doubt reinforced by his personal characteristics and his disdain for the squabbles of party politics, his general aloofness from politics was certainly supported by this position. The result was that, in practice, the relevance of sociology to the achievement of real social change remained obscure. Durkheim attempted to escape from this difficulty by placing stress upon the 'partial' character of sociological knowledge: the emphasis that the advance of sociology was slow and painstaking, because it had to conform to the rigorous criteria of scientific validation. Since the needs of life in an everyday social and political context required immediate decisions and policies, the relevance of the 'scientific' knowledge of the sociologist had definite limitations. But his own writing, often dealing with the broadest issues of social organization and social change, belied this sort of modest prescription – as, indeed, did the more abstract analysis of the 'therapeutic' role of sociology in diagnosing what was 'normal' and what was 'pathological' at given stages of societal evolution.

In Durkheim's writings this uneasy tension between theory and practice finds expression in a constant tendency to shift from the analytical to the optative. Durkheim's discussions of extant reality frequently slide into a portrayal of what he expects to be the case in the future, because of what is supposedly entailed by the 'normal' conditions of functioning of a society or social institution. Thus the development and strengthening of the occupational associations was due to occur because this was demanded by the 'normal' operation of the division of labour. This analysis was not based upon an empirical demonstration that there was a discern-

ible trend towards the emergence of such *corporations*: it derived
from the attempt to implement the notion that the functionally
necessary supplied the criterion of what was desirable – in this
case, that 'the absence of all corporative institution creates ... a
void whose importance it is difficult to exaggerate.' As with all of
Durkheim's attempts to diagnose 'normality', this barely avoids
degenerating into crude teleology: the 'evil', the 'malady *totius
substantiæ*' of the anomic division of labour, calls into being the
'remedy' of the development of the *corporations*.[87]

The shortcomings of Durkheim's writings in these very general
respects are undoubtedly related to inadequacies in his conceptual
treatment of the state and political power. While it is not the case
that he 'ignored' the problem of power, or more specifically the
role of force, in society, it is true that he established the basic
framework of his thought, in *The Division of Labour*, before he
developed a systematic analysis of the state and politics. His subsequent exposition of the partial 'independence' of state power
only effected a restricted modification of the theory of the division
of labour. While this enabled him to deal more adequately with
the existence of coercive power it failed to deal with a really
consequential point: what were the *conditions* which generated
the development of an absolute state? The analyses given in
Leçons de sociologie and *Deux lois de l'évolution pénale* left this as
a residual factor: Durkheim nowhere undertook to show what
determined the degree to which the state was able to 'separate
itself' from society. He continually underlined the point that every
form of state, weak or strong, was rooted in civil society, and
nourished from it; but he failed to analyse in any detail at all the
nature of these connections. Consequently there is in Durkheim's
writings no systematic treatment of the mechanisms of legitimation in politics.[88] Political power was implicitly assumed to be an
outcome of a pre-established moral ascendancy of the state: the
more transcendent or 'religious' the moral basis of the state, the
more absolute its power. But this conception allows no means of
dealing with the tension between legitimation and power which is
of crucial importance in all political systems: power, and force, in
other words, are frequently *means* for the creation of values by
dominant strata.

In this Durkheim certainly remained a prisoner of the intellectual sources in which his thought was steeped. The concept
of the state which he employed is a clear indication of this, and

while he used it to attempt to break away from Comte's treatment of the state, his own conceptual formulation actually here resembled that of Comte. The state was defined as the 'organ of social thought', the 'ego' of the *conscience collective*. Durkheim specifically rejected the notion that the state was primarily an executive agency. The main task of the state was to be 'a special organ whose responsibility it is to work out certain representations which hold good for the collectivity'; the 'true meaning' of the state 'consists not in exterior action, in making changes, but in deliberation.'[89] His treatment of democracy, of course, is intimately tied in with this conceptualization. In analysing the role of the occupational associations, he certainly saw them as 'balancing' the power of the state. But the view that an essential element in democratic government was the sharing of power, as he made fully explicit, was to him not a viable one. He rejected not only the classical conception of 'direct democracy', but also what later came to be called the 'theory of democratic élitism'. A minority had to govern, in any developed society, and it made little odds how this minority came to power: the activities of an aristocracy might often conform more closely to the will of the people than that of an elected elite. The difference between a system in which 'the governing minority are established once and for all', and one in which 'the minority that carries the day may be beaten tomorrow and replaced by another' is only 'slight'.[90] Democracy, for Durkheim, thus becomes a matter of the interplay of sentiments and ideas between government and mass; his discussion of democratic government contains no developed examination of the functioning of political parties; or of parliament, or of the franchise, and indeed these considerations are regarded as of purely minor significance.

The weaknesses inherent in this viewpoint are nowhere more clearly exposed than in Durkheim's discussion of the German state in *L'Allemagne au-dessus de tout*. As has been indicated previously, the weight of Durkheim's theoretical perspective directed his thinking towards asserting the basic compatibility, in the modern world, between national ideals, patriotism, and the growth of a pan-national European community. Characteristically, his response to the growth of German militarism – since the latter fell outside the expectations generated by his standpoint – was to treat it as a 'pathological' phenomenon. This 'pathology' was explained by Durkheim as a 'moral disorder' manifest in a grandiosity of national ambition such as was revealed in the ideological writings of Treitschke. The effect of Durkheim's analysis, however, is to consider power *itself* only from the moral aspect, in terms of the immoderate emphasis which Treitschke placed upon the supremacy of the state. In point of fact, German militarism can only be properly interpreted in terms of the structural properties of the nineteenth-century German state – of the leading part played by Prussian military strength in securing the political unification of the country, and the continued domination of the landowning elite in government. These made Germany into a 'power-state', as Max Weber well understood, and it is, of course, no accident that Weber's conceptualization of the state, which eschewed any possibility of defining the state in moral terms, placed primacy upon just those aspects which Durkheim underplayed: the successful claim to monopoly of the legitimate deployment of force, and the existence of fixed territorial boundaries.[91]

Unlike Weber, Durkheim undeniably belongs to those traditions of nineteenth-century social thought which subordinate the state to society. While he rejected the notion of the 'disappearance' of the state, and held instead that an expansion of the purview of the state was inevitable in modern society, he did not substantially break with the assumption that it was the movement of the 'infrastructure' which was of decisive significance in analysing social change. 'Infrastructure' here, of course, refers to the division of labour. In assessing Durkheim's theory of the division of labour in relation to his political sociology, it is important to evaluate what he shared with socialism (as he defined it).

Although Parsons claimed that, according to his own definition of these terms, Durkheim's political sociology marks him out as being closer to 'communism' than to 'socialism',[92] it is surely evident that the reverse is true. Communism, for Durkheim, expressed the constantly reappearing, but ultimately futile, hope that human egoism could be eradicated: it was thus essentially both ahistorical and unrealizable. Socialism, on the other hand, according to Durkheim, was an expression of the consciousness that radical changes had occurred and were occurring in contemporary societies, and that these changes had brought about a condition of crisis which pressed for resolution. This consciousness was filtered by the social circumstances of which it was an expression. That is to say, it reflected a condition of society in which economic relationships had come to dominate social life; hence it assumed that the remedy for the modern crisis must be purely economic. The flaw in all socialist doctrines was that they failed to see that the resolution of the crisis must entail moral reorganization, whereby the primacy of the 'economic' over the 'social' would be readjusted in favour of the latter.[93] But they were correct in holding that regulation of the capitalist market was necessary. Although Durkheim rejected the possibility of reorganizing capitalism by revolutionary means, he did argue that the forced division of labour, the exploitative relationship of capital and wage-labour, had to be contested. This was to be accomplished by the disappearance of the inheritance of property:

> Now inheritance as an institution results in men being born rich or poor; that is to say, there are two main classes of society, linked by all sorts of intermediate classes: the one which in order to live has to make its services acceptable to the other at whatever the cost; the other class which can do without these services, because it can call upon certain resources . . . as long as such sharp class differences exist in society, fairly effective palliatives may lessen the injustices of contracts; but in principle, the system operates in conditions which do not allow of justice.[94]

The abolition of inherited property was a process which was to take place through the action of the state. Although Durkheim was not entirely unambiguous on this point, it seems that he did not envisage the abolition of private property as such,[95] but rather that differentials in possession of property should be entirely determined by differences in the services which individuals rendered to society. Functional importance in the division of labour was to govern property rights. This was a 'work of justice' which had to be accomplished if the morality of individualism was to have regulative force in modern society: the advance of moral individualism was incompatible with a social order in which class situation determined from birth an individual's position in the occupational structure. Thus there was an intrinsic connection between the elimination of the 'forced' division of labour and the overcoming of the 'anomic' division of labour. What was required in order to reduce anomie was not simply the imposition of regulation upon the existing market system: this would only lead to an intensification of class conflict. 'It is not sufficient that there be rules . . . for sometimes the rules themselves are the cause of evil.' The morality of organic solidarity demanded major economic changes, which created a system in which there was a free or 'spontaneous' ordering of individuals in the division of labour, such that no 'obstacle, of whatever nature, prevents them from occupying the place in the social framework which is compatible with their faculties'.[96]

Conclusion

Durkheim's sociology had its origins in an attempt to reinterpret the claims of political liberalism in the face of a twin challenge: from an anti-rationalist conservatism on the one hand, and from socialism on the other. Each of these constituted a major tradition in French social thought, and each of them, in the early part of the nineteenth century, represented a response to the legacy of the French Revolution. Durkheim borrowed elements from both in an attempt to transcend them through a revitalized liberal republicanism which would fully realize the structural changes in society which had been promised, but not achieved, by the Revolution. What has been remarked of Jaurès is an apt and exact description of Durkheim's viewpoint: he was concerned with, 'not the negation but the completion of the bourgeois Republic, the extension of the Rights of Man from the political to the economic and social spheres'.[97]

4 Durkheim and the Question of Individualism

During his lifetime, Durkheim's methodological writings were notoriously subject to controversy, and his 'sociologism' was widely condemned. These early critiques, often involving quite inaccurate versions of Durkheim's views, have long since ceded place to critical interpretations of Durkheim's writings which are founded upon a more adequate understanding of the themes and the dilemmas inherent in his sociology.[1] None the less, it is arguable that we still await a treatment which fully explores the strengths and weaknesses of Durkheim's method. One main reason for this is that most secondary interpreters of Durkheim have failed to connect his *analytical* discussion (and rejection) of individualism as a methodological approach to social theory with his *developmental* conception of the emergence of individualism as a morality brought into being by the growth of the differentiated division of labour. It is commonly accepted – and, indeed, he himself stressed this very strongly – that Durkheim's methodological ideas must be evaluated in relation to their concrete implementation in his more empirical works. But this is generally taken to mean showing how successfully or otherwise he 'applied' his methodological views in his other studies. I wish in this discussion to establish a reciprocal relationship between Durkheim's substantive discussion of the development of individualism and his abstract formulations of sociological method. Durkheim is often regarded as being fervently 'anti-individualist'. But in fact his works contain a vigorous defence of individualism – understood in a specific way. In other words, Durkheim's writings represent an attempt to detach 'liberal individualism', regarded as a conception of the characteristics of the modern social order, from 'methodological individualism'.

We must first of all try to specify the main senses in which the term 'individualism' appears in Durkheim's writings. In his very earliest works, such as his long review article devoted to a study of certain leading contemporary German thinkers,[2] he used the term indiscriminately to refer to any branch of social philosophy which accorded the 'individual' some sort of definite primacy over 'society' – whether in ethical terms (as in Kant) or in methodological terms (as in utilitarian philosophy). But he soon came to perceive more clearly that there was an essential difference between these two types of 'individualist' philosophy, and the elaboration of the precise nature of this difference became a dominant theme in his own sociological viewpoint. Whereas utilitarian individualism had to be rejected as a methodology – sociology could not be based upon a theory which treated the individual as a *starting point* of analysis – ethical or 'moral individualism' referred to a social process which was very important in modern society. The latter form, which Durkheim also frequently referred to as the 'cult of the individual', was created by society: it was this very fact which demonstrated the inadequacy of utilitarianism as a social theory, because what it took as its premise was actually the outcome of a long-term process of social development.

Durkheim's discussion of the origins and nature of moral individualism thus constitutes one major dimension of his attempt to meet the age-old question of the relationship between the individual and society. The general framework of this position was set out in *The Division of Labour in Society*, but it was substantially clarified in later writings.[3] The primary question which Durkheim set himself in the former work was as follows:

'How is it that, at the same time as the individual becomes more autonomous, he depends more closely on society? How can he be at the same time more individuated [*personnel*] and more solidary? For it is indisputable that these two developments, contradictory though it may appear, occur in a parallel way.'[4] The formulation of the problem has become famous; its resolution, however, has frequently been represented as ambiguous by those who have sought to render the substance of Durkheim's argument. For it has seemed as though, while mechanical solidarity refers to a *moral* attachment between the individual and society, organic solidarity refers to a purely economic relation – functional interdependence within the division of labour. Thus it appears as though it is only somewhere near the end of the work that Durkheim perceived that organic solidarity must have a moral underpinning in the same way as mechanical solidarity does, and hence that there is a crucial shift in his argument from the first to the concluding half of the book. But in Durkheim's eyes at least there was no such transition in his thinking in the work. Some years prior to the publication of *The Division of Labour*, Durkheim made just this point in criticizing Tönnies's differentiation of *Gemeinschaft und Gesellschaft*: that, while Tönnies recognized the moral basis of solidarity in traditional societies, his portrayal of *Gesellschaft* treated modern society in a way comparable to that of the utilitarians, as lacking the moral character of the traditional type. Where, then, is the main line of Durkheim's argument? It seems to be as follows. In mechanical solidarity each individual remained largely unconscious of his or her 'separateness' as an individual since, dominated by the *conscience collective*, he or she shared similar traits with the other members of society; the limits of his or her autonomy were strictly bounded. The strength of the moral integration of the *conscience collective* was directly related to the strength of the ties which attached the individual to the group: like a simple organism, such a society could shed individuals, and even whole segments of itself, without difficulty. The characteristic of organic solidarity, on the other hand, was that the attachment of the individual to the *conscience collective* was mediated by his or her ties to other groups: especially, of course, those created by occupational specialization in the division of labour. Durkheim was never in any doubt that these were moral ties – that is, that there was a 'non-contractual element' which governed the negotiation of contracts. The point is that this presupposed moral diversity rather than uniformity: the 'universal man' of traditional society was replaced by modern 'specialist man'. The greater autonomy which was not only allowed for, but thereby *demanded*, of the individual, however, did not detach him or her from society, but actually increased the strength of the reciprocal tie between them. The main issue which was not fully clarified in *The Division of Labour* is not the nature of organic solidarity itself, but the relationship between the 'morality of specialization' generated by organic solidarity, and the morality of the *conscience collective*, which became focused upon the 'cult of the individual'; because Durkheim made it clear that 'there will always remain, at the very least, this cult of the person, of individual dignity . . . which now has become the focal rallying-point for so many.'[5] What does this 'cult of the individual' refer to, and how is it compatible, as a general shared morality, with the moral specialization enjoined by organic solidarity?

While all the main elements of Durkheim's answer were present in *The Division of Labour*, he did not elaborate upon them fully until later, in the context of his subsequent appreciation of the intimate connections between religion and moral authority. In these later writings, three important characteristics of moral individualism were worked out in some detail: what was 'the individual' referred to in the 'cult of the individual'; why it was a 'cult'; and what was the ideological source from which that cult derived. 'The individual' who was the subject of the ideals embodied in moral individualism was not the concrete individual, the particular personality, but 'man' in general. The morality of the 'cult of the individual' was composed of those values given intellectual expression by the eighteenth-century philosophers and which inspired the French Revolution. These were values which emphasized the dignity and worth of 'man' in the abstract; as such, not only did they not derive from the 'egoism' of the utilitarians, but they were its direct opposite. Egoism is the pursuit of self-interest. But these values implied sentiments of sympathy for others and for human suffering.[6] Precisely because they were created by society, they had a religious quality – although, if Durkheim's definition of religion given in *The Elementary Forms* be strictly applied, it is by no means clear what corresponded to the 'church' in relation to the 'sacred' beliefs of moral individualism. Finally, it can be shown, as Durkheim indicated in *L'Evolution pédagogique en France*, that the ideals of moral individualism had their immediate origin in Protestantism, and were more generally founded upon conceptions common to all forms of Christianity.[7]

Understood in these terms, moral individualism was not merely compatible with the moral diversification of organic solidarity, but directly stimulated its development. Respect for the individual, and the concomitant demand for equality, became moral imperatives: as such, they implied that the welfare and self-fulfilment of every member of society should be sought after. Human life could no longer be contained within the narrow limits enforced in traditional society. Specialization of occupational function according to talent and capacity was the principal mode in which the (concrete) individual could realize him- or herself. Hence the emergence and strengthening of the 'cult of the individual' progressed hand in hand with the diversification of the division of labour. Now Durkheim's theory of moral authority held that *all* moral norms have two components: they commanded respect, and had a positive attraction; but they also had a 'dutiful' character, and were supported by sanctions against deviation. It did not follow from this, however, that the *form* of moral authority was everywhere the same. The moral authority of mechanical solidarity was repressive: the individual was subject to the 'tyranny of the group'. Human freedom, according to Durkheim, consisted in the autonomy of individual action. This was acquired not by the dissolution of moral codes, but by the transformations implicit in the development of moral individualism:

> Rights and . . . liberties are not things inherent in the nature of the individual as such. Analyse the given constitution of man, and you will find there no trace of the sacred character with which he is today invested and from which his rights are derived. He owes this character to society. It is society that has consecrated the individual, and made of him the thing to be respected above all. The progressive emancipation of the individual thus does not imply a weakening, but a transformation of the social bond.[8]

Durkheim's conception of anomie connected directly with each of the two types of 'individualism' distinguished above: in a positive sense, it provided an important reinforcement to his analysis of moral individualism; negatively it constituted a major aspect of his critique of utilitarian philosophy. The notion of anomie, as Durkheim employed it in his writings, appears at first sight to be fairly simple in form; further investigation of it, however, discloses various overlapping strands which entered into his formulation. As an element in his critical evaluation of utilitarianism, it rested first of all upon a set of empirical observations, which seem to have been the main basis of Durkheim's first appreciation of its significance.[9] These observations concerned the finding that there was no direct correlation and, under certain circumstances, an inverse correlation, between the growth of economic prosperity and the advance of human happiness. The evidence from the analysis of suicide rates provided the clearest empirical index of this. In an early study of suicide, Durkheim noted that, if human wants were not simply 'given', but were plastic, then the rising capacity of society to provide for the needs of its members might in turn generate new needs, and thereby increase the gap between wants and their satisfaction.[10] This conclusion was affirmed in *The Division of Labour*. The theoretical side of this, however, remained obscure until the publication of *Suicide*. In that work, the empirical observations (concerning, for example, the rising rate of suicide with the advance of material civilization, and the relation between suicide and socio-economic position within the occupational system) were drawn together in terms of a coherent theoretical analysis. Durkheim's discussion of anomie in *Suicide* is far from unambiguous, but one major point can be gleaned from it. There was an essential distinction between biological needs and those which were engendered by society. The former were fixed in their *object* and in their *limits*: these two aspects might vary independently in the case of socially produced needs. That is to say, whereas biological needs were specific in what they demanded of motivated action (for example, hunger: food) and in their point of satiation (there were given organic reactions which reduced appetite in relation to the intake of nourishment), neither of these was fixed in a determinate fashion in the case of socially created needs or desires. The importance of the differentiation between these two aspects was never clearly brought out in any of the discussions of anomie which appeared at various places in Durkheim's work: as will be shown below, it is a source of certain basic difficulties in his writings. For the present, however, it is sufficient to note the significance of this theoretical position for the critique of utilitarianism. This critique was also twofold. First, human wants could not be taken as givens, but were socially created and thus historically variable. Second, and equally important, the creation of wants did not automatically produce the circumstances which made possible their realization. This latter point became focal to Durkheim's critical assessment of socialist doctrines. Socialism was superior to utilitarianism in recognizing that human wants were not simply 'contained' in the individual, but were socially created; however, it shared with utilitarianism the notion that society did not have to intervene in the satisfaction of needs. According to socialist theory, production thus had to be regulated, but consumption had to be freed from social control.

The positive connections between the conceptions of moral individualism and anomie, apart from the early formulation in *The Division of Labour*, were nowhere explicitly stated in any detail by Durkheim, and thus have tended to be among the most frequently misunderstood parts of his writings. As I have tried to show elsewhere, faulty interpretation of Durkheim on this matter has helped to sustain two of the most prevalent misrepresentations of Durkheim's sociology in the secondary literature: that which sees his work as primarily concerned with an abstract 'problem of order', and the closely related view of his writings as advancing a heavily authoritarian theory of moral discipline.[11] If there is a basic opposition in all of Durkheim's work, it is not that of social integration (normative control) versus social disintegration (lack of normative regulation: anomie), but, as with virtually all leading social thinkers of his time, that of 'traditional' versus 'modern' society, with all the profound social transformations which this latter distinction implies. It does not seem to have been generally appreciated that there is necessarily an historical dimension to Durkheim's treatment of anomie: this is integral to the very conception of 'socially generated need', but it is also important in regard to the second aspect of anomie, that of *provision* for wants. In the traditional social order, human faculties and needs were kept to a low level, and therefore were readily provided for. The dominance of the *conscience collective* played a role in each of these respects: on the one hand, by restricting the development of 'individualism' – the liberation of the individual personality – and, on the other, by setting strict limits to what might legitimately be striven for by an individual in a given social position. The process of evolution away from traditionalism both increased the level of individuation and at the same time undermined the fixed moral boundaries characteristic of previous ages. It was these *twin* developments which created the important theoretical problem – which Durkheim sought to resolve in terms of his analysis of the emergence of moral individualism. Anomie, therefore, was a phenomenon specific to the modern order (as was indexed by the documentation of the growth of anomic suicide in *Suicide*); it was to be understood in relation to individuation and moral individualism. Although Durkheim conceded that 'a certain level' of anomie was inevitable in modern society, which was committed to rapid and continuous change, anomie as pathology was to be traced to the temporarily inadequate development of moral individualism. The upsurge of anomie found in the contemporary age was mainly centred in economic life, which had broken away from the confines of tradition, but had not yet been sufficiently penetrated by the new morality of individualism

It might be useful at this juncture to summarize what has been said so far:

1 There are two, connected, aspects of Durkheim's discussion of the relationship between the 'individual' and 'society': a defence of the essential place of moral individualism in modern society, coupled with a disavowal that this means that 'individualism' as developed in utilitarian philosophy, forms a viable methodological basis for sociology.
2 Moral individualism is consequently quite distinct from 'egoism': the increasing range of individual autonomy (in the sense of 'individuation') was contingent upon the emergence of the 'cult of the individual', in conjunction with the other social changes involved in the transition from mechanical to organic solidarity.
3 Both the critique of utilitarianism and the analysis of moral individualism are grounded in an elaboration of the theory of anomie; the remedy for anomie consists not in the reimposition of traditional, repressive moral discipline, but in the further advance of the liberal morality of individualism.

With these points in mind, it is possible to turn to Durkheim's critique of 'methodological individualism', as set out in his discussion of 'social facts' in *The Rules of Sociological Method*. Like the rest of the work, much of this analysis is polemical: while its impact upon the reader is correspondingly powerful and convincing, the positive elements in the exposition of the characteristics of social facts are in fact difficult to unearth. As in Durkheim's analysis of the difference between egoism and moral individualism, there are two conceptions of the 'individual' implied in what he has to say: but whereas in the former case he himself specified the nature of the distinction, in his treatment of social facts this is not clearly brought out. This time it is a distinction between the concrete, flesh-and-blood individual, on the one hand, and the abstractly conceived 'social actor' on the other. The concrete individual is necessarily, of course, the 'carrier' of society: remove all human organisms, and there is no society. In holding that social facts were 'external' to the individual, Durkheim had in mind the concrete individual; there would be no role for sociology as an independent discipline if we accepted the utilitarian premise. But the manner in which this was expressed is such that it is hardly surprising that Durkheim has been accused of an illegitimate reification of the 'social'. A similar ambiguity arises in relation to the second criterion which he applied: that of 'obligation' or 'constraint'. If Durkheim's 'individual' is the 'concrete individual', then his analysis of the 'constraining' character of social facts in *The Rules* is, to say the least, unsatisfactory; for other phenomena 'external' to the concrete individual share the same character – such as those given in the geographical environment. Social facts would be merely residual, placed 'outside' the individual and resistant to his or her will.[12] But it is evident that Durkheim did not wish to hold this. Social facts were distinct from those of the physical world, because 'they consist in ideas and actions.'[13] In what sense, then, are social facts 'constraining'?

Much hangs on the answer to this question, of course, since it has been commonly accepted, even by those generally sympathetic to Durkheim's viewpoint, that his stress upon the constraining nature of social facts leaves no place for the social actor as a conscious willing agent. In *The Rules*, Durkheim offered two sorts of example to support his argument – without clearly recognizing the difference between them:

> If I attempt to contravene legal rules, they react against me in such a way as to prevent my act if that is possible; or to annul or re-establish it in its normal form if this can be done after it has been carried out; or to demand expiation if there is no way of repairing what has been done ... Moreover, constraint is no less effective if it is indirect ... If I am an industrialist, nothing prevents me from working with the procedures and methods of a hundred years ago: but if I do so, I shall surely be ruined.[14]

In the examples mentioned in the first part of the quotation, law and custom, constraint involves moral obligation (supported by sanctions). In those given in the second part, constraint does not involve any sort of moral commitment but only factors which comprise a 'factual' element in the horizon of the social actor. Thus the industrialist who ignores certain technical requisites of production fails to prosper. If Durkheim realized the full significance of this distinction at the time at which he wrote *The Rules*, he gave little sign of it, and it is clear that he tended to identify social facts primarily as moral obligations. Later, he became more clearly aware of the importance of the difference between these two sorts of social 'constraint', seeing that the moral sanction was different in character from the constraining factor which was present in the other type. The feature of moral sanctions was that they were not intrinsic to the act which was sanctioned: they could not be deduced from the properties of that act itself. The same act which was morally reprehensible in one type of society, for instance, might be tolerated or even actively encouraged in another. This was not the case with the consequences which stemmed from failure to adhere to prescriptions or practices which were not moral obligations.[15] Here the 'constraint' was an undesired consequence which followed automatically from the transgression of the rule   as in the case of the industrialist who fails to observe the rules of efficient business practice.

The distinctive character of moral obligation had two implications for Durkheim's sociology. One was that the content of moral obligations varied in different forms of society; the second was that, according to the theory of anomie, moral obligation not only set limits to human action, but also focused it and gave it defined form. Each of these actually indicated, in a differing way, that 'obligation' was not to be identified with 'restriction' *tout court*, as might be suggested by Durkheim's habit of using 'obligation', 'constraint' and even, occasionally, 'coercion' as interchangeable terms. To be sure, moral obligations were always constraining in the sense that deviation produced sanctions: but the degree to which acceptance of obligation was 'restrictive' upon the actor was contingent upon the moral form in question. The moral obligations involved in the 'cult of the individual' conferred increased autonomy of action, as compared to the rigid discipline of traditional society. This was possible precisely because moral codes defined the content of human motivation, at least with regard to socially generated needs. While Durkheim no doubt did not achieve complete clarity on the latter point until after he had written his account of the nature of social facts in *The Rules*, he did specifically point out in the book that his understanding of moral obligation diverged from the 'constraint' of Hobbes and Rousseau, who neglected the 'spontaneous' character of moral life. These thinkers, according to Durkheim, assumed that there was a dislocation between society and its component individuals: the human being was treated as naturally hostile to social life. Society, therefore, could only exist if people were compelled, by the action of the state, to adapt themselves to it. Their views contrasted with those of the utilitarians, who saw social life as a spontaneous phenomenon. In the first conception, 'constraint' was seen as fundamental to social life, but was considered as a purely 'external' sort of coercion. The second standpoint eliminated constraint, in any form, from the operation of society. His own position, Durkheim said, comprised elements of each of these, and also rejected both: there was no contradiction in holding that social life was both 'constraining' and 'spontaneous'.

These considerations are surely enough to suggest that Durkheim may be absolved from the cruder type of criticism which has frequently been directed against his methodological writings: that he accorded society 'objective' reality only at the expense of denying any reality to the active subject. Nor is there much substance in the equally common assertion that Durkheim's work should be ranged with that of those thinkers (mainly of a broadly conservative persuasion) who hold that there is an inherent antinomy between the individual and society, such that the continuation of social life depends upon the strict repression of individual desires. He clearly recognized that what the (concrete) individual was depended upon 'internalized' norms which were, in part, the *condition* of freedom of action. But his treatment of this matter involved definite inconsistencies. This can be seen quite plainly in his various discussions of 'egoism'. In his earlier writings, 'egoism' has reference to the utilitarian model of self-interest. In Durkheim's view, this presupposed a 'pre-social' man, and his critique of this conception in *The Rules* took this as its foil. But he evidently soon came to perceive that according to the position which he had taken in criticizing utilitarian individualism, egoism itself must be a product of sociology. That is to say, there could be socially created self-interest. He even gave a specific illustration of this. Moral individualism, he emphasized, did not derive from egoism: but the growth of moral individualism none the less produced, as an offshoot, an expansion in the range of egoistic inclinations:

> Undoubtedly pity for others and pity for ourselves are not foreign to one another, since they progress or decline in tandem; but the one does not derive from the other. There exists a tie of common origin between them, because they both originate in, and are only different aspects of, the same state of the *conscience collective*. They both express the way in which the moral value of the individual has come to be esteemed. Any social judgement which is collectively valued is applied to others at the same time as to ourselves; their person, like our own, becomes more highly valued in our eyes, and we become just as sensitive to what affects everyone individually as to what affects us particularly . . . Thus it is the case that even the sentiments which seem to belong most directly to the personal makeup of the individual depend upon the causes which go beyond him! Our egoism itself is, in large part, a product of society.[16]

Yet, in other writings, Durkheim reverted to a conception of 'egoism' which counterposed it in a direct way to social learning as if the two were necessarily mutually exclusive. The human being, he argued, everywhere conceived of him- or herself as *homo duplex*, as being composed of two beings, which were usually represented in religious thought as the body and the soul.[17] This corresponded to a psychological division between sensations, on the one side, and concepts and moral activity on the other. Sensations and sensory needs, according to Durkheim, were necessarily egoistic, because they originated from, and referred to, conditions of the biological organism. Conceptual thought and moral activity were 'impersonal'; they were social products, and did not 'belong' to any particular person who used them. These, therefore, were two opposed aspects of personality. They were not merely separate from one another, but were in constant conflict. 'Egoism' was thus identified solely with the 'pre-social', and was portrayed as wholly foreign to the 'penetration of the individual by society'.

The implications of this will be further discussed below. But it is worth pointing out that a similar inconsistency appears in various other parts of Durkheim's writings, which have reference to the connection between the 'biological' and the 'social' components of personality. An example may be given from his work on suicide.[18] The main thesis which Durkheim developed in *Suicide* was that the suicide rate, as compared with particular cases of suicide, 'constitutes in itself a new fact, *sui generis*, which has its own unity and individuality', and had to be explained sociologically.[19] To this end, he developed his typology of the social factors underlying observed differences in suicide rates. To hold that the suicide rate could only be explained in sociological terms did not mean, however, he went on to say, that there was no place for psychological studies of suicide. It was the role of the psychologist to examine the particular characteristics which caused one person, rather than another, to kill himself or herself, when placed in a given set of social circumstances: not everyone who was exposed to a situation of anomie actually committed suicide. While this may be a neat division of tasks between sociology and psychology, it is a clearly inadequate position, because it implicitly assumes that the traits of the 'suicidal personality' formed outside of society. The (social) factors which cause a certain *rate* of suicide were presented by Durkheim as separate from those relevant to the aetiology of the individual case. But this would only be so if it were true that the characteristics of suicidal personality were 'pre-social': that is, settled in the biological constitution of the organism. In fact, Durkheim accepted that this was not the case, showing that the 'individual type' of suicide was strongly influenced by the 'social type'. If this be admitted, however, the explanatory model which Durkheim set up in the book is immediately defective. It follows that there is a complicated interplay between society and personality in the aetiology of rates of suicide: the social conditions which he treated as simply acting 'directly' upon 'suicide-prone' individuals must also have an influence in *producing* that 'suicide-proneness' as a complex of personality characteristics.

Enough has been said this far to indicate that, although Durkheim's attempt to detach moral from methodological individualism was perhaps more subtle than has been assumed by many of his critics, what resulted is a brittle synthesis and essentially an unsatisfactory one. The ambiguities, and the very serious deficiencies, which run through his works, however, have to be understood in the light of this attempt. As happens so often with a writer whose works are strongly polemical in tone, ultimately he was unable to abandon certain of the very premises of which he was most critical in the writings of his opponents. In this discussion I have given most prominence to Durkheim's critique of utilitarian individualism, but this was not his only target of attack. A second tradition of thought that he sought to evaluate critically, while also being strongly influenced by it, was that of 'idealist holism'. A variety of substantively quite different doctrines, of course, may be subsumed under such a rubric. But the most important element in these doctrines which formed a negative frame of reference for the development of Durkheim's thought was the notion that a 'universal' moral consensus was the condition of the existence of society, of whatever type. As Durkheim attempted to show in *The Division of Labour*, this was a mistaken view. While this was indeed the condition of unity in traditional society, moral diversity was the necessary concomitant of the modern societal type. If modern society was, and had to be, a moral order, it was distinct from the traditional form. In developing this standpoint, as is plainly evident in his early critical articles and reviews, Durkheim was, in a certain sense, positively influenced by utilitarianism, especially as it was adapted by such writers as Spencer. These authors at least recognized that the character of modern social life was distinctively different from human life in traditional society, and their version of 'individualism' gave expression to this awareness. In exploring the insufficiencies of utilitarian individualism, however, Durkheim borrowed heavily from the other school of thought, asserting that moral ideals were irreducible to individual motivations or interests.

Along the *historical* dimension, therefore, Durkheim leaned partly upon utilitarianism in rejecting the conception of the relationship between the individual and society implicit in holistic idealism – that the individual was merely a 'microcosm' of society. This might be, in a sense, an apt characterization of the situation in traditional society, in mechanical solidarity, but it was quite inappropriate to the modern order, in which 'the individual personality develops with the division of labour.'[20] This showed, of course, that idealism is *methodologically* wanting. The individual in society was not simply a passive imprint of social forms, but an active agent. But, even while he recognized this, Durkheim relied upon the holistic standpoint in working out his critique of utilitarian individualism. From each of these two aspects, historical and methodological, this view rested upon the proposition that society was not a creation of the (pre-social) individual, but existed 'prior' to and moulds him or her. How, then, was it possible that the (concrete) individual was an active agent? It is at this point that the two dimensions, the historical and the methodological, in Durkheim's thought diverge. The answer which he reached via his study of the evolution of solidarity, and his analysis of moral conduct more generally, was that it was possible because the cognitive and motivational personality of the individual was shaped by social learning. The individual was not just moulded by society; the active orientation of his or her conduct was framed by 'internalized' moral norms. But there was a second answer, to which Durkheim's thought constantly tended to revert, and which undoubtedly derived from his preoccupation with utilitarianism. This was that whatever was actively willed by the individual was a 'pre-social' impulsion. In other words, in seeking to reject utilitarianism, Durkheim tended to deal with it in its own terms. Society could not be conceived as the outcome of pre-formed individual wills – because society made, and had to make, demands upon the individual which were foreign to his or her own wishes. Hence we reach the position that there was irremediable conflict between the ('egoistic') inclinations of the individual, and the moral commands which society enjoined upon him or her.

Durkheim never managed adequately to reconcile these two strands of his thought, and this is reflected in several of the ambiguities noted previously. Thus his discussion of social facts in *The Rules*, as has been mentioned, shifted from one meaning of 'individual' to another. His discussion easily lends itself to the interpretation that social facts are empirically 'external' to individual conduct, and exert a constraining force over that conduct which is of the same kind as that produced by geographical or climatic forces. The same kind of enforced polarization between the 'internal' and the 'external' appears in Durkheim's use of *argumentum per eliminationem* in *Suicide*.[21] Various sorts of 'external' or 'pre-social' factor (such as the influence of climate) are eliminated separately as explaining observed differentials in suicide rates. These include the influence of inherited insanity. Now the assumption that this is an 'external' factor is acceptable if it be granted that insanity is wholly inherited, and thus is built into the constitution of the organism. But Durkheim explicitly pointed out that this was not so: social factors had a definite role in the aetiology of mental disorder. The insight was, however, allowed to remain undeveloped. Yet, as has been indicated above, Durkheim at no time advocated what he called at one juncture the 'absurd notion' that society was 'external' to the individual in the same sense as the geographical environment was; and most of his argument in *The Rules* is only understandable if his 'individual' is the 'concrete individual'.

A similar point may be made about the concept of anomie. It has already been shown that, in Durkheim's formulation, the concept involved two components, which tended to be merged in his own use of it. One of these referred to the degree to which human action was provided with definite objectives; the other concerned how far these ends were realizable. The distinction is a fundamental one, yet Durkheim glossed over it. It is easy to see how closely this is tied in to the ambiguity in his treatment of social facts. In so far as one uses the concept of anomie to refer primarily to the first element – the lack of coherent norms which provide firm objectives for a person to strive for – one is talking of the 'concrete individual'. This is certainly the type case in most of Durkheim's abstract discussion of anomie. But many of the examples of anomie which he applied in his more empirical analyses (for example, in relation to class conflict) actually concentrated upon the second element: the objectives of conduct might be clearly defined, but could not be *attained*. In such cases his argument again tended to slip back into a direct opposition to the utilitarian position: utilitarian theory was mistaken because an external limitation (which could only come from society) had to be placed upon individual desires. It might be pointed out that Durkheim's illustrations often referred to cases of *biological* drives; for instance, that 'an insatiable thirst cannot be quenched.'

Durkheim's failure to utilize the distinction between the two aspects of anomie is a source of some of the most basic flaws in his sociology. As more recent literature employing the notion of anomie demonstrated, the concept takes on quite divergent theoretical applications according to which aspect is emphasized. If anomie is taken to refer mainly to 'normlessness' – the first aspect – then it tends to support a standpoint emphasizing the dimension of 'meaning'/'lack of meaning' in individual conduct.[22] The end

result of this is likely to be a position which, implicitly or otherwise, treats social conflict as 'pathological' – that is to say, which
links conflict to 'deviance' produced by 'imperfect socialization'.
Although, as I have argued elsewhere,[23] it is quite mistaken to
hold that Durkheim regarded all social conflict in this way, there
are obviously strong elements of this viewpoint in his writings. If
the other aspect is emphasized, on the other hand, it tends to lead
to a conception of 'normative strain', rather than 'normlessness'.
Here the objectives of conduct may be quite clear to the actor, and
there is not the strong overtone of irrationality which appears to
characterize the conduct of the individual where the first aspect is
stressed. The importance of this conception, then, is that it allows
a much greater scope for conceptualizing conflicts which derive
from divisions of interest in society. Durkheim undoubtedly minimized the significance of this form of conflict in his writings. There
are two respects in which it is possible to claim that a given
objective is not 'realizable'. One is that there exist barriers in a
society which prevent its realization. This *may* mean that it cannot
be achieved – that it involves some good which, in any conceivable
form of society, is simply impossible of attainment; or it may mean
that its realization demands some kind of *change* in the existing
organization of society. This perspective certainly has a substantial place in Durkheim's writings. Thus he emphasized that, in
order to overcome the class conflict which characterized modern
industry, social change (involving mainly removing barriers to
equality of occupational opportunity) was necessary. But there is
another sense in which an objective may be said to be
'unrealizable', and Durkheim continually reverted to this – for
reasons explained above – in his anxiety to refute the utilitarian
position. This is where the objective in question has no limits: the
insatiable appetite. We can now grasp more clearly the significance of another ambiguity which has been referred to in a previous part of this chapter, concerning Durkheim's treatment of
moral obligation and 'factual' constraint. Although he did not
seem to attach any importance to this distinction in *The Rules*, he
did later recognize that moral constraint was quite different in
character from the 'factual' consequences of actions. But he only
elucidated one dimension of this difference – the difference in the
nature of the sanction involved. He failed to consider the theoretical significance of the possibility that moral obligations *themselves*

might be 'factual' elements in the horizon of the acting individual. A person (or a group) may acknowledge the existence of the obligations, and take account of them in orienting his or her conduct, without feeling any strong commitment to them. Such action is not necessarily 'criminal', in the sense of directly flouting the moral prescriptions in question. But it rests neither solely upon fear of the sanctions which would be invoked as punishment for transgression, nor solely upon moral commitment. While Durkheim accepted that there were varying degrees of attachment to moral norms,[74] he had no place for this in his theoretical analysis of the nature of moral obligation. Nor was there any recognition of the differential 'interpretation' of moral norms.

These inadequacies can also be seen at the level of Durkheim's historical analysis and, indeed, partly derive from that analysis. It is perhaps significant that Durkheim has been called both a 'materialist' and an 'idealist'. The first label, so it has been thought, can be readily applied to his standpoint as expressed in *The Division of Labour*. In that work he argued that

> [Civilization] is itself a necessary consequence of changes which take place in the volume and density of societies. If science, art and economic activity develop, it is as a result of a necessity imposed on men; it is because there is no other way for them to live in the new conditions in which they are placed. From the moment that the number of individuals among whom social relations are established reaches a certain point, they can only sustain themselves if they specialize more, work more, and stimulate their mental capacities; and from this general stimulation there inevitably results a higher level of culture. From this point of view, civilization thus appears, not as a goal which moves people by the hold that it exerts over them, not as a good perceived and desired in advance, which they strive to create as fully as possible. Rather, it is the effect of a cause, the necessary result of a determinate state of affairs.[25]

The apparent theme of such statements is that the transformation of society from mechanical to organic solidarity is wholly a matter of changes in the social 'infrastructure'; that the changes which occur in the character of moral conduct are simply 'effects' of these 'causes'. The perspective developed in *The Elementary Forms* seems to contrast markedly with this. In the latter work, so it would appear, Durkheim treated moral ideals as the *force dirigeante* in social life. It is mainly by reference to this work that he has been regarded as advancing an 'idealist' position. Thus it seems as though, if one follows through the stages of his intellectual career, he began from a 'materialistic' standpoint, and moved later towards a view which is directly opposed to that which he initially adopted. In fact, however, throughout his writings Durkheim frequently and specifically denied that he wished to adopt either of these positions. In *The Division of Labour*, for example, the section which has just been quoted is immediately followed by the assertion that 'a mechanistic conception of society does not exclude ideals', and that 'it is mistaken to suppose that this conception reduces man to a mere inactive witness of his own history.' On the other hand, while his later writings are full of statements such as 'society is the ideal', he was always careful to insist that such propositions must be interpreted to mean that ideals were *creations* of human society, not 'given' forces which determined social conduct. This is, after all, the main proposition developed in *The Elementary Forms*, and Durkheim himself evidently still considered that his critics would regard it as another version of his earlier 'materialism'. Near the end of the book, he took pains to make clear that this was not what he was proposing: there was, he emphasized, an active interplay between the *conscience collective* and its 'infrastructure'.

But he never solved the problems which the analysis of this interplay presents, and, where he discussed social change, it is often as if there are two quite independent sets of processes going on: those in the 'infrastructure', on the one hand, and those in the sphere of moral ideals on the other. This is undoubtedly one reason which explains the apparent 'break' in the argument in *The Division of Labour*, mentioned earlier. The only direct connections which Durkheim was able to establish between the expansion of the division of labour and the changing nature of the *conscience collective* were those whereby the influence of the latter was *weakened*. It is not at all clear why its content should become changed: what factors promote the emergence of the 'cult of the individual'? Even in the theory developed in *The Elementary Forms*, the origin of the content of religious beliefs remained obscure. These beliefs were created in the fervour of collective ceremonial. But sacred beliefs, while framed in terms of categories ('space', 'time', etc.) which were based upon the characteristics of society, were essentially 'random': any object might become sacred, and there was, applying Durkheim's theory, a practically infinite range of potential primitive classifications. Durkheim's sociology lacks any systematic theoretical treatment of the social mechanisms which mediate the relationship between infrastructure and *conscience collective*.

The reasons for this touch upon weaknesses in Durkheim's thought which have not been explored here. But the analysis given earlier is certainly of basic importance: for it helps to show how, as a result of the theoretical impasse in which his thought became wedged, he was unable to deal in a satisfactory way with *socially generated* interests, and more especially with conflicts which stem from opposition of such interests.

5 Comte, Popper and Positivism

'Positivism' over recent years has become more a term of abuse than a technical term of philosophy. The indiscriminate way in which the word has been used, however, makes all the more important a study of the influence of positivistic philosophies in the social sciences.

I shall distinguish two main ways in which 'positivism' may be taken, one quite specific, the other much more general. In the more restrictive sense, the term may be taken to apply to the writings of those who have actively called themselves positivists, or at least have been prepared to accept the label. This yields two major phases in the development of positivism, one centred mainly on social theory, the other concerned more specifically with epistemology. The earlier phase is that dominated by the works of the author who coined the term 'positive philosophy', Auguste Comte. Although there are obvious contrasts between Comte's positivism and the 'logical positivism' of the Vienna Circle, there are equally clear connections – both historical and intellectual – between the two. Second, the term may be employed more broadly and diffusely to refer to the writings of philosophers who have adopted most or all of a cluster of connected perspectives: phenomenalism – the thesis, which can be expressed in various ways, that 'reality' consists in sense-impressions; an aversion to metaphysics, the latter being condemned as sophistry or illusion; the representation of philosophy as a method of analysis, clearly separable from, yet at the same time parasitic upon, the findings of science; the duality of fact and value – the claim that empirical knowledge is logically discrepant from the pursuit of moral aims or the implementation of ethical standards; and the notion of the 'unity of science': the idea that the natural and social sciences share a common logical and perhaps even methodological foundation. Below I shall use the term *positivism* without qualification to refer, in the appropriate context, to the views of Comte and subsequently to those of the leading figures of the Vienna Circle, that is, to those who have been prepared to call themselves positivists. I shall use *positivistic philosophy* to designate views that embody important elements among those mentioned in the second category. In this sense, positivistic strains are much more widely represented in the history of philosophy, overlapping with empiricism, than would be suggested if attention were confined to self-proclaimed 'positivism'.

I want also, however, to distinguish a third category, which I shall call, for want of a better name, *'positivistic sociology'*. We owe to Comte both the term 'positivism' and the term 'sociology'; in his writings, the two are closely connected, since the coming into being of sociology is supposed to mark the final triumph of positivism in human thought. The connection has been a fateful one for the subsequent development of the social sciences, for certain leading traditions in social thought over the past hundred years have been considerably influenced by the kind of logical framework established by Comte in his *Cours de philosophie positive*. As interpreted by Durkheim, this framework is closely tied in to modern functionalism. But the influence of positivistic philosophy, as defined above, in sociology has ranged much more widely than this. Here sociology is conceived of as a 'natural science of society', which can hope to reproduce a system of laws directly similar in form to those achieved in the natural sciences. In positivistic sociologies, as formulated in the early post-war period, especially in the United States, all three senses of 'positivism' I have just distinguished to some extent recombine. Certain of the prominent members of the Vienna Circle emigrated to the United States, and have exerted a strong influence over the development of philosophy there, particularly in regard of the philosophy of science. Their conception of the philosophy of science was in turn appropriated, explicitly or otherwise, by many authors writing in the social sciences: and it proved particularly compatible with the views of those drawing heavily upon the ideas of Comte and Durkheim.

In this discussion, I shall begin by analysing the positivism of Comte, its similarities to and its differences from the logical positivism of the Vienna Circle. From there I shall move to consider two partly convergent critiques of positivistic philosophies more generally conceived: one, the so-called 'newer philosophy of science', emanating mainly from within the English-speaking world, the other, 'Frankfurt philosophy' or critical theory, originating primarily in long-established German philosophical traditions.

Auguste Comte: sociology and positivism

In crude summary, we may distinguish several major elements in the intellectual background of Comte's writings. One is the frontal assault on metaphysics undertaken in eighteenth-century philosophy, above all in the works of Hume and his followers in British empiricism, and sustained in different form in Kant's 'critical idealism'. Comte went further than such authors, in not only accepting the success of the destruction of transcendental illusions, but in formally embodying the metaphysical stage in the evolution of humanity as a phase superseded by the advent of positivist thought. In this respect, he accepted one of the fundamental aims of the writers of the Enlightenment, as he did important aspects of the rationalist critique of established religion. In Comte's scheme of history, the theological stage of thought was relegated to a phase prior to the metaphysical – both, to be sure, becoming regarded as necessary stages in social evolution, but both becoming dissolved once and for all when positivism triumphed. If Comte himself came to the rediscovery of religion, it was because his acceptance of these aspects of Enlightenment philosophy went along with a deep-rooted aversion to the methodical critique of inherited authority basic to the writings of the *philosophes*. Comte rejected an essential idea of Enlightenment itself: that the Middle Ages were also the Dark Ages, whose passing opened up the way to revolutionary changes in human intellectual and social life. In place of this view Comte substituted a progressivism influenced by the 'retrograde school' of authors – conservative apologists for Catholicism, reacting against Enlightenment radicalism and against the 1789 Revolution which was its heir: Bonald, de Maistre and others. Comte's positivism preserved the theme of progress, but questioned the radicalism with which this was associated in Enlightenment philosophy. 'Progress' and 'order' were more than reconciled: the one became dependent upon the other. Positive thought replaced the 'negative' outlook of the *philosophes*, the perspective that a new dawn could be achieved through the shattering of the past.

Of course, Comte owed many of his ideas most immediately to Saint-Simon, who in turn was considerably indebted to Condorcet and Montesquieu, both of whom had tempered the enthusiasms of the Enlightenment with a rigidly applied version of the subservience of society to natural laws of development. Condorcet assigned to history the same kinds of potentiality that Comte was later to allocate to the positive science of sociology, expressed in the famous phrase *savoir pour prévoir, prévoir pour pouvoir*. Condorcet looked to the past to supply the moving principles of evolution whereby the future could be made open to human intervention. Hence he took to task those who arrogantly supposed that it is possible to achieve large-scale social change *ex nihilo*. The progress of humanity achieved equilibrium in such a way that, while the pace of development could be speeded or retarded by active human intervention, such development formed an autonomous force for betterment. I shall not take up the vexed issue of just how directly Comte plundered Saint-Simon's ideas in constructing his own system, a matter of great acrimony in the relations between the two thinkers after Comte broke away from the tutelage of his mentor. Whatever their immediate provenance, one can say without undue simplification that Comte's writings constitute one direction of development out of Saint-Simon, that which gave 'sociology' its name, and established a logical framework for the supposedly new science; the other direction was that taken by Marx, in which elements of Saint-Simon's ideas were reconnected to revolutionary social transformation.[1]

That Comte entitled the first of his two major works *Cours de philosophie positive* should not blind us to the fact that the work actually declared an end to philosophy as previously practised: as an independent enterprise separable from the achievements of science. 'Positive philosophy' is perhaps not, as Marcuse suggested, a contradiction *in adjecto*.[2] But it does reduce philosophy to expressing the emergent synthesis of scientific knowledge. The 'true philosophic spirit', Comte said, incorporated the 'essential attributes . . . summed up in the word *positive*'. These included, first of all, an orientation to 'reality' and to 'utility': the useless endeavours of speculative philosophy to penetrate behind appearances were disavowed. But the term also implied – in all the European languages, according to Comte – 'certainty' and 'precision', attributes which similarly distinguished the intellectual life of modern humanity from that of its predecessors. Finally, also suggested by the term were an 'organic tendency' and a 'relativist outlook'. The former of these referred to the constructive character of the positivist spirit: by contrast, 'the metaphysical spirit is incapable of organizing; it can only criticize.' The latter sealed the rejection of absolutism, as practised in metaphysical philosophy: the laws that governed the co-variance of phenomena always retained a provisional character, since they were induced on the basis of empirical observation, rather than being posited as 'absolute essences'.[3]

In the *Cours*, the relation between the various sciences was claimed to be hierarchical, in both an analytical and a historical sense, the second being explained in terms of the celebrated law of the three stages of human intellectual development. Analytically, Comte made clear, the sciences formed a hierarchy of decreasing generality but increasing complexity; each particular science logically depended upon the ones below it in the hierarchy, and yet at the same time dealt with an emergent order of properties that could not be reduced to those with which the other sciences were concerned. Thus biology, for example, presupposed the laws of physics and chemistry in so far as all organisms were physical entities which obeyed the laws governing the composition of matter; on the other hand, the behaviour of organisms, as complex beings, could not be derived directly from those laws. Sociology, at the apex of the hierarchy of sciences, logically presupposed the laws of each of the other scientific disciplines, while at the same time similarly retaining its autonomous subject matter.

The logical relations between the sciences, according to Comte, provided the means of interpreting their successive formation as separate fields of study in the course of the evolution of human thought. The sciences which developed first, mathematics and astronomy, then physics, were those dealing with the most general or all-enveloping laws of nature, governing phenomena most removed from human involvement and manipulation. From there, science penetrated closer and closer to humanity itself, moving through chemistry and biology to its culmination in the science of human conduct – originally labelled by Comte 'social physics', then redubbed 'sociology'. The process was not achieved without struggle; scientific understanding lay at the end of the progression of intellectual life through the theological and metaphysical stages, through which all branches of thought had to move. Human thought as a whole, as well as each science taken separately, progressed through the theological, the metaphysical and the positive stages. In the theological stage, the universe was experienced as determined by the agency of spiritual beings; this stage, *l'état fictif*, as Comte called it, was 'the necessary point of departure of the human intellect', and it reached its climax in Christianity with its recognition of one all-powerful deity.[4] The metaphysical phase replaced these moving spirits with abstract essences, thereby, however, clearing the ground for the advent of science, *l'état fixe et définitif* of thought. The enunciation of the law of the three stages, Comte said, was enough 'that its correctness should be immediately confirmed by anyone who has a sufficiently profound knowledge of the general history of the sciences'. (Comte later claimed to have achieved personal verification of the law of the three stages in his periods of insanity, which he had experienced, he claimed, as a regression back through from positivism to metaphysics to theology on the level of his own personality, in his recovery retracing these stages forwards again.)

The task of the *Cours* was not only to analyse the transmutation of human thought by science, but also to *complete* it. For humanity's understanding of itself was still in substantial part in its pre-scientific phase:

> Everything can be reduced to a simple question of fact: does positive philosophy, which over the two past centuries has gradually become so widespread, today embrace all orders of phenomena? It is evident that such is not the case and that consequently there still remains the major scientific undertaking of giving to positive philosophy the universal character that is indispensable to its proper constitution . . . Now that the human mind has founded astronomy, and terrestrial physics – both mechanical and chemical – and organic physics – both botanical and biological – it remains to finalize

the system of the sciences by founding *social physics*. Such is, in several capital respects, the greatest and the most pressing intellectual need today.[5]

Positivism supplied a general ground-plan for the formation of sociology: that is to say, the new science of society had to share the same overall logical form as the other sciences, as it was cut free of the residues of metaphysics. But since the phenomena with which it was concerned were more complex and specific than the sciences lying below it in the hierarchy, it also had to develop methodological procedures of its own. Like biology, sociology employed concepts that were 'synthetic' in character: that is to say, concepts which related to the properties of complex wholes, rather than to aggregates of elements as in the lower sciences. The two also shared a division into statics and dynamics. In sociology, the first consisted in the study of the functional interrelationship of institutions within society, the second in the study of the process of social evolution. The significance of dynamics in sociology, however, was more marked than in biology because – via the law of the three stages – it examined the intellectual development of positive thought as a whole. Sociology relied on three methodological elements, each of which involved features specific to it: observation, experiment and comparison. Comte held that a commitment to the essential importance of empirical observation was not the same as advocating empiricism. 'No logical dogma,' Comte said, 'could be more thoroughly irreconcilable with the spirit of positive philosophy, or with its special character in regard to the study of social phenomena, than this.'[6] Consequently, theory was basic to sociological investigations. On the other hand, the context of Comte's discussion makes it apparent that 'empiricism' here was understood in a limited sense; his point was not that all observations of objects or events were (to use Popper's term) 'theory-impregnated', but that 'scientifically speaking, all isolated empirical observation is idle.' 'Scientific and popular observation', Comte said, 'embrace the same facts'; but they regarded them from different points of view, because the former was guided by theory whereas the latter was not. Theories 'direct our attention towards certain facts rather than others.'[7] While experimentation in the laboratory sense was not possible in social physics, it could be replaced by indirect experimentation, that is, 'natural experiments' whose consequences could be analysed. But this was less important than the comparative method, which was the crucial foundation of sociological research.

Comte always intended sociology to be directed towards practical ends. If it is true that the strange extravagances of the immanent social future envisaged in the *Système de politique positive* are largely absent from Comte's earlier writings, it is still the case that main elements of his political programme already appear there. These were perhaps stated with greater clarity, in fact, in the *Cours* than in the later work. The overriding theme continued that of the intellectual diagnosis of the origins of positive philosophy: the mutual necessity of order and progress. For Comte it was precisely his insistence upon the conjunction of the two that allowed positivism to supersede both the 'revolutionary metaphysics' of the *philosophes* and the reactionary connotations of the Catholic apologists. The latter school wanted order, but was against progress; the former sought progress at the expense of order. The 'order' desired by the 'retrograde school' was nothing but a reversion to feudal hierocracy; while the 'progress' aspired to by the revolutionaries was nothing less than the subversion of any form of government as such. The sort of society Comte foresaw as guaranteeing order and progress none the less placed a heavy enough emphasis upon features that bulked large in the writings of the members of the 'retrograde school' – moral consensus, authority, and an antagonism to the 'chimera of equality' – even if stripped of their specific association with Catholicism. At first sight the call to establish a Religion of Humanity seems quite inconsistent with the positive philosophy advocated in the *Cours*, and many commentators have supposed that there is a major hiatus between Comte's earlier and later works.[8] But it is perhaps more plausible to argue that the *Système de politique positive* brought fully into the open the latent substratum of the positive spirit: we see that science cannot, after all, provide its own commitment.

How, even so, can a perspective which insisted that the course of human social development is governed by laws akin to laws of nature provide any leverage for rational human intervention in history? Does this not imply the adoption of fatalism in the face of the inevitable sweep of social change? According to Comte, the contrary was actually the case. For the rational facilitation of progress was only possible if the limiting conditions of intervention were known; the laws that controlled the movement of society were subject to considerable margins of variation in their operation, and such variation could be actively influenced by deliberate action.[9]

Comte's influence: the origins of logical positivism

Although his writings had rather little immediate influence in France, Comte's works attracted a considerable following abroad: in other European countries, the United States, and particularly Latin America. In Britain, the *Cours* acquired a notable admirer in John Stuart Mill, and Mill's *Logic* was in important respects its counterpart in English-speaking social thought. Many such followers were alienated, however, by the drift of Comte's thought in the later part of his career, as expressed in the *Système de politique positive*, which Mill called 'this melancholy decadence of a great intellect'. As a social movement, which Comte had all along tried to make it, positivism died with the withering of the groups of disciples who remained to celebrate the Festival of Humanity held in London in 1881. I shall not be concerned here to detail how far Comte's works were drawn upon by other authors, during his lifetime or after it: some prominent contemporaries, most notably Herbert Spencer, were anxious to claim greater contrasts between their ideas and those of Comte than seems in fact to have been the case.[10] I shall consider the influence of Comte only from two aspects: the ways in which his writings were utilized by Durkheim; and the extent to which Comte's views conformed intellectually to the philosophical programme developed in logical positivism.

The importance of the line of connection from Comte to Durkheim is easily documented. So far as social science in the twentieth century is concerned, the influence of Comte's writings derives less from their direct impact than from their reworking in Durkheim's version of sociological method. Durkheim's works provided the proximate source of functionalism in both anthropology and sociology. But Durkheim's work also had a more broad-ranging and diffuse effect, as a stimulus to those central traditions of contemporary social thought in which the goal of achieving a 'natural science of society' is considered both desirable and feasible.

In Durkheim, the methodological framework of Comte's positivism, which was sustained, was separated from the global theory of historical change, which was largely abandoned. Durkheim made this view quite explicit. Comte regarded Condorcet and Montesquieu as forerunners who established the groundwork of the positivist spirit, but none the less were unable to detach themselves adequately from the speculative philosophy of history. Durkheim had much the same attitude to the two former thinkers, but lumped Comte along with them as belonging to the pre-scientific phase in the history of sociology. The 'law of the three stages', according to Durkheim, was proclaimed by *fiat* rather than corroborated empirically: a massive research undertaking, well beyond the capacity of any single scholar, would be required to document adequately such a principle of social change.[11] In this respect, Durkheim's comments concurred with the judgement of Mill: 'M. Comte, at bottom, was not so solicitous about completeness of proof as becomes a positive philosopher.'[12]

Durkheim's discussions of social evolution, and his diagnosis of the trend of development of modern industrial civilization, owed as much to Saint-Simon and to the German 'academic socialists' as they did to Comte. But the influence of Boutroux and others notwithstanding, it was undeniably the legacy of Comte that loomed largest in the methodological scheme of sociology which Durkheim set out. While Durkheim did not endorse the 'hierarchy of the sciences' as such, he insisted perhaps even more strongly than Comte upon the autonomy of sociology as a distinctive field of endeavour. Like Comte, he held that recognition of such autonomy did not imply that the study of human social conduct was logically discrepant from natural science; social facts had a moral dimension that was absent in nature, but had 'to be treated as things' in the same manner as natural objects. The aim of sociology was to arrive at the formulation of principles that had the same objective status as natural scientific laws. In Durkheim, a Baconian version of scientific method is perhaps more apparent than in Comte. Every science, Durkheim said, including sociology, advanced only slowly and cautiously, through the patient inductive generalization on the basis of observed regularities in social facts. This was, indeed, why he was critical of Comte's claims to have established a positivist account of history. When Durkheim rejected the 'positivism', in favour of 'naturalism', he sought to dissociate his general position from that of Comte, while reaffirming the character of sociology as a natural science of society. Durkheim's account of the emergence of the scientific spirit, although not elaborated in anything like the historical detail attempted by Comte, actually followed the outline of Comte's discussion very closely. All thought, Durkheim held (and tried to explain concretely how this was so in *Les formes élémentaires de la vie religieuse*), originated in religion; it could be demonstrated that even the Kantian categories were first of all religious concepts.[13] The key differences between pre-scientific and scientific thought were methodological; 'thought and reflection are prior to science, which merely uses them methodologically.'[14] As religious concepts became secularized in the form of metaphysical philosophy, they became more precise, but they were finally rendered scientific only by being anchored in empirical observation, and thereby transformed.

It is clear that Durkheim derived his conception of functionalist method from Comte and not from Spencer. Durkheim followed Comte closely in separating out functional explanation (statics) from historical explanation (dynamics), although he criticized Comte along with Spencer for reifying 'progress': treating the impetus to self-betterment as if it were a general cause of the evolution of society. As in Comte's writings, and of course in those of many other nineteenth-century writers also, Durkheim's stress upon the significance of functional explanation in sociology came fairly directly from the model of biology, as did his acceptance of 'holistic' concepts as basic to sociological analysis. The biological parallel also provided, however, another very important element in Durkheim's works, bearing immediately upon the practical implications of social science. In claiming that the scientific study of society could offer the means of distinguishing what was normal from what was pathological, in any particular type of society, Durkheim upheld the most intrinsic part of Comte's programme for positivism. For just as natural science showed us that the development of knowledge could only be achieved incrementally, so sociology showed us that all truly progressive social change occurred only cumulatively. The mutual dependence of progress and order is as much a theme of Durkheim's writings as it is of those of Comte. Durkheim's antagonism to revolution continued that of Comte, and was likewise held to be grounded scientifically: political revolution expressed the inability of a society to generate progressive change, rather than itself providing a possible instrument of securing social transformation. However, while the form of the account is similar, the content is not wholly the same: that is to say, in identifying what is normal, and what is pathological, in contemporary society, and thus specifying the immanent trend of social development, Durkheim moved away substantially from Comte.[15]

In mentioning these respects in which Durkheim was indebted to Comte, I do not, of course, want to claim that Durkheim's works can be regarded as little more than an extension of those of the earlier thinker. But Durkheim's writings have been more influential than those of any other author in academic social science in the spread of 'positivistic sociology', as I have defined that term previously. Through them, Comte's 'positivism' has had a major influence upon the more diffuse development of such positivistic sociology. This is one line of filiation leading from Comte through to twentieth-century thought. The other is less direct, and is that connecting Comte to the logical positivism of the Vienna Circle.

The principal mediator between Comte's positivism and the positivism of the Vienna Circle is normally held to be Ernst Mach, the physicist and physiologist. Mach, like Durkheim, rejected the label 'positivist' and, unlike Durkheim, was not directly influenced by Comte save in minor respects. The importance of Comte in relation to Mach is really in helping to further the intellectual currents that were in the background of Mach's work as a natural scientist. The following elements in Comte's thought are relevant in this respect:

1 The reconstruction of history as the realization of the positive spirit. In this scheme of things, religion and metaphysics had a definite place, but only as prior phases of mystification, to be broken through by the advent of science. With the development of the scientific outlook, the 'pre-history' of the human species was completed; the positive stage of thought was not a transitional one, like the others.

2 The final dissolution of metaphysics, closely linked to the idea of the supersession of philosophy itself. In Comte's positivism,

science replaced philosophy: 'positive philosophy' was the logical explication of the canons of scientific method. Metaphysics was not accorded the status of being open to philosophical discussion in its own right: it was consigned to the lumber-room of history on the basis that the questions posed in metaphysical philosophy were empty of content.

3 The existence of a clear and definable boundary between the factual, or the 'observable', and the imaginary, or the 'fictitious'. Comte did not provide an ontological justification of what counted as factual, but rather a methodological one. It is in this regard, his disavowals notwithstanding, that Comte adopted the standpoint of empiricism. Systematic observation supposedly distinguished positive science from other types of claim to knowledge, and such observation, according to Comte, depended upon the evidence of sense-perception; this was the ground of certainty in science. The rationalist features of Comte's thought did not enter in at this level, but only at the level of the selective organization of facts within theories: theories provided for the *connection* of facts to universal propositions or laws.

4 The 'relativism' of scientific knowledge. 'Relativism' here was not used in the sense which it has subsequently come to acquire: the acceptance, in some form or other, of multiple worlds of reality. That is to say, it was again not an ontological term, but referred to the thesis that science confined itself to explaining the interdependence of phenomena: it did not claim to discover essences or final causes. Scientific knowledge was never 'finished', but constantly open to modification and improvement.

5 The integral tie between science and the moral and material progress of humanity. Comte's adoption of the Baconian formula that the foreknowledge yielded by science made possible technological control, the integration of *prévoir* and *pouvoir*, expressed this exactly. This not only unified science and technology, but extended the realm of the technological to human social development itself; as Comte said quite explicitly, technology would no longer be exclusively associated with the physical, but would become 'political and moral'.[16]

Each of these views reappears in Mach's writings, although not of course in identical form to their expression in Comte's works.

There is nothing in Mach comparable to Comte's massive endeavour to synthesize scientific knowledge within a scheme that is simultaneously historical and analytical. But Mach was directly influenced by theories of evolution, and saw in Darwin and Lamarck a basis for explaining the emerging hegemony of scientific thought from the entanglements of metaphysics. For Mach, the scientific outlook triumphed historically, and found its moral justification in facilitating the survival and welfare of the human species.[17] Mach used the term 'philosophy' with the same double meaning as Comte. When he wrote that he was not a philosopher, and that science did not rely on any particular type or system of philosophy, Mach echoed Comte's theme of the abolition of philosophy. 'Philosophy' here was used to mean transcendental or 'metaphysical philosophy': both Comte and Mach proclaimed an end to philosophy in this sense. Where Comte and Mach spoke of the retention of philosophy, on the other hand, it was as *philosophie positive*: philosophy here was the logical clarification of the basis of science. 'There is above all *no* Machian philosophy', Mach emphasized, there was at the most 'a natural-scientific methodology and a psychology of knowledge'; these latter 'are like all scientific theories provisional, incomplete attempts'.[18] Mach's dismissal of metaphysics was as complete as that of Comte, although linked to a more thorough going phenomenalism than Comte ever adopted:

> I should like the scientists to realize that my view eliminates all metaphysical questions indifferently, whether they be only regarded as insoluble at the present moment, or whether they be regarded as meaningless for all time. I should like then, further, to reflect that everything that we can know about the world is necessarily expressed in the sensations, which can be set free from the individual influence of the observer in a precisely definable manner ... Everything that we can want to know is given by the solution of a problem in mathematical form, by the ascertainment of the functional dependency of the sensational elements on one another. This knowledge exhausts the knowledge of 'reality'.[19]

For Mach, scientific knowledge was 'relative' in Comte's sense; the object of science was to discover relations between phenomena. According to Mach, however, this carried the implication that theory had a purely heuristic role in scientific investigations. The precise identification of the mathematical functions that expressed the dependencies between phenomena in nature rendered theory obsolete. In Mach's phrase, theories resembled dead leaves which fell away when the tree of science no longer had a need to breathe through them. Although this is distinct from Comte's view, it is not as far removed from it as may seem at first blush. In his discussion of the positive method of science, Comte commingled empiricism and rationalism: as I have already mentioned, however, he did so by treating theory as the mode of organizing fact in a way relevant to scientific procedure.

In Comte's positivism, no place was found for the reflexive subject; psychology did not even appear in the hierarchy of the sciences, and the notion of subjective experience was regarded as a metaphysical fiction. In this regard Comte stands in direct line of descent from Hume. But this is a standpoint that was taken for granted in Comte's writings rather than defended in detail. Mach, however, confronted the issue directly, and his stand upon it was quite unequivocal. The self or ego did not exist as a unity; it was merely an aggregate of sensations. According to Mach, if such a view was accepted, it disposed of the accusation of solipsism, frequently made against phenomenalism; since the self did not exist, there could be no question of the isolation of the self in the universe. Mach saw no discrepancy between this view and either the existence of morality or the role of science in furthering the betterment of humanity. It was anti-religious in so far as it had the consequence that there could be no survival of the soul after death, since 'I' had no unitary existence anyway – although in the latter part of his career Mach came to see affinities between his standpoint and the world-view of Buddhism. Mach believed that his view, far from rejecting the ethical value of the individual personality, enhanced it by preventing an over-evaluation of the 'self'; it placed the emphasis on the moral welfare of humanity as a whole. This linked back to Mach's conception of the relation between science and human progress: the triumph of the scientific spirit provided both a technological and a moral basis for human evolutionary advancement.

Mach's writings and teachings both helped to foster a climate of opinion in Vienna propitious for the development of what came to be known as logical positivism or logical empiricism (the latter being the term preferred by Schlick), and also directly influenced the ideas of the most prominent members of the Vienna Circle.[20]

But the logical positivists drew heavily upon other sources also, and in certain respects their work contrasts quite clearly with that of Mach. Beginning with the group formed in 1907 around Frank, a physicist, Neurath, an economist, and Hahn, a mathematician, the logical positivists sought to develop a view of science which would recognize the vital significance of logic and mathematics, as systems of symbolic representations, in scientific thought. This led them to acknowledge the central importance of language: a theme which connects their writings to the major thrust of development of philosophy as a whole in the twentieth century. One line of thought leading in this direction within the philosophy of science was that provided by Poincaré's conventionalism, sometimes referred to as the 'new positivism'. Schlick and others were critical of conventionalism, but recognized the force of the claim that scientific theories embodied linguistic conventions. The thesis that theories were languages for the representation of facts, stripped of some of the sceptical features of conventionalism, was taken over as a key element of logical positivism.

But in their approach to the mode of analysing the content of such languages, the logical positivists were indebted to British philosophy. What has been called the 'revolution in British philosophy',[21] led by Moore and Russell, was initiated by them as a reaction to the Hegelianism of Bradley, McTaggart and others. It was both a return to the traditions of British empiricism and a new departure. Russell himself did not set out to discredit metaphysics; rather, he believed that philosophy should become rigorous and precise, and that the way to achieve this goal lay through the logical elucidation of the language in which scientific theories were couched. Philosophy was to reveal the logical structure which underlay the superficial play of appearances. Russell's object was not, like that of Husserl's transcendental reduction, eventually to recover the everyday world of common sense or of the 'natural attitude', but to provide an account that would conform to established scientific knowledge. Russell's 'logical atomism' had a strong influence on the young Wittgenstein, and it was partly through Wittgenstein's personal contacts with some of the Vienna Circle, and through his *Tractatus*, that these ideas were communicated. Wittgenstein's impact upon the members of the Circle has been so frequently emphasized, however, that it is worthwhile pointing out that Carnap, ultimately the most influential of the group, acknowledged Frege and Russell as having had the strongest effect upon his philosophical development. He attended Frege's lectures in Jena, and through them was introduced to the *Principia Mathematica*; Hahn had independently acquainted the members of the Circle with the latter work.

In retrospect, it has become clear that the logical positivists read Wittgenstein's *Tractatus* against a Machian background which led them to disregard crucial features of it. The book is not an exposition which as a whole could be said to exemplify the traditional tenets of empiricism; it is rather, as Wittgenstein remarked subsequently, a sort of 'Platonic myth', a metaphor in its own right. This undoubtedly separates the early Wittgenstein decisively from the main line of development of logical positivism, even if Schlick and his associates saw themselves as continuing along the path Wittgenstein had opened up.[22] The *Tractatus* influenced the growth of logical positivism particularly in respect of the argument for the distinction between the analytic and the synthetic. There were no synthetic *a priori* judgements. Systems of logic or mathematics, deductively derived from axioms, were essentially tautological; any other general claim to knowledge was synthetic, which meant that it could be counterfactually shown to be false.

Logical positivism and modern empiricism

The members of the Vienna Circle, in its early days, saw themselves as the enthusiastic progenitors of a new Enlightenment: as Feigl described it, as carrying on 'in the spirit of Hume and Comte, but equipped with more fully developed logical tools'.[23] In the writings of the logical positivists the differentiation of what was scientific and what was not became convergent with what was meaningful and what was meaningless. What came to be called the 'Verification Principle' went through numerous versions, as the inadequacy of Schlick's original formulation, that the meaning of (synthetic) statements consisted in the method of their verification, became very rapidly apparent. In these later versions, 'testability' was substituted for 'verification'. Obviously it would be mistaken to hold that a statement was meaningful only when we had managed to test its validity: otherwise, with improvements in empirical techniques of validation, previously meaningless statements would suddenly become meaningful ones. So the Verification Principle was altered to hold that a statement was meaningful if there was some means of potentially testing, or 'confirming', it. But various major difficulties still remained evident, the most debated being the status of the Principle itself. For if it could not be subjected to the criterion of testability, if it could not itself be tested, it should seemingly be dismissed as meaningless.

To attempt to get around this difficulty, the Verification Principle was declared to be a procedural rule, not itself a statement. This helped to indicate that what was at issue was, in some part, a problem of the nature of statements: of what constituted a statement. This can be illustrated by reference to another dilemma in the early formulations of the Verification Principle, concerning the breadth of its application. If taken as a criterion to be applied very generally to all kinds of moral prescription or aesthetic judgement, it had the consequence of eliminating these as meaningless, along with metaphysics and theology. But if it concerned only the meaningfulness of 'statements', the implication could be drawn that it supplied a criterion for distinguishing statements from other kinds of judgement, command, etc. The first, more 'radical', version of logical positivism gradually became abandoned in favour of the second, more 'liberal' one – especially in the hands of Carnap.[24] The view that the 'pseudo-sentences' of metaphysics were meaningless came to be supplanted by the more sophisticated notion that metaphysical doctrines lacked cognitive meaning, although they might have emotive meaning. To borrow an expression of Ayer's, originally applied in a slightly different context, the metaphysician was treated less like a criminal than like a patient.[25]

The logical positivists initially classified most of the traditional ontological and epistemological dilemmas of philosophy as belonging to metaphysics, and hence as outside the scope of rational discussion. The disputes between phenomenalism, realism, idealism, and so on were dismissed as meaningless, since there was no way that they could be made to submit to any characterization of the Verification Principle. However, they believed that certain issues relevant to these long-established debates could be sustained, and resolved, if they were treated as debates about appropriate philosophical languages. In this way the back door was left

ajar for the incorporation of features within the writings of the
logical positivists that were denied public admittance at the front.
Carnap's earlier work sets out a version of phenomenalism, although he claimed to be discussing only the relevance of 'a
phenomenalistic language' to scientific procedures. His major
work in the first part of his intellectual career, *Der logische
Aufbau der Welt*, pursued the theme that the aim of philosophy
was to express knowledge as a logical structure of basic certainties.
Here Carnap advocated a phenomenalistic grounding of such certainties. The only sure knowledge was that which was immediately
given as sense-data; our knowledge of material objects was secondary and derived.[26] Neurath was mainly instrumental in persuading Carnap to abandon this position, the first of several
substantial alterations the latter was to introduce into his views
over the course of the years. In order to skirt the suggestion that
he was again becoming involved in the sorts of epistemological
debate that were prohibited, Carnap referred to his shift from
phenomenalism to physicalism as a change of 'attitude', and not
one of 'belief', since this would require a theoretical defence of the
falsity of the first and the truth of the latter. However, it is clear
enough that there was an underlying theoretical justification of the
change which both Neurath and Carnap accepted: that whereas
phenomenalism led to solipsistic paradoxes, physicalism provided
more readily for an intersubjective language in which reports of
observations were communicated between observers.

Neurath and Carnap developed their physicalist thesis in some
part in direct opposition to the tradition of the *Geisteswissenschaften*, which insisted upon the existence of logical and methodological differences between the natural and the social sciences.
Everything, Neurath held, occurred in nature, as part of the physical world. Carnap attempted to express this as a thesis about
language: that is, to show that all knowledge could be reduced to
the propositions of a physicalist language. This applied as much to
our knowledge of minds as to that of happenings in nature. All
statements in psychology, according to Carnap, whether they were
about a mental state of one's own or that of others, could be
translated into a language which referred to physical events in the
body of the person or persons concerned.

On these grounds, psychology is a part of the domain of
unified science based on physics. By 'physics' we wish to mean,

not the system of currently known physical laws, but rather the science characterized by a mode of concept formation which traces every concept back to state-coordinates, that is, to systematic assignments of numbers to space–time points. Understanding 'physics' in this way, we can rephrase our thesis in a particular thesis of physicalism – as follows: psychology is a branch of physics.[27]

The members of the Vienna Circle were already divided quite considerably among themselves prior to their enforced scattering into exile and Schlick's death in 1936. Hahn, Neurath and Carnap, the so-called 'left wing' of the Circle, were the main figures in the shift away from the dogmatic views of the earlier days, whereas Schlick and Waismann were more inclined to hold fast to their established ideas. In later times, the core of the movement was continued in the United States, and to a lesser extent in Britain. 'Logical positivism' lost the clear-cut identity that it previously had, and devolved into a more general stream of positivistic philosophy, finding ready contacts with, and having a great deal of influence upon, the traditions of empiricism and pragmatism already strongly engrained in Anglo-Saxon philosophy. Among the members of the Vienna Circle, Carnap, Neurath, Frank, Gödel and Feigl went to the United States, as did Reichenbach, von Mises and Hempel from the Berlin group of philosophers who shared much with them, and the Polish logician Tarski, whose ideas influenced both Carnap and Popper (who came to Britain after a spell of time in New Zealand). The sway of these authors over the development of certain core areas of analytic philosophy in the English-speaking world has been very considerable indeed, although tempered in Britain particularly by the influence of 'ordinary-language philosophy' and the later Wittgenstein. I shall be concerned with two principal, connected aspects of the influence of the former group of authors: in respect of the philosophy of natural science, the dominance of what has been variously called (by Feigl) the 'orthodox' or (by Putnam) the 'received' model of science; and the elaboration, in the light of these views, of the thesis of the unity of science in respect of the logic of the social sciences.

The orthodox model of science derives from the liberalization of the original logical positivist doctrines, especially as led by Carnap; but it also preserves features that stretch back through to Mach's writings. Mach wanted to reduce experience to relations between simple elements. These elements were sensations, not statements about sensations, such as appeared in scientific theories. Hence Mach failed to recognize the difference between 'formal' and 'material' modes of speaking. Statements are frequently couched in such a form that they seem to concern experiences, while in fact they are assertions about other statements: these were called by Carnap 'syntactical sentences'. Mach's positivistic philosophy was transformed into logical positivism by treating Mach's 'elements' syntactically, as components not of experience but of a formal language in which experience was described. Mach's elements became 'elementary sentences' or 'protocol sentences': the simplest sentences, not further reducible, in which the formal language was expressed.[28] A protocol sentence, as in legal transcription of protocols, was supposed to be a statement of experience, immediately recorded. Carnap regarded the problem of the form of protocol statements as the basic issue in the logic of science, and his attempts to grapple with it provide the key to some of the major changes in his ideas from his early phenomenalist viewpoint onwards. The original view of most of the Vienna Circle was that scientific knowledge rests upon a bedrock of indubitable fact, expressed in the immediacy of sensations as specified by Mach: this is the theme of the *Aufbau*. But just as Neurath rejected phenomenalism, he never accepted the existence of the bedrock of certainty as ordered by protocol statements. In his famous analogy, knowledge was like a ship that had to be continually rebuilt even while it remained afloat. Carnap was influenced by this, and also came to acknowledge that the thesis that scientific theories could in a fairly simple sense be 'reduced' to protocol statements had to be revised and made more elaborate.

Carnap was thus led to place a much greater emphasis upon the role of theoretical concepts in the advancement of scientific knowledge than in his very early work, upon the incompleteness of such concepts, and upon their differentiation from the language of observation protocols. Theoretical concepts, one part of the system of scientific knowledge, could not be directly derived from, or reduced to, the other part, the language of observation. The theoretical language and the observation language, however, were connected by 'correspondence rules', whereby observations might be interpreted in the light of theories, and vice versa. This conception was the core of the orthodox model. A science such as physics was conceived to be a calculus, whose axioms were the fundamental physical laws. The calculus was not directly interpreted, but was a 'freely floating system', in relation to which other theoretical terms were defined. Some of the latter could be interpreted by semantic rules that related them to a groundwork of observable fact; but interpretation of the theoretical terms was never complete. The theoretical cohesion of the system was provided by its hypothetico-deductive character, in which theorems could be deduced from the axioms and hence, via the rules of correspondence, particular observations could be 'explained'. This is some way from the original emphases of logical positivism in so far as the criterion of 'testability' only applied in an immediate way at the level of the observation language – although in the final works of his career Carnap still expressed the belief that a means could be found for differentiating cognitively meaningful theoretical terms from meaningless ones.

The precise nature of correspondence rules has proved a controversial matter among positivistically minded philosophers. The usual overall picture of the relation between the observational and theoretical languages is something akin to Braithwaite's analogy: correspondence rules are the 'zip' that fastens together theory and observation; the fastener progressively pulls the two elements of a system of knowledge together as uninterpreted theorems are transformed into observation statements, expanding the empirical content of the theoretical constructs.[29] Allowing of a detachment between theoretical concepts and observation statements – representing the abandonment of the Verification Principle in anything at all close to its original form – had the virtue, Carnap claimed, of allowing for the creative scope of scientific innovation and the wide explanatory power that abstract theory could possess.[30] On the other hand, since it had become generally recognized that observation statements were not unchallengeable, the implication might be drawn that the claimed differentiation between the theoretical and the observation language could not be drawn clearly at all. For, as Feigl says, most positivistically inclined authors, even those involved in or close to the original Vienna group, came to recognize that observation statements cannot be entirely 'theory-free'.[31]

The dominant account of scientific explanation developed in modern empiricism is that given clearest shape in a famous article by Hempel and Oppenheim.[32] It stimulated a wide-ranging debate, and a very large literature, in response to which Hempel modified and elaborated upon his views as first set out. I shall only summarize its main features briefly here; since its possible application to the social sciences and history provoked as much discussion as its relevance to natural science, it provides an appropriate transition point from which to move to an appraisal of the influence of positivistic philosophy in sociology. The core idea was that the most precise, although not only, form of scientific explanation was 'deductive-nomological' (this also, following Dray, came to be called the 'covering-law model' of explanation). Explanation of an event here involved reference to information supplied by two types of statement, which were brought together. These were, first, general laws; and, second, statements that specified particular circumstances in which those laws had application. The statement referring to the event or phenomenon to be explained (the 'explanandum') was deduced as a necessity from the conjunction of these two.[33] The objective testing of a scientific explanation hence involved empirical confirmation of the statement describing the initial or 'boundary' conditions; empirical confirmation of the laws in relation to which the explanandum was deduced; and logical confirmation of the deduction made. According to Hempel, there was a symmetry or a 'structural equality' between explanation and prediction, since the logical form of the two was the same: a prediction consisted in deducing a statement about a future rather than a past event. Deductive-nomological explanation was held to be integral to all 'empirical sciences', save that in the social sciences and history it was often less clearly manifested than in natural science. Hempel offered two reasons for this: the universal laws in question were frequently common-sense ones that were taken for granted implicitly rather than formulated as explicit statements; and, partly because of this, not enough was known about the empirical basis of such laws for us to be able to state them with precision. Historians mostly offered what Hempel called 'explanation sketches', in which the relevant laws and boundary conditions were only vaguely hinted at: explanation sketches could be made more complete, and thus more 'scientifically acceptable', in Hempel's words, through being filled out by empirical testing of the laws and conditions on which they were based.

This theory of explanation in social science was justified by Hempel in conscious opposition to the tradition of 'interpretative understanding' of the *Geisteswissenschaften* – thus echoing one of the persistent themes of logical positivism. *Verstehen*, or what Hempel referred to as 'the method of empathic understanding', was admitted as a component in the method of the social sciences only as a mode of suggesting hypotheses. It was not indispensable for social or historical explanation, and any hypotheses arrived at empathically had then to be established in deductive form, and tested empirically. Hempel made it clear that an empiricist criterion of cognitive meaning had to be applied in the same way here as in the natural sciences. Interpretations of 'meaning' that were made in sociology and history

> consist either in subsuming the phenomena in question under a scientific explanation or explanation sketch; or in an attempt to subsume them under some general idea which is not amenable to any empirical test. In the former case, interpretation clearly is explanation by means of universal hypotheses; in the latter, it amounts to a pseudo-explanation which may have emotive appeal and evoke vivid pictorial associations, but which does not further our theoretical understanding of the phenomena under consideration.[34]

Positivistic philosophy and modern sociology

Of the members of the Vienna Circle, Neurath wrote most extensively on social issues, and made the most sustained attempt to apply logical positivist views to sociology, which he approached from a self-professedly Marxist standpoint. While Neurath was a strong supporter of, and a major influence upon, the thesis that the 'scientific way of thinking' in philosophy marked the way ahead in the evolution of human thought, he was more inclined than the other members of the group to emphasize the importance of the social context of particular philosophical traditions in explaining the hold that such traditions may have over their adherents. Neurath was the main figure who kept logical positivism tied to the general interest in the promotion of social progress character-

istic of Comte and of Mach. His Marxism, however, was unobtrus-
ive theoretically, save in respect of his advocacy of physicalism; he
rejected dialectical logic, the Hegelian legacy in Marx, no less
completely than did his colleagues.

For Neurath sociology was regarded as one segment of the
division of labour in the totality of unified science: like every other
science, it was 'free of any world view'.[35] He envisaged the coming
into being of a system of the sciences in which the laws of each
particular science, such as sociology, would be connected with the
laws of all the other sciences in a uniform logical structure. Laws,
Neurath said, were abstract means of passing from observation
statements to predictions; the concept of observation was in turn
analysed in terms of physicalism, as involving a 'social behaviourism'. Neurath's behaviourism bore close affinities with
operationalism, which of course had in various general respects
run parallel to logical positivism as a whole. In deciding whether a
term such as 'religious ethos' might be legitimately employed in
sociology, according to Neurath, we had to infer the sorts of
observation statement it presupposed, as concrete modes of behaviour. 'Let him [the sociologist] not speak of the "spirit of the
age" if it is not completely clear that he means by it certain verbal
combinations, forms of worship, modes of architecture, fashions,
styles of painting, etc.'[36]

Neurath's writings seem to have had little direct impact on
sociology as such. The influence of the work of the logical positivists has been brought into sociology in a much more important
and pervasive way through a general acceptance of the model of
scientific explanation developed in the phase of the devolution of
logical positivism into positivistic philosophy. Since this is so diffuse, it would be out of the question to analyse it in any detail
here. I shall therefore indicate some of the connections between
positivistic philosophy and positivistic sociology by illustration.
Such illustration is easy to find. One aspect of the broad influence
which positivistic philosophy has enjoyed within the social sciences, in the English-speaking world at least, is reflected in the
replacement of the term 'method' by 'methodology'. The latter
has come to mean nothing more than the analysis of procedures of
research; it has little explicit relation to the broader process
of reflection on the form and concerns of sociology, which is
hived off as the proper task of the 'philosophy of the social

sciences'. Methodology is often presumed to involve no particular philosophical commitments; but most of the leading texts offer a few positivistic trimmings to the package. Thus Lazarsfeld and Rosenberg, for example, quoted Bridgman and Hempel with approval, accepting the positivist programme of effecting the substitution of a precise, formal language of observation for everyday language as the first demand of a scientific sociology.[37]

Rather than attempting to multiply such examples, I shall concentrate upon discussing the direction of emphasis of three authors whose work was widely adopted within the mainstream of contemporary sociology. First, Ernest Nagel, whose book *The Structure of Science* served as a stock reference for innumerable sociological texts and discussions; second, Zetterberg's *On Theory and Verification in Sociology*, a representative and influential discussion of the methodology of social science; and third, Hempel's analysis of functionalism, which connects functional explanation to the deductive-nomological model, thereby re-establishing direct contact between 'positivism' in its modern form and 'positivism' in the tradition of Comte and Durkheim.

Nagel's book was explicitly indebted to Carnap and Frank (as well as to M.R. Cohen). The work followed something of a Comtean outline: the discussion proceeded from mechanics through physics to biology and the social sciences. The account was anchored in terms of an exposition of deductive-nomological explanation, and the differentiation of languages of observation and theory connected by correspondence rules; biology and the social sciences were distinct from the rest of natural science in so far as the former might make use of teleological or functional explanations. Nagel denied that 'teleology' was specifically dependent upon the activities of conscious, reasoning agents, or that teleological explanation involved a presumption of final causes. The question of the 'subjective' or 'meaningful' character of human conduct was taken up at some length. 'Interpretative understanding', according to Nagel, involved two characteristics: the assumption that one or more particular individuals were, at a certain time, in certain psychological states; and the assumption of a general principle or law stating the ways in which such states were related both to each other and to 'overt behaviour'. Observational evidence was required for both of these, rather than any kind of emphatic identification with the actors whose conduct was to be explained:

> We can *know* that a man fleeing from a pursuing crowd that is animated by hatred towards him is in a state of fear, without our having experienced such violent fears and hatred or without imaginatively recreating such emotions in ourselves – just as we can *know* that the temperature of a piece of wire is rising because the velocities of its constituent molecules are increasing, without having to imagine what it is like to be a rapidly moving molecule.[38]

Like Hempel, Nagel accepted that empathy might play a part in the derivation of hypotheses; but such hypotheses had then to be tested by 'controlled sensory observation'.

Most of the generalizations in the social sciences, Nagel said, were statistical uniformities rather than universal laws. This was not, however, because of any specific features of human behaviour as such, but was primarily because of the relatively youthful stage of development of sociology, which had not yet developed the conceptual and observational precision necessary for determining exactly the limiting conditions of its generalizations; while he had strong reservations about functionalist theories in the social sciences, Nagel apparently believed that such precision might be achieved in principle, although there were various factors likely to prevent its full realization in practice. In any case, statistical, rather than universal, laws were typical of many areas of natural science. Statistical generalizations were complemented in the social sciences by functional ones, the latter explaining the maintenance of system states through regulative feedback. The advance of functional explanations in sociology and anthropology was, as in the case of deductive explanations, hindered by the as yet diffuse character of most social scientific concepts.

In Nagel's view, the fact that human beings can modify their conduct in the light of their knowledge, including their knowledge of generalizations made by sociologists, was not a major source of 'difficulty' for social science. It was not in fact something which was unique to the social sciences: in natural science also the observation of a phenomenon could alter the character of that phenomenon. The very statement of the latter implied some awareness of the extent to which what was observed was altered by the process of observation; hence the effects produced by the interaction would either be small, and could be ignored, or if large could be calculated and corrected for. The logical character of the 'interference' was the same in nature and society, although the 'mechanisms involved' were different.[39] The possibility of self-fulfilling and self-negating predictions in the social sciences similarly found direct analogy in natural science. A computer, for example, which guided the firing of a gun might be defective such that it just missed the target; however, the oscillations produced by the transmitting of the (erroneous) calculations could cause the gun in fact to hit the target just because it was originally aimed wrongly.

Nagel's work was consciously directed to a spelling out of 'liberalized logical positivism'; that of Zetterberg, on the other hand, was more concerned to describe the conduct of research in sociology, and the connection between such research and what he called 'theoretical sociology'.[40] It was an attempt, the author said, to complement the insistence of authors such as Lundberg that sociology should match the scientific rigour of the natural sciences with a fuller appreciation than Lundberg expressed of the basic importance of theory in science. Zetterberg made due obeisance to the 'humanistic content' of the social sciences, but the main emphasis of his argument was upon the continuity between physics, biology and sociology. Explanation in sociology, if at any rate it was to advance beyond lay knowledge or lay beliefs, had to assume the same deductive-nomological form which it had in natural science. 'Theory' in sociology was often used very broadly, as virtually equivalent to 'social thought', Zetterberg said; in his usage, however, it meant a set of deductively connected laws, to which any particular event, within boundary conditions, could be referred. Zetterberg's description of the formalized language which sociology needed if it was to meet the demands of being an empirical science, in which he drew upon Hempel's analysis of cognitive meaning, implied a strict criterion of reducibility of theoretical terms to the terms of the observation language. In an ideal theory, it would be possible to reduce the content of all second-order theoretical concepts to a set of 'primitive terms', utilizing the procedures of formal logic. The primitive terms of theoretical sociology as a whole referred to observations of the behaviour of actors in interaction.[41]

Zetterberg answered affirmatively the age-old question: are there sociological laws parallel to those discovered in the natural sciences? There were many such laws or theoretical propositions that had been turned up by social science; for example 'persons tend to issue prescriptions that maintain the rank they enjoy in the social structure'; or, 'the more favourable evaluations rank-and-file members receive in a group, the more their ideas converge with those of other group members.'[42] Two factors influenced the specification of such laws in the sociological literature: the conditions of their application were often only vaguely indicated, and it was not made clear what procedures were necessary to confirm or 'verify' them. Everyday life abounded with generalizations that people made of their own conduct or of the activities of others; the task of sociology was to test these so as to turn them from lay hypotheses into confirmed findings and laws, discarding those shown to be invalid.

> I think sociology should make a more serious effort to incorporate in its theories the best thoughts (theoretical hypotheses) of the human conditions found in Homer, Dante, Shakespeare, Cervantes, Twain and other great writers, who now provide the lion's share of any educated layman's conception of the human drama. In the end, however, the outcome of the theoretical enterprise should be 'high informative content, well backed by experience', that is, laws.[43]

Zetterberg's discussion touched only marginally on functionalism, and did not elucidate the bearing of what he had to say upon the issue of functional explanation in sociology. Nagel had treated the question at some length; but here I shall consider the account provided by Hempel, which was concerned to connect deductive-nomological to functional explanation.[44] According to Hempel, functional analysis was a form of teleological explanation, the latter referring not to the causes of an event, but to the ends to which it was directed. Teleological explanation, however, had traditionally been impervious to empirical testing: Hempel quoted the example of entelechy or vital force as a metaphysical principle which, in biology, had been involved in unacceptable teleological theories. The problem was to strip functional analysis away from any association with such non-testable vitalistic principles.

In biology, Hempel said, functional analysis was concerned with the explanation of a recurrent activity (such as the beating of the heart) in terms of its contribution to a state (such as the circulation of the blood through the body) of the organism required for the maintenance of life. In the social sciences, the objects of analysis were similarly patterned and repetitive modes of social conduct examined in relation to states of the larger social system. But what was the explanatory element in functional explanation? It was not to be found in the type of nomology characteristic of either deductive-nomological or inductive-statistical explanation. There was a close similarity in logical form nevertheless. When, in giving physical explanations, we say that an ice cube melted because it was put into warm water, we are able to justify this as an explanation of the melting by reference to general laws of which the specific case is an instance. In a similar way, the 'because' of functional explanation implied a principle such that, within specified conditions, a system would either invariably or with a high degree of probability meet the functional exigencies needed for its survival in the face of forces threatening to change it. That is to say, the general propositions involved in functional analysis referred to the self-regulation of biological or social systems; thus understood, they yielded predictions which could be objectively tested.[15] This depended upon defining concepts like 'system need' operationally.

> It will no doubt be one of the most important tasks of functional analysis in psychology and the social sciences to ascertain to what extent such phenomena of self-regulation can be found, and can be represented by corresponding laws. Whatever specific laws might be discovered by research along these lines, the kind of explanation and prediction made possible by them does not differ in its logical character from that of the physical sciences.[16]

The three examples I have chosen here are arbitrary, in so far as they could have been replaced by many others expressing similar views – although each has been influential in its own right. I do not want to claim, of course, that the general standpoint they represent has ever become an unrivalled one, but it has undoubtedly been the dominant approach in English-speaking sociology. This is not just because the main tradition has insisted that the social sciences should model their aspirations on the sciences of nature:

rather, many authors in the former field have accepted, explicitly or implicitly, that 'science' can be identified with the positivistic philosophy of science. Functionalism has played an important part in this, as the conceptual vehicle of the continuity between natural and social science: the division between the physical and the life sciences appears as great as, if not larger than, that between biology and sociology.

The post-positivistic philosophy of science

In the philosophy of science, as contrasted to the methodological self-understanding of the social sciences, the 'orthodox model' has long since become subject to broad-ranging attack, led by such authors as Toulmin, Feyerabend, Hesse, Kuhn and others. While these writers disagreed about the conclusions that should be drawn from their critical analyses of positivistic philosophy, it is clear that they successfully displaced the orthodox model. The work of Karl Popper, however, is both prior to theirs and in some part one of its sources; a tracing of the critical views which Popper expressed of logical positivism, as well as the evident themes which connect his writings to those of the Vienna Circle, necessarily precedes any commentary on the 'newer philosophy of science.'

The relation between Popper's views and those of the leading members of the Vienna Circle, particularly Carnap, has been a controversial one from the beginning. Popper was not himself a member of the Circle, but had a close intellectual contact with it. His first and still his major work, *Logik der Forschung*, was discussed within the group, and regarded as basically in accord with the perspective of logical positivism. Popper, on the other hand, emphasized that the work was radically critical of the philosophy of logical positivism, and since its first publication has continued to stress the differences between his position and any kind of empiricism or positivistic philosophy. The points at issue are not easy to disentangle. In assessing the differences between Popper's ideas and those of logical positivism, even in its more liberalized versions, one should mention the following of Popper's views as the most distinctive sources of contrast: his complete rejection of induction, and his concomitant rejection of 'sensory certainty', whether manifest as phenomenalism or as physicalism; his substitution of falsification for verification, with the corresponding stress upon boldness and ingenuity in the framing of scientific hypotheses; his defence of tradition which, in conjunction with the operation of the critical spirit, is integral to science; and his replacement of the logical-positivist ambition of putting an end to metaphysics, by revealing it as nonsense, with the aim of securing criteria of demarcation between science and pseudo-science. These differences are certainly considerable, and underlie Popper's continual insistence that not only is he not a 'positivist', but that he is one of its foremost critics in the philosophy of science. However, some major overall similarities between Popper's writings and those of the logical positivists are clearly apparent. Popper shares the conviction that scientific knowledge, imperfect though it may be, is the most certain and reliable knowledge to which human beings can aspire; his endeavour to establish clear criteria of demarcation between science and pseudo-science has much of the same impetus as the concerns of the logical positivists to free science from mystifying, empty word-play; and, like the logical positivists, his characterization of science is a procedural one: science is separated from other forms of tradition in so far as its theories and findings are capable of being exposed to empirical testing and therefore to potential falsification.

Popper's first formulation of the principle of falsification as the key to the demarcation between science and non-science was arrived at, according to his own testimony, as a result of reflection upon the gulf between certain types of social theory – especially Marxism and psychoanalysis – and the physical sciences. The former, Popper came to the conclusion, had more in common with primitive myths than with science; they were more like astrology than astronomy. The reason for this, according to Popper, lay less in their lack of precision, as compared to physics, than in what to their adherents was their most attractive characteristic: the range of their explanatory power. As total systems of thought, they gained their support from a quasi-religious experience of conversion or revelation, and, once converted, the believer was able to explain any event in terms of them. Since they could explain anything or everything, there was no source or type of empirical evidence that could be pointed to as a basis of showing the ideas involved to be mistaken. This stood in marked contrast to relativity theory in physics, which generated specific predictions about the movement of material entities, and delivered itself as a hostage to the outcome of the testing of those predictions; such an element of risk was absent from theories such as Marxism and psychoanalysis, which protected themselves against counterfactual evidence. The distinctive characteristic of science, therefore, was that instead of merely seeking confirmation or verification of a theory, the scientist attempted to refute it. Confirmation, or what Popper subsequently came to call 'corroborating evidence', of a theory resulted from its successful withstanding of empirical assaults which had the aim of falsifying it. 'One can sum up all this by saying that *the criterion of the scientific status of a theory is its falsifiability, or refutability, or testability.*'[47]

Popper's emphasis upon falsification stands in the closest possible relation to the critique of inductive logic with which he began his *Logik der Forschung*. A major tension had always existed at the heart of empiricist philosophies of science. Science was supposed to yield certain knowledge; on the other hand, the logical form of the induction of laws from observations precluded certainty. However many tests we might make confirming a theoretical proposition, there always remained the possibility that the next test would disconfirm it were it to be made: hence the validity of scientific laws could never be conclusively verified. Popper's response to this classical problem of empiricism was to deny the premise on which it rests: that is to say, he denied that science proceeded through induction at all, and accepted as inevitable that no abstract proposition in science could ever be finally verified. There was, as Popper put it, an asymmetry between verification and falsification. No matter how many white swans we might observe, this did not justify the conclusion 'all swans are white'; but while such a universal statement could not ever be derived from singular statements reporting observations, it could be contradicted or shown to be wrong by singular statements. Thus although Popper's philosophy of science was sceptical in the sense that it accepted that no scientific law, even that which scientists might feel was completely securely founded, could be conclusively proved, it insisted that scientific advance was possible through the empirical refutation of hypotheses. The object of science was still conceived of in a traditional manner as the securing of abstract generalizations that were true in so far as they corresponded to facts; but we could never be logically certain that we had attained truth, although we could approach closer and closer to such certainty by the elimination of false theories.

Just as scientific theories were not tested inductively, neither were they arrived at inductively: the manner in which a theory was discovered or invented had nothing to do with its scientific status, which depended solely upon its being able to specify falsifying conditions and being able to withstand empirical testing of those conditions. There was no 'logic of discovery', since new ideas might be conceived as a flash of intuition, or as the result of religious reflection, or in many other contexts. Nor was there any 'observation' which was prior to 'theory' in the manner integral to the notion of inductive logic, and fundamental to logical positivism in the form of protocol statements. All observations were 'theory-impregnated', and were interpretations of facts. There could be no foundation of certain or incorrigible knowledge upon which science built, as logical positivism, and positivistic philosophy more generally, assumed. Scientific knowledge was built on shifting sand, and what was important was not where we began but how far we were able to subject our conjectures to empirical test, and hence to rational criticism. This also supplied the guiding thread in Popper's social philosophy. An 'open society' was one in which no single system of ideas was able to monopolize the social order: where freedom was ensured by the critical confrontation of diverse ideas and policies, whose outcomes could thus be rationally assessed.

Popper consistently attempted to separate his thought from the preoccupation with language characteristic of so much contemporary philosophy, holding that the latter obscured the true nature of the scientific enterprise, which was above all concerned with the relation between hypotheses and the world of real objects and events. Terminology, Popper argued, did not matter, save in so far as clarity and unambiguousness of expression were demanded for the rigorous testing of scientific theories. The same ideas could be expressed in different words; all that mattered was that they should be clearly expressed, and formulated in such a way that the circumstances in which they could be declared to be falsified were known. Popper's philosophy possesses the boldness of formulation that he requires of science itself: the appeal of his substitution of falsification for verification derives in large part from the simple and incisive way in which it disposes at a stroke of the traditional dilemmas of induction. But the simplicity of the notion is belied by difficulties which it conceals, consideration of which forces us to confront more directly issues of language which Popper tended to dismiss as being at most of only marginal importance.

In the first place, the notion of falsification sits uneasily in Popper's writings with his commitment to a correspondence theory of truth. The aim of science, according to Popper, was more accurately described as concerned with 'verisimilitude' than as with truth. But the idea of verisimilitude is only defensible if we assume that there are a finite number of possible conjectures or theories about nature, such that by progressively refuting them we get nearer and nearer to the truth. There seems no warrant for such an assumption, all the less so given Popper's injunction that it was incumbent on the scientist to look for 'unlikely' hypotheses since these were the easiest to test. Second, the very idea of falsification, which looks so concise and clear presented as a logical solution to difficulties of induction, when applied to the analysis of actual scientific activities of testing and the comparison of theories, becomes quite murky. Popper, of course, acknowledged that the logic of falsification was in some part separable from its implementation in scientific procedures. The universal statement 'all swans are white' is in principle contradicted by the discovery of a black swan, but in practice matters are not so simple because we have to decide, for one thing, what is to count as a black swan, that is, as a falsifying observation. It would be possible, for example, for someone accepting the universal statement 'all swans are white' to discount any case of a black swan that might be found as not being a swan at all, and hence place it outside the scope of the law. Popper's response to such a tactic was to declare it unscientific, as alien to the spirit in which science should be carried on. But this is not very convincing, and one could claim that here Popper is hoist with his own petard, because such an argument seems to do just what it criticizes: namely, to propose that any instance which does not accord with the thesis should be disregarded as 'unscientific procedure'. One of the consequences of Kuhn's work was to affirm that this would not do, and the same holds for that of Feyerabend and Lakatos – in spite of the fact that the latter author regarded Popper as the main originator of what he called 'sophisticated falsificationism'.

Kuhn's most important study, *The Structure of Scientific Revolutions*, has become very well known indeed, and there is no need to do more than refer in the most cursory manner here to its main themes. Kuhn's views may differ considerably in certain respects from those of Popper, but they also connect up closely with them, because both authors recognized the significance of the history of science for the philosophy of science (and vice versa). This has not been true, by and large, of the logical positivists, who have concentrated primarily upon producing abstract, formal analyses without giving any detailed attention to the historical study of the development of science. Hence, as Kuhn pointed out, they have tended to operate with accounts of scientific discoveries as finished achievements, as they are recorded in textbooks: but these no more satisfactorily describe the substance of what actually happens in science than tourist brochures do the culture into which they initiate the traveller.

Kuhn's work was partly stimulated by his awareness of a contrast between the natural and social sciences, not of the kind traditionally stressed in the *Geisteswissenschaften*, but concerning the lack of agreement among social scientists over the basic character of their intellectual endeavours. The social sciences, in short, lacked 'paradigms'. Thus they did not show the characteristic pattern of development of the natural sciences, which was one of periods of relatively stable 'normal science', involving puzzle-solving activity within the confines of a shared paradigm, interspersed with periods of revolutionary change as a result of which a new paradigm came to supersede the old. Revolutions were written out of textbooks of science, or rather never written in: a textbook expressed a paradigm as the consolidated achievements of a particular science to date. Periods of revolutionary change in science were none the less a consequence of the activities of normal science, for it was through the puzzle-solving activities of normal science that contradictions or anomalies emerged within the existing framework of knowledge. A revolution in science was a change in world-view, a *Gestalt*-switch: the conceptual transformation thus effected infused 'observation' itself.

Is sensory experience fixed and neutral? The epistemological view-point that has most often guided Western philosophy for three centuries dictates an immediate and unequivocal, Yes! In the absence of a developed alternative, I find it impossible to relinquish entirely that viewpoint. Yet it no longer functions effectively, and the attempts to make it do so through the introduction of a neutral language of observations now seem to me hopeless.[48]

The Structure of Scientific Revolutions has provoked a great deal of discussion, to which Popper, among many others, contributed. In the course of this debate, Kuhn has attempted to clear up ambiguities in the original work, and to elaborate upon it in various ways. I shall concentrate only upon mentioning issues relevant to the subsequent sections of this study. The most useful way to identify these is to indicate some of the differences of emphasis in Kuhn's work as compared to that of Popper. Three such differences are the following:

1 For Kuhn, 'normal science' was integral to scientific progress, since the suspension of criticism involved in the common acceptance of a paradigm made possible a concentration of effort upon clearly defined problems. Constant critical assessment of the most basic elements of a 'disciplinary matrix' would prevent such a concentration of effort: this was just what occurred in pre-paradigmatic disciplines, such as the social sciences, in which the inability to agree over basic premises of the substance and method of inquiry blocked the development of knowledge in the form achieved in many areas of natural science. The sort of 'permanent revolution' in science envisaged by Popper neither described the actual conduct of science, nor was a desirable framework for it; normal science was not merely deformed science. This view also separated Kuhn from Feyerabend's 'scientific anarchism': a proliferation of basic theories was only to be striven for in times of revolutionary crisis.

2 Kuhn's writings demonstrated the hazards in transferring the idea of falsification to the actual practice of science. He said he took the notion of 'the asymmetry of falsification and confirmation very seriously indeed',[49] but 'testing' had to be related to the conjunctions of normal and revolutionary science. Scientists working within a paradigm often either ignored or treated as

consistent with their accepted theories findings that were subsequently – following the dissolution of the paradigm – recognized as incompatible with, or as refuting, those theories.

3 Meaning-variance or the 'incommensurability' of paradigms
   appeared as a fundamental problem in Kuhn's work in a way in
   which it did not in that of Popper; partly as a consequence of
   this, Kuhn found Popper's account of verisimilitude unacceptable. Kuhn has consistently denied that he is a relativist, and
   it is quite obvious that he could not be one: for if the succession of paradigms is not regarded as 'progressive', in some
   sense, the differentiation between pre-paradigmatic and post
   paradigmatic sciences effectively loses its significance: on the
   logical level, successive paradigms would only be 'laterally' dis-
   tributed, each equivalent to any other – the same situation that
   is claimed to exist in the social sciences. On the other hand,
   Kuhn found some considerable difficulty in spelling out how
   scientific progress occurred through revolution, and what the
   consequences of the resolution of this problem were for a
   theory of truth.

The critique of positivism in Frankfurt philosophy

Since Hume, positivistic philosophers have generally adopted the
stance that the sensory experience which provides the basis of
scientific knowledge cannot be extended to encompass moral
judgements or ethical values. Disputes concerning morality cannot be settled by appeal to intersubjectively available observations as debates over factual issues can. In the social sciences,
this has long been the common assumption of most otherwise
divergent schools of thought, including various forms of revision-
ist Marxism (such as that led by Eduard Bernstein). Perhaps the
most well-known and influential exposition of the standpoint in
sociology is that of Max Weber, who perhaps more than any other
major writer pursued the implications of the 'fact–value dichotomy' to its furthest limits, and was prepared to accept these
implications in full. For Weber, who drew his views on this issue
from neo-Kantianism rather than from British empiricism, the
findings of natural or social science stood in a purely instrumental
connection to moral values. Science could show us which of a

given choice of means was the most effective way of achieving a certain end, and what other consequences of the achievement of that end were likely to be; but it could not give us the slightest degree of help in deciding to opt for that end itself (save in so far as that end might be in some part a means to other ends).[50] One consequence of this was that there could be no rational arbitration between the sets of 'ultimate values' upon which the major world civilizations rested, and which Weber set out to analyse in his studies of the 'world religions'; such a clash of values was settled in the area of power-struggles.[51]

The imposition of strict limits upon moral reason in positivistic philosophies is something which two generations of Frankfurt philosophers, from Horkheimer, Adorno and Marcuse to Habermas, have been concerned to criticize. The critique of positivism in this respect has been one of the most central preoccupations of what has come to be called 'critical theory'. If there is a single dominating element in critical theory, it is the defence of Reason (*Vernunft*) understood in the sense of Hegel and classical German philosophy: as the critical faculty which reconciles knowledge with the transformation of the world so as to further human fulfilment and freedom. Frankfurt philosophy attempts to follow Marx, and thereby to refurbish modern Marxism itself, by appealing to Hegel's transcendence of Kantian dualisms: not only that of pure and practical Reason, but that of the apperception of phenomena and the unknowable 'things in themselves'. Such dualisms are regarded as both expression and source of a passive, contemplative attitude to knowledge: an attitude which reduces the practical import of knowledge to 'technology' or 'technique' robbed of the unifying potentialities of historical Reason. Whereas in Hegel, as Horkheimer put it, Reason was seen to be inherent in reality, in Hume and in Kant, as well as in Cartesian philosophy it became a 'subjective faculty of the mind'.[52] The individual subject is the sole possessor of reason, and the latter concept is taken to mean merely the calculative relating of means to ends.

The origins of the 'Frankfurt School' were contemporaneous with those of the Vienna Circle, and the members of the former group sharpened their critical assessment of the influence of empiricism in the past by means of onslaughts upon its most prominent representatives in the present. In one such discussion, written in the late 1930s, Horkheimer connected up logical positivism to the tradition of Hume and Locke, but argued that the critical character which the writings of these authors possessed had been sacrificed by the modern logical positivists.[53] The sceptical empiricism of Hume was directed subversively against the prevailing dogmas in order to forge a new beginning, in which rationalism would prevail over the forces of unenlightened mythology. In this sense, the Enlightenment had a moral impetus which in actuality cut across the belief of Hume that facts could be separated from values. This was largely absent from logical positivism, which sought only to complete and to sanction the domination of science as the contemplative reduction of experience to a logically coherent order of laws. Such a view might be thought unfair to Neurath and untrue to the Marxist leanings of various members of the Vienna Circle. But for Horkheimer this comment would be largely beside the point, because Marxism had not stood apart from the positivistic nature of much modern philosophy. On the contrary, the relapse of Marxism into positivistic philosophy was the origin of the twin characteristics of Marxism in the twentieth century: its quietism when in opposition (as in Germany) and its transformation into bureaucratic domination when in power (as in the Soviet Union).

The Frankfurt philosophers attempted to diagnose the beginnings of 'positivistic Marxism' in the writings of Marx himself. What for Althusser and his followers was an 'epistemological break' separating the speculative, idealistic Marx from the first formation of scientific Marxism, for the critical theorists marked the phase of the incipient degeneration of Marxism into positivistic philosophy. The Frankfurt authors differed among themselves about their evaluations of the nature and origins of positivistic Marxism, but their analyses – including that of Habermas in the 'younger generation' – had major overall points of agreement. The critical inspiration of Marxism derived from the dialectic of subject and object, and was lost where 'materialism' meant the denial of the active intervention of the subject in history, or the reduction of culture and cultural ideals to epiphenomena of physical events. Monistic materialism, which regarded all change as the interplay of natural occurrences, converged directly with non-Marxist positivistic philosophy. Several of the critical theorists had doubts about the use of the notion of labour in Marx's writings: in so far as this referred merely to the material transformation of nature, to which the critique of contemporary society was tied, socialism came to be conceived of merely as a technically more efficient version of capitalism. According to Habermas, in 'turning Hegel back on his feet', Marx compressed two elements of Hegel's philosophy into one: the individual's reflexive awareness as the maker of history, and the self-constitution of humanity through labour. When the former is reduced to the latter, the integral tie between history and freedom is dissolved.[54]

In critical theory, 'positivism' has a much broader and more diffuse meaning than it does for most other writers, wider even than what I have distinguished as 'positivistic philosophy'. This use of the term has to be understood against the background of the attempts of the Frankfurt philosophers to effect an ambitious critique of the tendency of development of Western culture since the Enlightenment, and indeed in certain basic respects since classical times. The progenitors of the Enlightenment set out to disenchant the world, to replace myth by solidly founded knowledge, and by the application of that knowledge in technology. In so doing they prepared the way for the domination of modern culture by technical rationality: the undermining of Reason against which Hegel struggled and which, with the disintegration of the Hegelian system, became largely lost to philosophy. In the name of freedom from the domination of myth, the Enlightenment created a new form of domination, hidden from view by its own philosophy: domination by instrumental rationality.

> Subject and object are both rendered ineffectual. The abstract self, which justifies record-making and systematization, has nothing set over against it but the abstract material which possesses no other quality than to be a substrate of such possession. The equation of spirit and world arises eventually, but only with a mutual restriction of both sides. The reduction of thought to a mathematical apparatus conceals the sanction of the world as its own yardstick. What appears to be the triumph of subjective rationality, the subjection of all reality to formalism, is paid for by the obedient subjection of reason to what is directly given. What is abandoned is the whole claim and approach of knowledge: to comprehend the given as such; not merely to determine the abstract spatio-temporal re-

lations of the facts which allow them just to be grasped, but on the contrary to conceive them as the superficies, as mediated conceptual moments which come to fulfilment only in the development of their social, historical, and human significance.[55]

Critical theory is a defence of just those traditions of philosophy which the logical positivists wished to show consist largely of empty metaphysics. It is not surprising that the two schools kept each other at arm's length, and that their mutual influence was slight indeed. However, with the increasing strains to which the positivistic philosophy of science was subject, the influence of the philosophy of the later Wittgenstein and Austin's 'ordinary-language philosophy' in Britain and the United States, and of hermeneutic phenomenology on the Continent, the situation in philosophy (as in social theory) became much more fluid. Among the younger Frankfurt philosophers, Habermas was particularly influential in connecting critical theory to each of the types of philosophy mentioned above, as well as to pragmatism – while sustaining most of its established themes. Habermas, together with Adorno, played the central part in the controversy over Popper's views that came to be called (following the usage of critical theory rather than that of Popper) the 'positivism debate' in German sociology. The debate was an odd one, in so far as none of the participants saw themselves as defending positivistic philosophy, much less described themselves as positivist; given the standpoint of critical theory, however, in which the term 'positivism' is applied very broadly to traditions of thought that would not ordinarily be thus designated, it is not difficult to appreciate that the contested meaning of the term is at the heart of the matters at issue, not merely a linguistic curiosity of the controversy. The initial origin of the dispute was Popper's presentation of 'twenty-seven theses' on the logic of the social sciences at the meeting of the German Sociological Association at Tübingen in 1961; this was followed by a paper by Adorno. Popper and Adorno did not attack each other's contributions directly, however, and their confrontation only ramified into a wide-ranging debate through the subsequent interventions of Habermas, Albert and others.[56]

In his paper, Popper reiterated his well-known view that the aim of the social sciences was the explanation of conduct through the 'situational logic' of action: that is to say, through the rational reconstruction of the circumstances (goals and knowledge) under which individuals acted, and of the consequences of their behaviour. This was an 'interpretative sociology', but not one, according to Popper, that retained any residue of the subjective, empathic qualities with which it had characteristically been associated. It was a 'purely objective method'.[57] As such, it differed in content but not in logical form from the methods of the natural sciences, which Popper described in terms made familiar by the general corpus of his writings. He rejected what he called 'naturalism' in the social sciences, on the same basis as he rejected 'positivism' in natural science: naturalism supposed that sociology began by collecting observations and measurements, and induced generalizations from these which then became incorporated within theories. This derived from a mistaken (positivistic) philosophy of natural science; the 'objectivity' of science lay in its critical method of trial and error. Popper thus affirmed his support of 'critical rationalism', meaning by this his advocacy of falsification as the most integral procedure of science.

Habermas's critique of Popper concentrated mainly upon the limits of Popper's critical rationalism which, according to the former author, still contained a strong residue of positivistic philosophy. Popper's theory of science was an analytical, as opposed to a dialectical, one. Habermas suggested that the 'objectivity' of natural science could not be transferred directly to the social sciences, since the latter were concerned with a pre-interpreted universe of occurrences: that is to say, with a social world in which the categories of experience were already formed by and in the 'meaningful conduct' of human subjects. Hermeneutic understanding, involving the sustaining of communication between the social scientist and those whose conduct he or she studied, was an essential element of procedure in the social sciences, and could not be grasped by simple appeal to the 'observation' of events in nature, even if transposed as 'situational logic'. To conceive of the aim of sociology as that of discovering laws had the practical implication of making of it a social technology.

> In contrast, dialectical theory of society must indicate the gaping discrepancy between practical questions and the accomplishment of technical tasks – not to mention the realization of a meaning which, far beyond the domination of nature achieved by manipula-

tion of a reified relation, no matter how skilful that may be – would relate to the structure of a social life-context as a whole and would, in fact, demand its emancipation.[58]

To accomplish this, a dialectical or critical theory had to transcend the boundaries of critical rationalism as expressed by Popper.

The separation between fact and value, or cognition and evaluation, made in positivistic philosophies, Habermas said, condemned practical questions to irrationality, or to the 'closed world' of myth which it was supposedly the object of positivism to dispel. Unlike most philosophers, Popper openly acknowledged this by declaring that his adherence to rationalism was an article of faith. This made the adoption of rationalism an arbitrary initial decision. Some followers of Popper, notably Bartley, accepted that there could not be a deductive foundation for rationalism, but tried to ground critical rationalism by reference to itself: that is to say, by holding that the commitment to critical method as formulated by Popper could itself in principle be criticized.[59] But this will hardly do: Bartley was unable to specify the conditions under which the commitment to rationality would have rationally to be abandoned; this is because what was understood as 'criticism' here was too narrow, and was not grounded in the historical conditions of human social life and communication. Habermas pointed to the connection between Popper's adherence to a correspondence theory of truth and the thesis of the dualism of fact and value. Popper shielded himself against some of the problems which the correspondence theory raised, when combined with his acceptance of the theory-impregnated character of observation statements, by stressing the difference between knowing what truth meant and having a criterion for deciding the truth or falsity of a statement. According to the notion of falsification, we could not have such a criterion or standard of truth, all we could achieve was the progressive elimination of false views. What this involved, however, Habermas said, was the surreptitious incorporation of standards of evaluation that were uncritically taken over from everyday life: the hermeneutic understanding of ordinary language and intersubjective experience was taken for granted. Critical discussion, as formulated by Habermas, involved three uses of language: the description of a state of affairs; the postulating of rules of procedure; and the critical justification of the former two.[60] Criticism thus could not be contained within the sphere of science itself, but had to concern itself with the standards or values which structured science as one mode of activity among others. So far as the historical context of modern science was concerned, positivistic acceptance of the dualism of fact and value led to a failure to appreciate that technical rationality supported a system of domination as its legitimating ideology.

Neither Albert, defending Popper, nor Popper himself in his commentary on the debate, accepted that these views did place the sort of bounds upon critical rationalism that Habermas claimed. According to Albert, the empirical sciences were able to deal with the type of experience Habermas allotted to hermeneutics, and could represent these as 'facts' like any others. This was, for Albert, potentially a more profoundly critical standpoint than that of Habermas, since it was a more sceptical one, which found its critical impetus in the premise that science often showed that assumptions made within the ordinary day-to-day world were erroneous. Popper's theory of science as myth that was self-critical was the only way of avoiding the twin dilemmas of an infinite regress on the one hand, and the supplying of 'foundations' through sheer dogma on the other.[61] Popper's critical rationalism, he repeated, was quite distinct from positivism in all major respects; the critical theorists used the term in such a lax way that they were able to blanket out these differences, and hence obliquely charge Popper with some of the very same weaknesses that he had in fact shown to be characteristic of positivistic philosophy. In his comments, Popper concurred:

> The fact is that throughout my life I have combated positivist epistemology, under the name of 'positivism'. I do not deny, of course, the possibility of stretching the term 'positivist' until it covers anybody who takes any interest in natural science, so that it can be applied even to opponents of positivism, such as myself. I only contend that such a procedure is neither honest nor apt to clarify matters.[62]

Comments on the philosophy of natural science

It would obviously be out of the question in this context to attempt a comprehensive discussion of the issues raised in the previous sections. I shall confine my comments to a few problems in two major categories: the philosophy of natural science, and the relation between the natural and social sciences.

So far as the first of these is concerned, there are two issues raised by the post-positivistic philosophy of science that loom particularly large. One is the status of falsification, as elaborated by Popper and his disciples (particularly Lakatos), and more generally that of deductivist accounts of scientific knowledge, including within this the 'deductive-nomological model'; the other is the problem of the 'incommensurability' of paradigms such as derives from the writings of Kuhn.

Popper's 'solution to the problem of induction', which he relentlessly advocated from his earlier works, gained much of its attractiveness from its simplicity: the idea that it took only a single disconfirming instance to falsify a universal statement. But the logic of falsification, he had to admit, was discrepant from the practice. Lakatos's studies, although nominally directed at supporting main elements of the Popperian standpoint, showed how wide the discrepancy is. Lakatos distinguished three kinds of falsificationism: dogmatic falsificationism, naive and sophisticated 'methodological falsificationism'. The first was the weakest, treating the logical form of falsification as equivalent to its practice: as if a simple observed event, or unequivocally defined finite set of events, provided the means of refuting scientific theories. This was an empiricist version of falsificationism, in contrast to methodological falsificationism, which accepted the theory-impregnated character of observations. All testing of theories depended upon acceptance of a theoretical framework which, in any given context, represented unproblematic background knowledge.[63] Naive methodological falsificationism, however, still maintained the view that theories could be refuted, and therefore should be abandoned, in the light of 'observations' thus conceived. This would not do because a defender of a theory could always, if he or she was prepared to be ingenious enough, 'rescue' it from any number of apparently contravening instances. Sophisticated methodological falsificationism recognized this, and stated that there was no falsification where the discarded theory was not replaced by a superior one, where superiority was indexed by the following factors: the second theory had surplus empirical content over the first, predicting facts excluded by or improbable in the light of the theory it replaced; the second theory explained all that was explained successfully by the first; and some of the surplus content of the second theory was corroborated (in Popper's sense of that term). If these criteria were met, in any given circumstance of the abandonment of a theory for another, we might speak of a 'progressive problem-shift'. If they were not met, the problem-shift was a 'degenerating' one; it did not in effect constitute the falsification of the pre-existing theory by the one which supplanted it.

Lakatos's sophisticated methodological falsificationism was self-confessedly an attempt to reconcile a version of Popper's philosophy of science with some of the major difficulties created for the latter by the works of Kuhn and others. As such, as Kuhn pointed out, it actually expressed a standpoint quite close to his own.[64] One of the consequences of Lakatos's emendation of Popper was to downplay the decisionism that bulked large in Popper's own writings (which Habermas emphasized), and to provide standards for the critical comparison of theories; Lakatos argued that such standards, or 'rules of acceptance and falsification' were in fact not provided, or at least not made explicit, by Kuhn. But the question then arises whether Lakatos, having originally rejected justificationism in favour of fallibilism, did not in the end arrive at a justificationist position, which could better be defended and expanded by discarding falsificationism altogether. For Lakatos admits:

'Falsification' in the sense of naive falsificationism (corroborated counter-evidence) is not a *sufficient* condition for eliminating a specific theory: in spite of hundreds of known anomalies we do not regard it as falsified (that is, eliminated) until we have a better one. Nor is 'falsification' in the naive sense *necessary* for falsification in the sophisticated sense: a progressive problem-shift does not have to be interspersed with 'refutations'. Science can grow without any 'refutations' leading the way.[65]

As Lakatos used it, 'falsification' (1) only applied to the 'degenerating phase of research programmes' (in other cases anomalies are largely ignored, or accommodated to the existing theory), and (2) only was effective when a better theory superseded the existing one. It is clear that here refutation no longer forms the main substance of falsification. Lakatos has to all intents and purposes accepted the two major flaws in falsificationism, where that term is used in a sense that still retains any connection with Popper's critique of inductive logic. These two objections to falsificationism are the following. First, in deciding among theories, scientists do not do what Popper's account suggests: that is to say, look for the most bizarre, 'unlikely' theory on the grounds that it is the most easily falsifiable. Nor could there be any defence of the thesis that they should do so. Popper's usage here seems to trade on two different senses of what is 'unlikely'. A theory may be 'unlikely' in so far as it is highly innovative; or it may be 'unlikely' in the sense that it appears very improbable in the light of what is currently regarded as the relevant empirical evidence. Scientists would be wasting their time if they deliberately sought out as often as they could the latter type of unlikely hypothesis. The fact that they do not, however, indicates that they operate with an implicit notion of inductive inference. Second, as I have mentioned earlier, Popper's attempt to provide a plausible analysis of scientific progress in terms of 'verisimilitude' is unsuccessful, since there is no reason to suppose, within Popper's epistemology, that there is a finite number of potential theories available to interpret any specific range of occurrences.

In rejecting falsificationism, we also at the same time reject the Popperian criterion of the demarcation between science and nonscience, and the rigid dislocation between the psychology of discovery and the logic of testing. But how can we do so without reverting to the ideas that Popper set out to criticize: those involved in positivistic philosophies of science? In attempting to provide the beginnings of an answer to this question, it is helpful to reconsider the problems that came to light with early formulations of the Verification Principle, and subsequently with the liberalized version of logical positivism. The early formulations were based upon the thesis, which stands in direct line of descent from Hume and Mach, that the meaning of scientific concepts can always be in principle reduced to empirical observations. The later differentiation between observation and theoretical statements abandoned this standpoint, replacing it with the notion of correspondence rules linking observations and theories; the liberalized model retained the same image of science as a hierarchy of statements built upon a secure foundation of observations. Some of the difficulties created by the distinction between observational and theoretical terms can, as Shapere pointed out, be linked to this context in which the distinction was elaborated.[66] One such difficulty is that of the ontological status of 'theoretical entities'. What was no problem in the earlier phase of logical positivism emerges as a major difficulty in its liberalized version. A phenomenalist or physicalist standpoint connects observation terms unproblematically to entities that exist; but it is not clear in what sense a theoretical entity such as an 'electron' exists, or is some sort of handy fiction. The 'surplus content' of a theoretical term, that is, that which cannot be directly expressed in the observation language, is supposed to be created by the place of the term in the deductive hierarchy of statements. This seems to lead to the uncomfortable and unsatisfactory conclusion that, as there is a continuum from the observable to the unobservable, so there is from objects that exist to ones which do not exist. A second, related, difficulty concerns the character of the deductive relations presumed to hold between the levels in the hierarchy of observational and theoretical statements as interpreted axiomatic systems. The 'correspondence rules' that intervene between observation and theory are conceived of in a manner parallel to the interpretation of formal systems of mathematical logic, as rules of logical derivation. But logical connections of this sort are obviously different from the connections that may pertain between entities, such as causal relations; and hence we are again led to conclude that theoretical terms are linked to observational ones in such a way that the former do not refer directly to the properties of existent things.

The outline of an alternative scheme, involving a revised model of inductive inference, was suggested by the writings of Quine, and elaborated in some detail by Hesse.[67] This drew upon Duhem's notion that scientific knowledge should be represented as a network of statements, while not accepting some of the aspects of Duhem's conventionalism.[68] Within such a network, what was 'observable' and what was 'theoretical' could only be distinguished in a pragmatic and relative way. The connecting statements in the network were laws, but laws were treated as pertaining to finite domains; hence one of the classical dilemmas of inductivism, that one could not move from particular statements to universal ones, was superseded, for all inductive inference involved movement from particulars to analogous particulars. Such a view of scientific laws, Hesse argued, did not imply that universal laws were statistical generalizations, or that statistical generalizations were to be regarded as preferable to universal laws in finite domains.[69] Nor did it imply an instrumentalist account of science, but rather a realist one in which the analogical character of theoretical innovation was made central. 'Scientific language', as Hesse put it, 'is therefore seen as a dynamic system which constantly grows by metaphorical extension of natural language, and which also changes with changing theory and with reinterpretation of some of the concepts of the natural language itself.'[70]

This view of scientific theory does away with the idea of correspondence rules. The network involves observational predicates, which are the 'knots' that attach it to the object-world, but these are not a fixed and invariable foundation; where the knots are depends upon the state of development of the theory and the form of its language, and they may be altered in the course of its transformation, especially where this is of the 'revolutionary' character described by Kuhn. Scientific theory does not involve two languages, a language of observation and a language of theoretical terms; rather, it involves two overlapping and intersecting uses of the same language. Nor is there an absolute differentiation between formal languages of science and natural languages, since the former proceed by metaphorical extension of the latter, and of experiences originally organized by the latter in the 'natural attitude'. In everyday life – and in learning scientific theories – we manage to get to understand observational terms and use them in their relevant contexts, but only by at the same time coming to grasp more abstract terms to which their meanings are connected. If the mode in which this is accomplished conforms to the process suggested by Quine, then all descriptive predicates, however 'theoretical', are learned in conjunction with definite stimulus-situations, or through sentences that contain such predicates (or the two combined). No such predicates, however, are learned by empirical association alone: they do not form an 'independent' class of observational terms such as is presupposed in positivistic philosophy. What counts as an observational term cannot be specified without presupposing a framework of accepted laws, which constitute the integrative elements of the network, but which in principle and in practice can be radically changed. It is not possible to know, at any given point of time, which laws and predicates may have to be revised or discarded in the light of research findings.

The network model of science provides a way of recognizing the poetics of theoretical innovation while at the same time offering a mode of distinguishing sense and reference in regard of 'paradigms'. Writings such as those of Kuhn, which show the importance of discontinuities in the development of science, push to the forefront two sorts of problem, each potentially posing dilemmas of relativism: one concerns how it is possible to make the transition from one paradigm to another, if they are distinct and different 'universes of meaning'; the other concerns how it is possible to sustain a notion of truth, given that the succession of paradigms involves transforming what are recognized as 'facts' within divergent systems of theory. The first, the so-called problem of 'meaning-variance', is in some part an outcome of exaggerating the internal unity of paradigms, or 'frames of meaning' more generally.[71] If paradigms are treated as closed systems of concepts, whose meanings are determined only by their mutual relation within the system, it becomes difficult to see how transference from one paradigm to another is achieved. The mediation of paradigms or frames of meaning should, however, be more aptly regarded as normal in human experience than as extraordinary: becoming a scientist, for example, involves distancing oneself from common-sense views of the world as part of the process of mastering scientific theories. The capacity to shift between what Schutz calls 'multiple realities', involving the control of allegory and metaphor, is a routine feature of everyday human activity, although placed in relief in so far as it is consciously organized as a process of learning new frames of meaning, or one of becoming able to move from one paradigm to another within the context of scientific activity. In this view the mediation of radically discrepant paradigms, such as is involved in scientific 'revolutions', is not qualitatively different from meaning-transformations required in moving between quite closely related theories; the role of learning by analogy and metaphor is central to both.

The relativistic implications of Kuhn's writing in respect of truth have been a core issue in the debate surrounding his work from the first publication of *The Structure of Scientific Revolutions* (although Kuhn himself consistently rejected relativism in this sense). Such implications also emerge in the writings of some philosophers not concerned specifically with the philosophy of science; for example, in the works of Gadamer in hermeneutics, and those of Winch in 'post-Wittgensteinian philosophy'; and are one focal point in the respective controversies to which these have given rise. The source of the strain towards relativism is easy to trace: it derives from the idealist leanings of these authors. If 'paradigms' ('traditions', 'language-games') are treated as constitutive of an object-world, rather than as modes of representing or relating to an object-world, there are as many 'realities' as there are meaning frames. Kuhn made it clear that he did not accept such a view, without, however, elaborating an account of what notion of truth should replace the versions of the correspondence theory of truth (including that of Popper) which he rejected.[72]

Hesse suggested that the network model of science involved breaking with the time-honoured dichotomy between correspondence and coherence theories of truth, borrowing elements from each while discarding some of their traditional features; and that this position was most appropriately connected to a realist ontology. Acceptance of the theory-impregnated character of observations seemed to some to foreclose altogether the possibility of doing what scientists usually claimed to be doing, that is comparing different theories in the light of the evidence, since what counted as 'evidence' was influenced by the theories themselves: the phenomena could always be saved by the interpretation and reinterpretation of observations. But in this view there lurks a strong residue of positivist philosophy. a purely instrumental account of science is the last refuge of the disillusioned positivist As against such a standpoint we can pose two integral elements of scientific procedure. One is an insistence upon the significance of sanctioned standards of criticism which help to separate science – although not to demarcate it cleanly – from religious cosmologies. Acknowledgement of the importance of science as self-critique has no necessary connection with a falsificationist epistemology. Indeed separating the one from the other helps to add force to Habermas's analysis of the shortcomings of Popperianism, by making it clear that the ' critical tradition' of science presupposes normative standards that cannot be validated as such in terms of the procedures of scientific testing, because they are the legitimating framework within which those procedures are organized. The second point is that the mediation of divergent theories, or paradigms, involves the conjunction of referential parameters which, given the normative orientation of science, always provide an 'empirical intersection' subject to disputation in respect of truth claims. This follows directly from the network model of science. The mediation of paradigms is a hermeneutic task, in the sense that it involves the capability of moving between frames of meaning; but such a capability cannot be acquired purely on the level of intension, since the terms comprising the network are tied in in a complex (and variable) way to extensional predicates.

Since the correspondence theory of truth was traditionally bound up with positivistic philosophies, it was usually presumed by critics of such philosophies that rejection of them necessitates discarding it also. There are several features of established correspondence theories of truth, however, which are a substantial part of the residue of positivistic philosophy, and which can be separated out without disavowing the correspondence notion altogether. One is the assumption that a correspondence theory presupposes at least some statements which are founded upon indisputable observations: which are not open to revision. This idea can be traced in large part to the thesis that the meaning of terms employed in a theoretical language can either be expressed directly as empirical observations, or must rest upon a foundation of such observations. The view of language involved here is an impoverished one, and muddies over the distinction between the relation of concepts within a theoretical network, and the relation between statements involving those concepts and the object-world. The former relation can be illuminated, in respect of truth-values, by the incorporation of coherence criteria or 'coherence conditions' as these are suggested by the network model. Such coherence criteria cannot be taken for granted, as in the positivistic scheme, where the connection between concepts is implicitly explained through the operation of correspondence rules. The criteria can be specified as a set of conditions providing for the interrelatedness of concepts within the networks. The interrelatedness of the components of the network only concerns the object-world with regard to its production as a system of classification: as such it pertains to the network as an organizing medium whereby truth as a relation between statements and the object-world is made possible, but does not provide the substance of that relation itself.

Two further assumptions deriving from the association of correspondence theory with positivistic philosophies are that advocacy of a correspondence theory presupposes the explication of 'correspondence' in some more basic philosophical terms; and that such advocacy necessarily involves providing an account of the existence of the object-world itself. The first gets to the nub of the objections that are traditionally raised against correspondence theory, which concern the difficulty of defining what 'correspondence' *is*. The presumption that such objections have to be answered by specifying the nature of correspondence in terms of some other type of relation, however, is bound up with the positivistic view of the character of observation statements, since observation is taken as a more 'primitive' relation than correspondence, that is, as one to which the latter can be in some way reduced. If we break with such a view of observation statements, we can also reject this mode of treating the correspondence relation; 'correspondence' then becomes the more primitive term, and as such is regarded as a necessary element of the extensional character of a knowledge claim.

The assumption that a correspondence theory has to provide a justification of the independent existence of the object-world is similarly connected with the central concerns of positivistic philosophies, because these are directed towards tying the conditions of knowledge to sensory experience, the latter being taken (in phenomenalism) actually to constitute the object-world. Rejection of positivistic philosophy frees us from the obligation to ground a correspondence version of truth in such a justification, or at least indicates that an account of the concept of truth does not logically entail it. To propose that the network model of science may be conjoined to a realist epistemology is therefore not to claim that the latter is necessarily the only view which could potentially be reconciled with a reworked theory of truth of the sort suggested here. Moreover, this in turn would involve a detailed reworking of pre-existing formulations of 'realism'.

The natural and the social sciences

The foregoing discussion of the philosophy of natural science does not provide, in and of itself, an adequate scheme for a treatment of the connections and divergencies between the natural and the social sciences. It rather indicates some elements of an approach to epistemological problems that span whatever differentiations may exist between them. But the formulation of a post-positivistic philosophy of natural science undoubtedly has direct implications for social scientific method, which has usually been analysed against a background of positivistic philosophy, explicitly stated or implicitly assumed. This is not only true of that tradition of thought I began by discussing, which links Comte, Durkheim and modern functionalism; it also applies to the 'counter-tradition' associated with the notion of the *Geisteswissenschaften*.

The contrast between *Erklären* (explaining) and *Verstehen* (understanding) as portrayed by Droysen and Dilthey, is at the heart of the tradition of the *Geisteswissenschaften*. In establishing his version of this contrast, Dilthey opposed his views to those of authors, such as Comte and J.S. Mill, who emphasized the continuity of the scientific study of nature and society, stressing instead that the subjective, meaningful character of human conduct had no counterpart in nature. The natural sciences developed causal explanations of 'outer' events; the human sciences, on the other hand, were concerned with the 'inner' understanding of 'meaningful conduct'. But Dilthey also accepted important elements of the ideas of Comte and Mill, emphasizing the need to make the human sciences as precise and empirical as the sciences of nature. The differences between the natural and the social sciences concerned not so much the logical form of their investigations and their results, as the content of their objects of investigation and the procedures whereby they might be studied.

Some of the main tensions in Dilthey's writings (and in those of Max Weber) stemmed from his attempt to combine elements of positivistic philosophy with the idealistic conception of 'life-philosophy' taken from the earlier development of the *Geisteswissenschaften* tradition. The 'understanding' of human action or cultural products was held to be, following Schleiermacher, a process of the re-experiencing or re-enactment of others' inner experiences. But at the same time, this process was not one of mere intuition: it was one which had to be made the basis of a scientific history, and which consequently formed the centrepiece of the method of the human sciences. Dilthey's term *Erlebnis* ('experience'), as Gadamer pointed out, expressed the strain between the positivistic and idealistic strands in his works.[73] Unlike the verb form *erleben*, the word *Erlebnis* only became common in historical works in the 1870s, largely because of Dilthey's use of it. The word is more restricted than the other German term that may also be translated as 'experience', *Erfahrung*, and in Dilthey's writings was introduced as the specific focus of the process of interpretative understanding; in understanding the meaning of what another person did, we grasped the content of that person's 'experience' of the world. *Erlebnis* constituted the fundamental content of consciousness, which Dilthey sometimes referred to as 'immediate lived experience'; it was prior to any act of reflection. The term thus tied together the influence of empiricism (only that which can be directly experienced was real) and the influence of life-philosophy (the meaningful character of human life was given in the inner experience of consciousness).

The critical response to the *Geisteswissenschaften* tradition on the part of the logical positivists, or those close to logical positivism, was a consistent one. *Verstehen* could not supply the sort of evidence necessary to scientific research, since it depended upon some sort of empathic identification with others. The observation language of social science had to refer to overt behaviour, not to hypothetical states of consciousness. No matter how much one might try to provide a concrete specification of *Erlebnis,* the latter remained inaccessible to the intersubjectively agreed observations upon which all the sciences had to depend. The value of *Verstehen,* if it had any at all, was as a mode of suggesting hypotheses; but such hypotheses had to be tested against observations of behaviour.[74] In this respect, the views of the logical positivists converged closely with behaviourism in the social sciences.

There are three ways in which this critique of *Verstehen* can be assessed: one is in terms of assessing what 'understanding' is; another is in terms of assessing what 'observable behaviour' should be taken to mean; a third is in terms of evaluating the significance of 'subjective' elements in conduct. In Dilthey's works, particularly in his earlier writings, *Verstehen* was represented as a procedure, or *the* procedure, whereby the human sciences gained access to their subject matter; and as founded upon some sort of empathic process of 're-enactment'. The notion that *Verstehen* was primarily a mode of procuring data was also taken for granted in positivistic critiques. Thus Abel said that *Verstehen* was an 'operation' that produced 'evidence', and went on to claim that such an intuitional mode of procedure simply begged the question of whether the process of 'understanding' that took place was a valid one.[75] Such an objection has definite force if the notion of *Verstehen* is represented as specific research procedure, and as involving some kind of empathic process; Dilthey indeed did not successfully manage to reconcile subjectivity and objectivity in the manner in which he sought to do, within a framework strongly influenced by empiricism. But the dismissal of *Verstehen* as a mere propaedeutic writes off major elements of the *Geisteswissenschaften* tradition; the preoccupation with the 'meaningful' character of human conduct and culture that characterized that tradition was abandoned in positivistic philosophy, which attempted to reduce this to the content of 'empirical observation'. Hence it is important to recognize that recent contributions from within the tradition, as revitalized by hermeneutic phenomenology, reworked the notion of *Verstehen* in such a way as to detach it from its dependence upon the idea of the 're-enactment' or 're-living' of the experiences of others. Thus for Gadamer *Verstehen* was to be treated, not as a special procedure of investigation appropriate to the study of social conduct, but as the ontological condition of intersubjectivity as such; and not as founded upon an empathic grasp of the experiences of others, but upon the mastery of language as the medium of the meaningful organization of human social life.

To associate the notion of *Verstehen* with language as the medium of intersubjectivity offers direct points of connection with the post-positivistic philosophy of science. Recognition of the significance of frames of meaning, and of their mediation, appears both in Gadamer and in Kuhn, although in the writings of the former this was incorporated into a broad exposition of hermeneutics. In so far as all 'understanding' occurs through the appropriation of frames of meaning, it is no longer regarded as a procedure that distinguishes the social from the natural sciences, but as common to both. The question of the relation between the social and natural sciences can then be seen in a new light. Natural science involves the development of frames of meaning, organized as networks, and discontinuities in the progression of scientific theories pose hermeneutic problems similar to those relating to the mediation of meaning frames in other spheres of activity. But the social sciences are concerned with a pre-interpreted world, in which meaning frames are integral to their 'subject-matter', that is, the intersubjectivity of practical social life. Social science thus involves a 'double hermeneutic', linking its theories, as frames of meaning, with those which are already a constituent part of social life.[76] The ramifications of this, of course, are complex and difficult to trace out, involving identifying the relations between lay beliefs and ordinary-language concepts on the one hand, and the concepts and theories of the social sciences on the other.

Let us move to the problem of what the notion of 'observable behaviour' should be taken to refer to. It should be clear that what has already been said about the reformulation of the concept of *Verstehen* connects with this, in so far as it helps to indicate the residual difficulties in the claim of positivistically minded critics that *Verstehen* is no more than a preliminary source of hypotheses that then have to be matched against behaviour. Abel explained this as follows. At the onset of a spell of freezing weather, a man saw his neighbour go out to his woodshed, chop some logs, carry them into the home and light them in his fireplace. He understood what his neighbour was doing as 'lighting a fire to warm himself because he feels chilly'. But he could not know, without further investigation, that this was correct; the neighbour might, for example, have lit the fire as a signal of some sort to someone else. Hence *Verstehen* only provides a plausible hypothesis as to what happened.[77] This conclusion, however, begs one type of question by assimilating it to others. It presupposes that the observer already understands the ordinary-language terms 'freezing weather', 'neighbour', 'woodshed', etc. Because such understanding is taken for granted, the question of how it is accomplished is not distinguished from the issues of how behaviour may be characterized, and in what sense, if any, 'subjective' elements are relevant to the explanation of human conduct in the social sciences.

The affiliation of positivistic philosophy with behaviourism stems from a common mistrust of features of conduct that are not 'observable', where the latter term means 'directly apprehended by the senses'. Rejection of phenomenalism or physicalism frees us from some of the restraints of this view, which has never managed to come to terms with the difference between 'behaviour' and 'agency', that is, between involuntary reactions and acts that are 'made to happen' by the individual. The notion of agency or action has been much discussed in the recent philosophical literature, in some substantial part as a result of the emphases of Wittgenstein's *Philosophical Investigations*. Some philosophers, particularly those strongly influenced by Wittgenstein, argued that human conduct could be described on two discrete levels, one being that of 'movements', employing something like the language of behaviourism, the other being that of 'actions'. To speak of 'an arm moving up' was to describe a movement; to speak of 'raising one's arm' was to redescribe the movement as an action. But this idea is misleading, if it assumes that these are two alternative modes of description that are equally applicable to any specific form of human conduct. They are more appropriately seen as rival, rather than complementary, types of predicate: to refer to action as if it were merely (reactive) behaviour is to *misdescribe* it. In the distinction between 'movement' and 'action' there is still a residue of the view that only 'overt behaviour' can be directly observed. But there is no warrant for this, if the positivistic view be relinquished; we observe 'actions' as directly as we do 'behaviour'.

This still leaves unresolved the status of 'subjective elements' in action. Abel's example makes it clear that he was referring to the purposes for which an act might be undertaken: the actor in question lit the fire in order to keep himself from feeling chilly. Abel employed a behaviouristic terminology to describe this situation, and held that the event of lighting the fire could only be adequately explained when it was made part of a type of deductive-nomological scheme. The explanation took the following form: low temperature reduces body temperature; heat is produced by making a fire; the 'stimulus' (freezing weather) was connected to the 'response' (lighting the fire) via the generalization, 'those feeling cold will seek warmth'. This, as it were, formalized the assimilation of reactive behaviour and action. The scheme recognized no difference between cases in which what Abel called the 'feeling-states' of an individual were connected by some kind of mechanical effect, and those which were within the scope of his or her agency. Hence the treatment of purposive components of conduct is thin and barren: purpose or intention appears only as a 'feeling-state' tying stimulus to response. There is no place for a conception of the actor as a reasoning agent, capable of using knowledge in a calculated fashion so as to achieve intended outcomes.

This is one of the major points at which the line of thought running from Comte and Durkheim to modern functionalism, and modern positivistic philosophy as stemming from logical positivism, coincide: in the absence of a theory of action. Each involves a deterministic form of social philosophy, although the logical positivists regarded as suspect the proclivity of the former for 'holistic' concepts such as *conscience collective, représentation collective*, etc.[78] The writings of Talcott Parsons played a major part in connecting Durkheim's works to modern functionalism. Parsons specifically sought to break with some of the main emphases of positivistic philosophy; he also formulated an 'action frame of reference', originally established in order to incorporate an important element of 'voluntarism' into social theory.[79] But the voluntaristic features of Parsons's scheme turned out to depend mainly upon the Durkheimian theorem that the collective values which facilitated social solidarity were also 'internalized' as motivational components of personality. The attempt to provide a treatment of voluntarism in the context of a theory of institutions became reduced to a stress that social analysis needed to embody a theory of motivation, rather than providing a framework that related motives to the rational monitoring of action.

A developed theory of action must deal with the relations between motives, reasons and purposes, but must also attempt to offer, as functional theorists have always tried to do, an account of institutional organization and change. For if it is the case that functionalism, even in its most sophisticated form in Parsons's writings, was not able to produce an adequate theory of action, it is also true that those schools of thought which have been most preoccupied with the philosophy of action, including particularly post-Wittgensteinian philosophy and existential phenomenology, have skirted problems of institutional orders and their transformation. I have suggested elsewhere, following Schutz, that the terms 'motive', 'reason' and 'purpose' are misleading as employed in ordinary terminology, because they presuppose a conceptual 'cutting into' or segmentation of the uninterrupted flow of action; such a cutting into the ongoing course of action is normally made only when an actor is queried about why he or she acted as he or she did, when he or she reflexively categorizes a segment of his or her action, or when an observer does.[80] Thus it is more appropriate to regard the above three terms as processual ones: the subjective orientation of action can then be regarded as directed purposively in conjunction with ongoing processes of the motivation and rationalization of action. The latter implies that the socially competent actor routinely monitors his or her action by 'keeping in touch' theoretically with the content of what he or she does; or, expressed in an alternative way, that when asked for an explanation of a specified 'segment' of his or her conduct, he or she is able to provide one. The problem of connecting the subjective orientation of action to institutional structures has always appeared an enormously difficult one, but this is at least in some part because 'structure' has usually been conceived of in a fundamental way as a *constraint* upon action. Durkheim explicitly made this the defining property of social structure separating 'social facts' from 'psychological facts'; if others have been less direct, they have accepted much the same notion.[81] Yet the structural properties of institutions are not just constraints upon action, they are enabling: a central issue facing social theory in this regard is that of developing a reformulation of the key concepts of 'structure' and 'system' in such a way as to acknowledge the enabling as well as the constraining aspect of institutional forms. In such a conception, the reflexive rationalization of action must be seen as operating through the mobilization of structural properties, and at the same time thereby contributing to their reproduction.[82]

Recognition of the central importance of such an approach to a theory of action involves rejecting the positivistic tendency to regard reflexivity as merely a 'nuisance', and also has direct consequences for the question of the status of laws in the social sciences. Nagel's discussion of self-influencing predictions, referred to previously, is typical in respect of the first of these issues, in so far as reflexivity was treated only from the point of view of prediction, and in so far as it was assumed that its influence was a 'problem' for the social sciences. Even within these terms of reference, however, 'self-fulfilling' and 'self-negating' prophecies do not have, as he claimed, direct analogies in the natural sciences. The point is the manner in which such things happen, not the fact of their happening, in society and in nature. That is to say, in the sphere of the former, as contrasted to the latter, self-influencing predictions occur because the predictions made come to be taken over and reacted to as part of the behaviour of reasoning agents: as an element of the 'knowledge' they employ in the reflexive rationalization of their conduct.

Human beings are reasoning agents who apply knowledge of their contexts of action reflexively in their production of action, or interaction. The 'predictability' of social life does not merely 'happen' but is 'made to happen' as an outcome of the consciously applied skills of social actors. But the scope of the reflexive rationalization of action of concrete individuals is bounded, in several ways; each indicates specific matters of concern for social science. One concerns the formalization of the knowledge that is applied in action. In producing a grammatical English utterance, for example, a speaker demonstrates and draws upon knowledge of syntactical and other rules involved in speaking English; but he or she is not likely to be able to give a formal account of what those rules are, although he or she does 'know' them, that is, know how to use them. However, the application of such 'knowledge' is made within a parameter of influences that are not part of the ongoing rationalization of his or her action. Such influences include repressions and unconscious elements of personality; but also external conditions, including the conduct of other actors. A third boundary of the reflexive rationalization of conduct is found in the unintended consequences of action. This connects closely to the second, in so far as the production and reproduction of institutional structures appears as the unintended outcome of the conduct of a multiplicity of actors.

A crucial point to recognize is that the boundaries between these three types of unacknowledged condition of action are fluid, as is the scope of the rationalization of action in relation to them. We then have a basis for an analysis of the question of the status of 'laws' in the social sciences. Zetterberg suggested that there was no shortage of generalizations in social science: the object of the latter should be to make their formulation more precise, and to verify them in the light of empirical research. His discussion followed the characteristic lines of positivistic sociology, in holding that such laws would derive from the progressive accumulation of research, and should form a deductive hierarchy. Adoption of the network model of natural science involves rejecting the latter. We can represent theories in social science, as in natural science, as networks involving laws or abstract generalizations . But in the second of these the network is not in interaction with the object-world it seeks to explain, whereas in the former it is. Generalizations in the social sciences are always in principle unstable in relation to their 'subject matter' – that is, social conduct and its institutional forms – in so far as their acceptance alters the relation between the rationalization of action and its unacknowledged grounds. This is distinct from the 'technical' possibilities of intervention in nature offered by laws in the natural sciences. Knowledge of laws in natural science allows people to alter the empirical incidence of the circumstances under which they apply: or, if this be desired, to extend their range. But while knowledge of the laws allows for material transformation in such ways, this does not alter the causal connections involved in or underlying them. In the social sciences, on the other hand, the causal connections that are specified or implied in generalizations depend upon particular alignments of the rationalization of action and its unacknowledged conditions, and hence are in principle mutable in the light of knowledge of those generalizations

The degree to which this happens, and its consequences, are of course limited by practical circumstances. But however this may be, the implication is unavoidable that the relation of social science and its subject matter cannot be handled within a differentiation between 'pure' and 'applied' science.

6 'Power' in the Writings of Talcott Parsons

Talcott Parsons was often attacked for his neglect of issues of conflict and power. Yet he devoted a number of his later writings to this subject and in fact made important contributions to it.

Parsons's later work on power involved a conscious modification of his previous views, where he accepted what he called the 'traditional' view of power. His newer theory of power was an attempt to develop a set of concepts which would overcome what he saw as important defects in the 'traditional' notion. One of the first places where Parsons explicitly confronted these issues was in a review article of C. Wright Mills's *The Power Elite*. There Parsons proffered a variety of criticisms of Mills's book, but also took issue with the conception of power which he saw as underlying Mills's work. Mills's thesis, Parsons argued, gained weight from a 'misleading and one-sided' view of the nature of power, which Parsons labelled the 'zero-sum' concept of power. That is, power was conceived to be possessed by one person or group to the degree that it was not possessed by a second person or group over whom the power was wielded. Power was thus defined in terms of mutually exclusive objectives, so that a party was conceived to hold power in so far as it could realize its own wishes at the expense of those of others. In terms of game theory, from which the phrase 'zero-sum' was taken, to the degree that one party won, the other necessarily lost. According to Parsons, this view tended to produce a perspective from which all exercise of power appeared as serving sectional interests.[1] Parsons then went on to suggest that power was more adequately conceived by analogy with a non-zero-sum game: in other words, as a relation from which both sides might gain.

Power, Parsons proposed, could be seen as being 'generated' by a social system, in much the same way as wealth was generated in the productive organization of an economy. It was true that wealth was a finite quantity, and to the degree that one party possessed a proportion of a given sum of money, a second party could only possess the remainder; but the actual amount of wealth produced varied with the structure and organization of different types of economy. In an industrial society, for example, there was typically more for all than in an agrarian one. Power similarly had these two aspects, and it was the collective aspect which was most crucial, according to Parsons, for sociological analysis. Parsons summed up his objections to Mills's views as follows:

> to Mills, power is not a facility for the performance of function in, and on behalf of, the society as a system, but is interpreted exclusively as a facility for getting what one group, the holders of power, wants by preventing another group, the 'outs', from getting what it wants.
> What this conclusion does is to elevate a secondary and derived aspect of a total phenomenon into the central place.[2]

Much of the substance of Parsons's later writings on power consists of a reaffirmation of this position, and an elaboration of the analogy between power and money.[3] The parallels which Parsons developed between the two were based upon the supposition that each had a similar role in two of the four 'functional subsystems' of society which Parsons had distinguished in previous works. Power had a parallel function in the polity (goal-attainment subsystem) to that of money in the economy (adaptive subsystem). The main function of money in the modern economy is as a 'circulating medium': that is, as a standardized medium of exchange in terms of which the value of products can be assessed and compared. Money itself has no intrinsic utility; it has 'value' only in so far as it is commonly recognized and accepted as a standard form of exchange. It is only in primitive monetary systems, when money is made of precious metal, that it comes close to being a good in its own right. In a developed economy, precious metal figures directly only in a very small proportion of exchange transactions. The sense in which the economy is 'founded' upon its holdings of gold is really a symbolic and an indirect one, and gold forms a 'reserve' to which resource is made only when the stability of the economy is for some reason threatened.

Power was conceived by Parsons as a 'circulating medium' in the same sense, 'generated' primarily within the political subsystem as money was generated in the economy, but also forming an 'output' into the three other functional subsystems of society. Power was defined, therefore, as 'generalized capacity to serve the performance of binding obligations by units in a system of collective organization when the obligations are legitimized with reference to their bearing on collective goals'.[4] By 'binding obligations' Parsons meant the conditions to which those in power, and those over whom power was exercised, were subject through the legitimation which allowed them that power; all power involved a certain 'mandate', which might be more or less extensive, which gave power-holders certain rights and imposed on them certain obligations towards those who were subject to their power. The collective goals rested upon the common value-system, which set out the major objectives which governed the actions of the majority in a society. Thus American society, according to Parsons, was characterized by the primacy of values of 'instrumental activism', which entailed that one main 'collective goal' of the society was the furtherance of economic productivity.

Just as money had 'value' because of common 'agreement' to use it as a standardized mode of exchange, so power became a facility for the achievement of collective goals through the 'agreement' of the members of a society to legitimize leadership positions – and to give those in such positions a mandate to develop policies and implement decisions in the furtherance of the goals of the system. Parsons emphasized that this conception of power was at variance with the more usual 'zero-sum' notion which had dominated thinking in the field. In Parsons's view, the net 'amount' of power in a system could be expanded 'if those who are ruled are prepared to place a considerable amount of trust in their rulers'. This process was conceived as a parallel to credit creation in the economy. Individuals 'invest' their 'confidence' in those who ruled them – through, say, voting in an election to put a certain government in power; in so far as those who had thus been put into power initiated new policies which effectively furthered 'collective goals', there was more than a zero-sum circular flow of power. Everybody gained from this process. Those who had 'invested' in the leaders received back, in the form of the effective realization of collective goals, an increased return on their investment. It was only if those in power took no more than 'routine' administrative decisions that there was no net gain to the system.

Power was thus for Parsons directly derivative of authority: authority was the institutionalized legitimation which underlay power, and was defined as 'the institutionalization of the rights of "leaders" to expect support from the members of the collectivity'.[5] By speaking of 'binding obligations', Parsons deliberately brought legitimation into the very definition of power, so that, for him, there was no such thing as 'illegitimate power'. As Parsons expressed it: 'the threat of coercive measures, or of compulsion, without legitimation or justification, should not properly be called the use of power at all, but is the limiting case where power, losing its symbolic character, merges into an intrinsic instrumentality of securing compliance with wishes, rather than obligations.'[6]

In line with his general approach, Parsons stressed that the use of power was only one among several different ways in which one party might secure the compliance of another to a desired course of action. The other ways of obtaining compliance should not be regarded, Parsons stressed, as forms of power; rather it was the case that the use of power (that is, the activation of 'binding obligations') was one among several ways of ensuring that a party produced a desired response. Parsons distinguished two main 'channels' through which one party might seek to command the actions of another, and two main 'modes' of such control, yielding a fourfold typology. Ego might try to control the 'situation' in which alter was placed, or try to control alter's 'intentions'; the 'modes' of control depended upon whether sanctions which might be applied were positive (that is, offer something which alter might desire) or negative (that is, held out the threat of punishment):

1 Situational channel, positive sanction: the offering of positive advantages to alter if he or she followed ego's wishes (*inducement*, such as the offering of money).
2 Situational channel, negative sanction: the threat of imposition

of disadvantages if alter did not comply (the use of *power*: in the extreme case, the use of force).

3 Intention channel, positive sanction: the offering of 'good reasons' why alter should comply (the use of *influence*).

4 Intention channel, negative sanction: the threat that it would be 'morally wrong' for alter not to comply (the appeal to *conscience* or other moral commitments).[7]

There was, Parsons pointed out, an 'asymmetry' between positive and negative sanctions. When compliance was secured through positive sanctions, because there was some definite reward, the sanctions were obvious. But, in the case of negative sanctions, compliance entailed that the sanction was not put into effect; the operation of negative sanctions was generally symbolic rather than actual. In most cases where power was being used, there was no overt sanction employed (instances where force was used, for example, were relatively rare in the exercise of power). It was quite misleading, Parsons emphasized, to speak of the use of power only when some form of negative sanction had actually been used: some writers who took the 'zero-sum' notion of power tended to do this, referring to 'power' only when some form of coercion had been applied. As Parsons said:

> [When things are 'running smoothly'] to speak of the holder of authority in these circumstances as not having or using power is, in our opinion, highly misleading. The question of his capacity to coerce or compel in case of non-compliance is an independent question that involves the question of handling unexpected or exceptional conditions for which the current power system may or may not be prepared.[8]

It was particularly necessary to stress, Parsons argued, that possession and use of power should not be identified directly with the use of force. In Parsons's view, force had to be seen as only one means among several, in only one type among several, modes of obtaining compliance. Force tended to be used in stable political systems only as a last resort when other sanctions had proved ineffective. Again using the analogy between money and power, Parsons drew a parallel between centralization of state control over gold, and state monopoly over the instruments of organized force in 'advanced and stable' societies. In the economy, there sometimes occurred deflations, in which loss of confidence in the value of money led to increasing reliance upon gold reserves in order to maintain the stability of the economy. In a similar way, Parsons held, 'power deflation' could occur when a progressive decrease of confidence in the agencies of political power developed. Such a 'loss of confidence' produced increasing reliance by such agencies upon force to preserve political integration. In both the economic and political cases, the undermining of the confidence which was the foundation of money and of power produced a 'regression' towards a 'primitive' standard.[9]

In the subsequent discussion, my main interest will be to comment on Parsons's analysis of power as such. I shall not attempt to assess in any detail the accuracy of the parallels which Parsons attempted to specify between the polity and economy as 'functional subsystems' of society. If Parsons's conceptual scheme, and the assumptions which underlie it, cannot satisfactorily handle problems of power, then many of these 'parallels' must in any case be declared either invalid or misleading.

Parsons's critique of the 'zero-sum' concept of power does contain a number of valuable contributions and insights. There is no doubt that Parsons was correct in pointing out that the 'zero-sum' concept of power sometimes reinforces a simplistic view which identifies power almost wholly with the use of coercion and force. Such a perspective tends to follow from, although it is not at all logically implied by, the Weberian definition of power, which has probably been the most influential in sociology. In Weber's familiar definition, power is regarded as 'the chance of a man or of a number of men to realize their own will in a communal action even against the resistance of others who are participating in the action'.[10] Such a definition tends to lead to a conception of power relations as inevitably involving incompatible and conflicting interests, since what is stressed is the capacity of a party to realize its *own* (implicitly, sectional) aims, and the main criterion for gauging the 'amount' of power is the 'resistance' which can be overcome.

As Parsons correctly emphasized, this can be extremely misleading, tending to produce an identification of power with the sanctions that are or can potentially be used by the power-holder. In fact, very often it is not those groups which have most frequent recourse to overt use of coercion who have most power; frequent use of coercive sanctions indicates an insecure basis of power. This is particularly true, as Parsons indicated, of the sanction of force. The power position of an individual group which has constant recourse to the use of force to secure compliance to its commands is usually weak and insecure. Far from being an index of the power held by a party, the amount of open force used rather is an indication of a shallow and unstable power base.

However, to regard the use of force in itself as a criterion of power is an error which only the more naive of social analysts would make. It is much more common to identify the power held by a party in a social relation with the coercive sanctions it is *capable* of employing against subordinates if called upon to do so – including primarily the capacity to use force. Again Parsons made an important comment here, pointing out that a party might wield considerable power while at the same time having few coercive sanctions with which to enforce its commands if they were questioned by subordinates. This is possible if the power-holding party enjoys a broad 'mandate' to take authoritative decisions ceded or acquiesced in by those subject to the decisions – that is, if those over whom the power is exercised 'agree' to subject themselves to that power. In such circumstances, the party in power depends, not on the possession of coercive sanctions with which it can override non-compliance, but sheerly upon the recognition by the subordinate party or parties of its legitimate right to take authoritative decisions. The latter in some sense acquiesce in their subordination. Thus when subordinates 'agree' to allow others to command their actions, and when at the same time those who receive this 'mandate' have few coercive sanctions to employ if their directives are not obeyed, then there exists a situation of power not based upon control of means to coerce. It is because of such a possibility that Parsons emphasized that the question of 'how much' power a party held, and the question of what sanctions it was able to bring into play in case of disobedience, were analytically separable. And it must be conceded that lack of capacity to command a defined range of sanctions does not necessarily entail a lack of power; the 'amount' of power held by a party cannot be assessed simply in terms of the effective sanctions it is able to enforce if faced with possible or actual non-compliance. At the same time, it should be pointed out that the 'amount' of power wielded in any concrete set of circumstances, and the effective sanctions that can be used to counter non-compliance, are usually closely related. Studies of all types of social structure, from small groups up to total societies, show that power-holders usually do command or develop sanctions which reinforce their position: in any group which has a continued existence over time, those in power face problems of dissensus and the possibility of rebellion. The very fact of possession of a 'mandate' from those subordinated to a power relation allows the dominant party to use this 'good will' to mobilize sanctions (even if only the scorn, ridicule, etc., of the conforming majority) against a deviant or potentially deviant minority. If a power-holding party does not possess sanctions to use in cases of disobedience, it tends rapidly to acquire them, and can in fact use its power to do so.

What Parsons was concerned to point out, then, was that the use of power frequently represented a facility for the achievement of objectives which *both* sides in a power relation desired. In this sense, it is clear that the creation of a power system does not *necessarily* entail the coercive subordination of the wishes or interests of one party to those of another. Nor is the use of power inevitably correlated with 'oppression' or 'exploitation'. Quite clearly, in any type of group, the existence of defined 'leadership' positions does 'generate' power which may be used to achieve aims desired by the majority of the members of the group. This possibility is, of course, envisaged in classic Marxist theory, and in most varieties of socialist theory, in the form of 'collective' direction of the instruments of government.

As Parsons recognized, this kind of power is necessarily legitimate, and so he made legitimacy part of his very definition of power. Parsons thus rejected the frequently held conception that authority is a 'form' of power, or is 'legitimate power'. This is again a useful emphasis. To regard authority as a 'type' of power leads to a neglect of its principal characteristic: namely that it concerns the *right* of a party to make binding prescriptions. Authority refers to the legitimate position of an individual or group, and is therefore properly regarded as a *basis* of power (for Parsons, the only basis of power), rather than as a kind of power. It is precisely the confusion of the forms with the bases of power which causes Parsons to specify a very restricted definition of power.

Authority is no more a form of power than force is a form of power.

A further valuable aspect of Parsons's analysis is the introduction of a typology of compliant behaviour. It is still quite common for social analysts naively to assert or to assume that conformity to any specific course of social action is founded *either* on 'internalization' of appropriate moral values *or* upon some form of coercion. This tendency is strong in the works of both those who follow Parsons and those who are highly critical. The isolation of various modes of securing compliance does allow for other mechanisms of conformity. The importance of the typology is diminished by the lack of any attempt to specify how these different ways of securing compliance are related together in social systems. Nevertheless, within the general context of Parsonian theory, this typology has some significance, marking a more definite recognition of the role of non-normative factors in social action.[11]

But there are other respects in which Parsons's discussion of power shares some of the basic difficulties and deficiencies of his general theory, and is at least as one-sided as the conception which he wished to replace. Parsons was above all concerned to emphasize that power did not necessarily entail the coercive imposition of one individual or group over another, and he did indeed point to some valuable correctives for the mainstream of sociological thinking on problems of power. But what slips away from sight almost completely in the Parsonian analysis is the very fact that power, even as Parsons defined it, is always exercised *over* someone! By treating power as necessarily (by definition) legitimate, and thus *starting* from the assumption of consensus of some kind between power-holders and those subordinate to them, Parsons virtually ignored, quite consciously and deliberately, the necessarily hierarchical character of power, and the divisions of interest which are frequently consequent upon it. However much it is true that power can rest upon 'agreement' to cede authority which can be used for collective aims, it is also true that interests of power-holders and those subject to that power often clash. It is undoubtedly the case that some 'zero-sum' theorists tend to argue as if power differentials *inevitably* entail conflicts of interest, and produce overt conflicts – and fail to give sufficient attention to specifying the conditions under which no conflict of either type is present. But it is surely beyond dispute that positions of power offer to their incumbents definite material and psychological rewards, and thereby stimulate conflicts between those who want power and those who have it. This brings into play, of course, a multiplicity of possible strategies of coercion, deceit and manipulation which can be used either to acquire, or to hold on to, power. If the use of power rests upon 'trust' or 'confidence', as Parsons emphasized, it also frequently rests upon deceit and hypocrisy. Indeed this is true of all social life; all stable social action, except perhaps for all-out total war, depends upon some kind of at least provisional 'trust' – but this very fact makes possible many sorts of violation and rejection of 'confidence'. *L'enfer c'est les autres.* 'Deceit' and 'mistrust' only have meaning in relation to 'trust' and 'confidence': the former are as ubiquitous a part of social life as the latter are, and will continue to be as long as people have desires or values which are exclusive of each other, and as long as there exist 'scarce resources' of whatever kind. Any sociological theory which treats such phenomena as 'incidental', or as 'secondary and derived', and not as structurally intrinsic to power differentials, is inadequate. To have power is to have potential access to valued scarce resources, and thus power *itself* becomes a scarce resource. Though the relationships between power and exploitation are not simple and direct, their existence can hardly be denied.

Parsons escaped dealing with such problems largely through a trick of definition, by considering only as 'power' the use of authoritative decisions to further 'collective goals'. Two obvious facts, that authoritative decisions very often do serve sectional interests and that the most profound conflicts in society often stem from struggles for power, are defined out of consideration – at least as phenomena connected with 'power'. The conceptualization of power which Parsons offered allowed him to shift the entire weight of his analysis away from power as expressing a relation between individuals or groups, towards seeing power solely as a 'system property'. That collective 'goals', or even the values which lay behind them, might be the outcome of a 'negotiated order' built on conflicts between parties holding differential power was ignored, since for Parsons 'power' assumed the prior existence of collective goals. The implications of this are clearly demonstrated in Parsons's short book, *Societies*, in which he tried to apply some of these ideas to social change in actual historical settings. Social change in its most general aspect, Parsons made clear, was fundamentally cultural evolution – that is, change in values, norms and idea systems. And the basic *sources* of change were to be traced to changes in cultural values, and norms *themselves*, not to any sort of 'lower-level' factors, which at the most exerted a 'conditioning' effect on social change. In spite of various qualifications and assertions to the contrary, Parsons's theory, as he applied it here, came down to little more than a kind of idealist orthodoxy. History was moved, societies changed, under the guiding direction of cultural values, which somehow changed independently of other elements in the structure of social systems, and exerted a 'cybernetic control' over them. This is hardly consonant with Parsons's conclusion that 'once the problem of causal imputation is formulated analytically, the old chicken and egg problems about the priorities of ideal and material factors simply lose significance.'[12] There is a great deal of difference between the sort of interpretation of social and historical change which Parsons presented in *Societies*, and one which follows a Marxist standpoint. Parsons's account was based very largely upon an examination of value-systems, and changes in them, and displayed practically no concern with non-normative factors as causative agencies in their formation, maintenance and diffusion. As in Parsons's more general theoretical expositions, such factors were formally recognized as of some importance, but no systematic discussion of the interplay between them and values was presented. As a consequence, Parsons tended to argue as if to show that some kind of logical relationship or 'fit' between a specific value, norm, or pattern of behaviour, and some more general value or set of values, constituted an 'explanation' of the former. This is characteristic also of Parsons's theoretical analysis of power and social change. Thus, for example, at one point in his discussion of political power, he traced 'political democracy' – that is, universal franchise – to 'the principle of equality before the law', which was a 'subordinate principle of universalistic normative organization', as if this were to explain why or how universal franchise came into being.

In Parsons's conceptualization of power there was one notion which had an explicitly dynamic reference: that of 'power deflation'. This did at least make a conceptual niche in the Parsonian system for the possibility of social revolution. It is characteristic, however, that this concept depended upon the prior assumption of consensual 'confidence' in the power system. Power deflation referred to a spiralling diminution of 'confidence' in the agencies of power, so that those subordinate to them came increasingly to question their position. Parsons did not suggest any answers to why power deflations occurred, except to indicate that once they got under way they resembled the 'vicious circle' of declining support characteristic of economic crisis. Now the parallel with economic deflation, in the terms in which Parsons discussed it, shows clearly that he conceives the process as basically a psychological one, which is a kind of generalization of the picture of deviance presented in *The Social System*. Power deflation is deviance writ large and in so far as it is focused on legitimate authority.[13] Thus the possibility of explaining power deflation in terms of the mutual interaction of interest groups is excluded. The opportunity for theoretically tying such factors to the mechanics of power deflation, via the typology of means of obtaining compliance, is left aside. The parallels which Parsons was determined to pursue between the polity and the economy serve, in fact, to separate political and economic processes from one another. That economic and other 'material' factors themselves play a key part in power deflation is ignored because Parsons was above all concerned to show how the polity and economy were 'analytically' similar, not how they intertwined. Parsons's many discussions of the relationships between sociology and economics, including his and Smelser's *Economy and Society*, were all stated in terms of highly formal typological categories, and rarely suggested any substantive generalizations linking the two. Parsons's method is well illustrated by the entirely abstract character of his typology of modes of securing compliance. A distinction was made between 'inducement' and 'power'. The rationale for the distinction was that these could be considered parallel 'media' in the subsystems of the economy and the polity. Now such a typological distinction might be useful, but the important sociological problem is to apply it. How do inducement and power operate as systematic properties of societies or other social structures? Obviously inducement is often a *basis* of power; and the reverse also may frequently be true – a person or group holding power is often in a position allowing access to various forms of inducement, including the offer of financial reward. The relationship between 'positive' and 'negative' sanctions may be quite complicated as they actually operate in social systems. Thus inducements, offering some definite rewards in exchange for compliance, always offer the possibility of being transformed into negative sanctions; the *withholding* of a reward represents a punishment, and represents a definite form of coercion. But Parsons made no attempt to draw out such possibilities and apply them to the analysis of power deflation, and in view of this, the process of power deflation was conceived purely as one of psychological 'loss of confidence' in the existing system.

Perhaps it is significant that Parsons made very little mention of what factors produce 'power inflation' – that is, the process whereby 'confidence' in a power system is *developed and expanded* in societies. It is just in this area that some of the most crucial problems in the study of power lie, and where conflict and coercion may play a major part. In Parsons's treatment of power, coercion and force were pictured as along the end of the line of a progression of corrective sanctions which could be applied to counter any tendency towards power deflation. Force was the sanction which was applied when all else had failed. It was only when the system showed a lack of 'confidence' that open use of power became frequent. Thus, Parsons argued, stable power systems were only based indirectly, or 'symbolically', on the use of force. But in power 'inflation', coercion and force may be the foundation of a consensual order in quite a different way. The history of societies shows again and again that particular social forms are often at first implemented by force, or by some other form of definite coercion, and coercive measures are used to *produce* and reinforce a new legitimacy. It is in this sense that power can grow out of the barrel of a gun. Force allows the manipulative control which can then be used to diminish dependence upon coercion. While this has been in previous ages probably only in part the result of conscious manipulation, in recent times, through the controlled diffusion of propaganda, it has become a much more deliberate process. But whether deliberate or not, it is not only the fact that stable power systems rest upon stable legitimation of authority which is the key to the analysis of power but, as the 'zero-sum' theorists have always recognized, just how legitimation is *achieved*. Through defining power as the activation of legitimate obligations, Parsons avoided dealing with the processes whereby legitimacy, and thereby authority and power, were established and maintained. Consensus was assumed, and power conceived to be derivative of it; the determinants of the consensual basis of power were regarded as non-problematic.

This means also that Parsons tended to accept the operations of authority at their face value, as if all 'obligations' of importance were open, public and legitimate. But it is an accepted fact of political life that those who occupy formal authority positions are sometimes puppets who have their strings pulled from behind the scenes. It is in the hidden processes of control that some of the crucial operations of power in modern societies are located. By defining power as 'the activation of *legitimate* obligations' Parsons would seem to have had to classify those processes as not involving 'power'. But the puppeteers behind the scenes may be the people who hold real control, and it is not a helpful concept of power which does not allow us to explore the often complicated relations which pertain between the 'unrecognized' or illegitimate, and the legitimate, in systems of power.

This may not necessarily stem from Parsons's definition of power *per se*, since it could be held that those who are *in fact* 'activating legitimate obligations' are those who are using the individuals in formal authority positions as a front – that it is the people behind the scenes who really control those 'legitimate obligations', and thus who really hold 'power'. But, at any rate, Parsons's own analysis showed an ingenuous tendency to see nothing beyond the processes which were overt. Parsons's account of how political support was derived, for example, was given in terms of a *prima facie* comparison between government and banking: 'political support should be conceived of as a generalized grant of power which, if it leads to electional success, puts elected leadership in a position analogous to a banker. The 'deposits' of power made by constituents are revocable, if not at will, at the next election.'[14] Thus those in positions of political power have the legitimized right to 'use' the power 'granted' to them by the electorate in the same way as a banker can invest money deposited with him or her. Parsons is presumably only arguing that these two processes are 'analytically' parallel, and would no doubt recognize the many substantive differences between them. But nevertheless his anxiety to develop formal similarities between the polity and economy, and correspondingly between money and power, seems to have blinded him to the realities of political manipulation.

Parsons's treatment of power, while marking in a few respects a greater formal recognition of the role of 'interests' in social action,[15] in the main represented a strong retrenchment of his general theoretical position as set out in *The Social System*. Power became simply an extension of consensus, the means which a society used to attain its 'goals'. But this is surely inadequate. Power extends as deeply into the roots of social life as do values or norms; if all social relations involve normative elements, so also do all social relations contain power differentials.

Conclusion

In the 'normative functionalism' of Durkheim and Parsons, the concept of interest tends to be conceived of only in relation to a traditional dichotomy of the individual and society, rather than as concerning divisions between groups within the social totality. Thus this type of social theory finds difficulty in allowing a conceptual space for the analysis of power as the instrument of sectional group interests. Power is conceived as the 'power of society' confronting the individual. While such a view, as is shown in Durkheim's political writings, can yield an account of the domination of the state over civil society, it cannot conceive of society itself as a system of power founded in entrenched divergencies of interest.

Nevertheless, the notions that power is not adequately treated as being a fixed quantum, and that it has no necessary tie to conflict, are important. Neither is dependent upon the sort of formulation of the concept that Parsons gave. The 'expandable' character of power actually has no logical connection with conceiving of power as concerned with the 'goals' of the collectivity. It is possible to sustain Parsons's critique of the zero-sum conception of power without following his reconstruction of the notion.

We can distinguish a broad and narrow sense of the term 'power', which parallel the differentiation between 'action' and 'interaction', where the latter refers to mutually oriented forms of conduct between two or a plurality of actors. Action or agency implies the intervention (or refraining) of an individual in a course of events in the world, of which it would be true to say that 'he or she could have done otherwise.' Defined in this way, action involves the application of 'means' to secure outcomes, these outcomes constituting the intervention in the ongoing course of events. Let us now define power as the use of resources, of whatever kind, to secure outcomes. Power then becomes an element of action, and refers to the *range* of interventions of which an agent is capable. Power in this broad sense is equivalent to the *transformative capacity* of human action: the capability of human beings to intervene in a series of events so as to alter their course. In this sense, power is closely bound up with the notion of *praxis*, as relating to the historically shaped, and historically mutable, conditions of social and material existence.

The production and reproduction of interaction of course involves power as transformative capacity: but in interaction we can distinguish a narrower, 'relational' sense of power, since action taken with the intention of securing particular outcomes then involves the responses, or the potential behaviour, of others (including their resistance to a course of action that one party wants to bring about). Power here is domination, but it would be quite mistaken to suppose, as zero-sum theories of power do, that even in this narrower sense the existence of power logically implies the existence of conflict, whether that latter term is taken to mean opposition of interest or actual struggle of some sort between two or more combatants. It is precisely the concept of interest that is most immediately linked to those of conflict and solidarity. The use of power is frequently accompanied by struggle; this is not because of a logical relation between the two, but because of a lack of coincidence of actors' interests in circumstances of the application of power. (In saying this, I do not want to propose the view that people are always aware of what their interests are, although the identification of interests on the part of the theorist always involves the imputation of wants to those persons. Nor do I want to claim either that division of interest always leads to open conflict, or conversely that the existence of such conflict *ipso facto* presupposes division of interest.) The concept of interest has to be understood as a metatheoretical one. That is to say, it has to be freed from any association with human needs in a state of nature, or for that matter with any unique connection to class divisions in society. The first leads to a situation in which interest is conceived solely in reference to the interests of the 'individual' as opposed to those of 'society' (or the state). The second, on the other hand, as expressed in certain readings of Marx, carries the implication that, with the transcendence of classes, divisions of interest in society thereby disappear. While we must recognize that particular interest oppositions may always be transcended by social transformation, this is altogether distinct from the presumption that divisions of interest in a society may be superseded altogether.

The same point applies to domination. Specific forms of domination, as historically located systems of power, are in every instance open to potential transformation. If power is seen as intrinsic to all interaction, there can be no question of transcending it in any empirical society. It would be possible to develop a model of emancipation based upon equality of power in interaction. But taken alone, this would be quite inadequate. For it would not deal with power, in the guise of transformative capacity, as the medium of the realization of collective human interests. From this aspect, freedom from domination in systems of interaction appears as a problem of building rationally defensible forms of authority.

7 The Improbable Guru: Re-reading Marcuse

'The improbable Guru of surrealistic politics': a phrase used in *Fortune* magazine in the late 1960s to describe Herbert Marcuse. Why improbable? Because Marcuse, already at that time seventy years old, had for many years laboured in relative obscurity, a writer less than limpid in style, whose works were known only to certain sectors of the academic community. One book above all others propelled Marcuse to a fame – or brought to him a notoriety – which stretched far beyond the bounds of the academy. First published in 1964, *One-Dimensional Man* coincided with the initial rise of the student movement in the USA, and became something of a manifesto for student activists associated with the New Left in many countries. Marcuse himself, of course, was far from wholly content with the ways in which his work was invoked by New Left radicals. Indeed, while lending his support to various of the radical activities of the period, Marcuse foresaw that the impact of the student movements might be limited; and he anticipated their dissolution. In 1969 he wrote that neither the students, nor the New Left more generally, could be seen as the progenitors of a new society; when their activities reached their limits, he feared, 'the Establishment may initiate a new order of totalitarian suppression.'[1]

It is not my object in this discussion to assess the influence of the New Left, or Marcuse's involvement with it. Neither shall I make any endeavour to examine the development of Marcuse's work as a whole. I shall concentrate my attention mainly upon *One-Dimensional Man*. What can a reading, a re-reading, of the book offer today? Was the book expressive of a transient phase in Western political life, or does it contain an analysis of contemporary society of enduring importance?

Marcuse's analysis: its leading themes

Naturally it would be misleading to sever *One-Dimensional Man* completely from Marcuse's other writings, for in some ways it represents a synthesis of them. It was written in English, and took the US as the prime focus of discussion. But the book continued and amplified notions first worked out some thirty years previously, in Marcuse's early writings, formed through the combined influences of Marx, Hegel and Heidegger.[2] Although Marcuse later repudiated certain of the views adopted from Heidegger, he remained more strongly influenced by that thinker than did either of the other two principals of the 'Frankfurt School', Horkheimer and Adorno.[3] Prepared to revise Marx in a thorough-going fashion where necessary, Marcuse retained a life-long affiliation to a philosophical anthropology drawing in a significant fashion upon the early Marxian texts — most notably the 'Paris Manuscripts' of 1844. From Hegel he took over a conception of the 'driving power of the dialectic' as 'the power of negative thinking', employed in order to disclose the 'internal inadequacies' of the given, empirical world.[4] The inadequacies of the given world are revealed by showing how the actual inhibits the development of immanent possibilities of change that would negate the existing state of affairs. Marcuse never took this view to imply negative dialectics shorn of any transcendental basis, in the manner of Adorno. Such a conception would be inconsistent precisely with Marcuse's philosophical anthropology in which, in the later phases of his work, of course, he conjoined Freud to Marx.

All these emphases are displayed in *One-Dimensional Man*, and constitute an essential background to understanding it. The book was explicitly introduced as a work of critical theory, an analysis of society which tried to assess the range of unrealized possibilities in circumstances of apparent industrial affluence. 'Negative thinking' and the positive goals of a philosophical anthropology were here shown by Marcuse to be connected elements of a single critical enterprise. He sought to formulate a critical theory of contemporary society, a theory which analyzes society in the light of its used and unused or abused capabilities for improving the human condition. [Such an analysis] implies value judgments ... the judgment that human life is worth living, or rather can be and ought to be made worth living ... [and] the judgment that, in a given society, specific possibilities exist for the amelioration of human life and specific ways of realizing these possibilities. Critical analysis has to demonstrate the objective validity of these judgments, and the demonstration has to proceed on empirical grounds.[5]

One-Dimensional Man was organized into three main sections. In the opening chapters of the book, Marcuse portrayed what he called the 'one-dimensional society', or what he often also referred to as 'advanced industrial society'. The second part was concerned with 'one-dimensional thought' – what Marcuse termed 'the defeat of the logic of protest' which resulted from the specific mode of development of the advanced industrial order. In conclusion, the author posed the question 'What alternatives are there?' What possibilities offered themselves for transcending a form of society which Marcuse saw as fundamentally repressive, but in which potential forms of protest had seemingly been undermined?

Basic to Marcuse's discussion of the first of these themes was his interpretation of social changes that have occurred since the nineteenth century. Marx's critique of political economy was constructed at a period in the development of capitalism when the two classes, bourgeoisie and proletariat, faced each other as contending antagonists. In its classical form, in Marx's texts, critical theory was anchored in the anticipation that the working class would bring about the demise of capitalism, and usher in a socialist society of a radically different character. Although these remained the basic classes, Marcuse argued, in the Western societies today, the working class could no longer be understood as the medium of historical transformation. The working class had ceased to be the 'material negation' of the advanced industrial order, but instead had become an integral part of that order. Advanced industrial society, according to Marcuse, was formed of a conjunction of the welfare state and the 'warfare state'. Internally, nineteenth-century competitive capitalism had ceded place to an organized industrial economy, in which the state, large corporations and unions co-ordinated their activities to further economic growth. But this was also an economy geared up to the threat of war, in which vast sums were spent on armaments, and where the threat of 'international Communism' was used to bolster a political unity between supposedly divergent political party programmes. 'Mobilized against this threat,' in Marcuse's words, 'capitalist society shows an internal union and cohesion unknown at previous stages of industrial civilization. It is a cohesion on very material grounds; mobilization against the enemy works as a mighty stimulus of production and employment, thus sustaining a high level of living.'[6]

Collaboration of unions with business leadership and the state was not by any means the most fundamental characteristic of advanced industrial society influencing the incorporation of the working class. More deep-rooted were changes in technology and the production process. The mechanization of production, in which labour power was increasingly part of the overall design of technology,[7] remained the focus of alienation. But the enslavement of the human being to the machine was concealed by the gradual disappearance of the more openly harsh, brutalizing work environments. Moreover, the machine itself became absorbed into much more encompassing systems of technical organization which cut across divisions between manual and non-manual labour. Class domination now appeared as merely neutral 'administration'. Capitalists and managers, Marcuse said, tended to lose their separate identity as a manifestly exploiting class, just as workers lost theirs as an exploited one. Class division and alienated labour were not eliminated, but became swamped by the expansion of organizational hierarchies. Political power, for Marcuse, also became merged with the technical apparatus of production. However much they might regard themselves as liberal democracies, contemporary societies were totalitarian. 'For "totalitarian"', in Marcuse's view, 'is not only a terroristic political coordination of society, but also a non-terroristic economic-technical coordination which operates through the manipulation of needs by vested interests.'[8]

The social and political cohesion of advanced industrial society gave rise to a corresponding cohesion, Marcuse continued, on the level of culture. In earlier times, 'high culture', or 'intellectual culture', as he often said, celebrated ideals distant from, and was thus explicitly or implicitly antagonistic towards, existing social realities. This was never, he admitted, a major stimulus to social change in and of itself; for high culture was the preserve of a minority, and operated at a distance from the mundane activities of day-to-day life. Nevertheless, it kept alive a range of alternative conceptions of the world that were today in the process of being swallowed up. The liquidation of 'two-dimensional culture' did not occur simply via the destruction of high culture, but rather through its appropriation within the established order. The values embodied in high culture were disseminated through the mass media and reduced to comfortable banalities stripped of their negating force. This was described as a process of 'repressive desublimation', a notion that connected directly with the views sketched by Marcuse in *Eros and Civilization*. Literature and art, as previously practised, rested upon the sublimation of instinctual impulses, mediated instinctual gratification. But the easy diffusion and trivializing of values and ideals permitted their immediate gratification. Such desublimation was repressive because it served only to reinforce the totalitarianism of the one-dimensional society. Sexuality was expressed within confines that repressed exactly that diffusion of the erotic which Marcuse saw as the precondition for the liberated society. The erotic had become reduced to permissive sexuality. This was a civilization whose discontents had been rendered palatable by a happy consciousness deriving from an absorption of the reality principle by the pleasure principle. Repressive desublimation 'manifests itself in all the manifold ways of fun, relaxation, and togetherness which practise the destruction of privacy, the contempt of form, the inability to tolerate silence, the proud exhibition of crudeness and brutality'.[9]

In advanced industrial society, technical reason became the only form of reason admitted as valid. Technical reason, the rationality of technology, defined reason purely instrumentally, in terms of the relation of means to ends. In seeing this conception as the foundation of positivism in intellectual discourse, and of contemporary ideology more generally, Marcuse's analysis at this point converged closely with that of the other members of the Frankfurt School. Reason, Marcuse said, rested upon the potentially subversive character of negation, as objectively linked to the revealing of 'internal inadequacies' of the existing world. But this subversive power of reason had itself become subverted in the 'one-dimensional thought' of technological rationality. In classical philosophy, as in a good deal of Western metaphysics until recent times, philosophy connected truth with the good life, with possible modes of living a free and rewarding existence. The quest for truth operated dialectically, exposing contradictions between thought and reality, and connecting such contradictions to the promise of the good life. But in instrumental reason truth concerned correspondence not contradiction, and truth (or 'fact') was separated from values.[10] Thus values could not be rationally justified in relation to the objective world, but became matters of subjective assessment. Instrumental reason was supposedly wholly neutral in respect of values, but actually preserved as an overriding value the one-dimensional world of technical progress.

The primacy of science, conceived of as a means of controlling nature, brought the actuality of technology into direct relation with philosophy, which was more and more dominated by positivism:

> The principles of modern science [Marcuse averred] were *a priori* structured in such a way that they could serve as conceptual instruments for a universe of self-propelling, productive control; theoretical operationalism came to correspond to practical operationalism. The scientific method which led to the ever-more-effective domination of nature thus came to provide the pure concepts as well as the instrumentalities for the ever-more-effective domination of man by man *through* the domination of nature. Theoretical reason, remaining pure and neutral, entered into the service of practical reason. The merger proved beneficial to both. Today, domination perpetuates and extends itself not only through technology but *as* technology, and the latter provides the great legitimation of the expanding political power, which absorbs all spheres of culture.[11]

The ordinary-language philosophy of Austin and others, and the philosophy of the later Wittgenstein, fell prey to such tendencies, however much they might superficially differ from positivism. For their aim was the freeing of philosophy from metaphysics, a cleansing operation which showed metaphysics to rest upon the misuse of language. The task of philosophy was again a 'technological' one, that of controlling its own past metaphysical excesses through the correction of language. As a therapeutic endeavour, Marcuse suggested, linguistic philosophy shared a common orientation with modern psychiatry. The unreason of madness was thus held to have an underlying affinity with the reason of metaphysics. For madness was a form of negation of the real, the concern of psychiatry being to 'adjust' the individual to the existing world, however insane that world might be. Like psychiatry, linguistic philosophy 'abhors transgression'.

A striking feature of *One-Dimensional Man* was the relative brevity of its third, concluding section: 'the chance of the alternatives' to the one-dimensional society and to one-dimensional thought. Much of what Marcuse had to say in this section was highly abstract, in a book which as a whole did not impress the reader with the detail of the discussions which it offered. The 'transcendent project' of the alternative society was spelled out in terms of its particular rationality, contrasting with the rationality of technique. The transcendent project, Marcuse claimed, must retain its connection with Marx's materialism in the sense that it must be concerned with real possibilities of change at the current level of material and intellectual culture. It must demonstrate its 'higher rationality', as contrasted to technological rationality, by showing that its negation of the present (compared, for example, with nihilism) affirmed values of human freedom and self-realization. Since technology, and technological rationality, were the underlying foundation of advanced industrial society, the transformative project must focus upon the development of a 'qualitatively new technics'. Technical reason had already become the basis of politics, and its reversal would necessarily imply a political reversal. The possibility of the transcendence of technological rationality, Marcuse argued, was built into its own progression, for it was approaching its limits within the repressive order of advanced industrialism. The furthering of the mechanization, and automation, of labour reached a phase at which it could no longer be contained within the one-dimensional society, but threatened its disintegration. It heralded a revolutionary rupture, a movement from quantity into quality:

It would open the possibility of an essentially new human reality – namely existence in free time on the basis of fulfilled vital needs.

Under such conditions, the scientific project itself would be free for trans-utilitarian ends, and free for the 'art of living' beyond the necessities and luxuries of domination. In other words, the completion of the technological reality would be not only the prerequisite, but also the rationale for *transcending* the technological reality.[12]

On its appearance, *One-Dimensional Man* was regarded by many of its critics as a profoundly pessimistic book, since its author appeared to hold out few concrete opportunities for social change, such was the seeming success of the one-dimensional society in closing off opposition. When, in *An Essay on Liberation* and other later writings, Marcuse made overtures towards student and other militants, this was widely seen as marking a change in posture towards a more optimistic outlook. But this was only partly the case, and rested upon a double misinterpretation. Marcuse did not regard the student movement and other militant tendencies of the time as the vanguard of a coming revolution, but rather as expressive of immanent tensions within the system. The chief basis of revolutionary transformation was not to be found in the activities of those not yet wholly incorporated within the one-dimensional society. It was to be found in the very centre of the one-dimensional society itself, in the potentially explosive consequences of that very force that was the origin of its coherence: the rationality of technique. In its own terms at least, *One-Dimensional Man* was a strongly revolutionary tract, and remained faithful to what Marcuse saw as an essential thread of Marxist thought, the tension between the relations of production (of the one-dimensional society) and emergent changes in the forces of production presaging a new society. The strands of pessimism that are to be found in the earlier works of Horkheimer and Adorno, and which eventually became strongly defined in their appraisal of the age of 'the end of the individual', are largely absent from Marcuse's writings from beginning to end. Moreover, the common assertion made against Marcuse that his works are merely 'utopian' ignores his reassessment of the meaning of 'utopia' in the contemporary age. What was utopian, he argued, had changed its character in virtue of the very level of development of technology in advanced industrial society. The utopian was no longer that which was specifically implausible, or had 'no place' in history;

utopian possibilities were contained in the very technical organization of the advanced industrial order.[13]

Some substantive comments

In some respects Marcuse was an easy target for critical attack, although he hardly deserved the short shrift he received from some adversaries on both right and left. However, it seems to me worth while recognizing two levels upon which *One-Dimensional Man* can be read. The book can be seen, as it were, as a 'substantive' text, which advanced certain theses about the nature of contemporary societies. On this level much of what Marcuse had to say is almost naively inadequate. But the work can also be taken, as one presumes Marcuse intended it to be taken, as a 'symptomatic' study: that is to say, as a defence of a critical theory of society in an era in which orthodox Marxism appeared seriously deficient. Reading the work from this second aspect, Marcuse's views retain their interest.

As a substantive analysis, Marcuse's work had a good deal in common with writers from whom his ideas in other respects diverged dramatically. Bell, Lipset and many others had written of the successful incorporation of the working class in what they called 'industrial society' rather than 'capitalism'. The shift in terminology, for these writers, was not a fortuitous one. According to their view, 'capitalism', as a form of society resembling that described by Marx, was at most a transitory social order, confined to the late nineteenth and early twentieth centuries. 'Capitalism' was a sub-category of the more generic type of 'industrial society' which had come to fruition in the twentieth century. In such a society, it was argued, a general consensus upon goals of economic advance and political liberalization replaced the old ideological disputes which polarized the social classes. The 'end of ideology' meant the end of radicalism, 'the defeat of the logic of protest' of which Marcuse also spoke.

In disputing the 'end of ideology' thesis, Marcuse confronted such views, in considerable degree, on their own terms. The one-dimensional society was a society in which the revolutionary subject of Marxist theory no longer carried the promise of radical change. The task Marcuse set himself was to demonstrate the validity, in some depth, of the remark by which C. Wright Mills almost casually dismissed the claims of the end-of-ideology thesis: that it itself was an ideology. *One-Dimensional Man* sought to show exactly how this could be so. The absorption of clashing opinions, of the driving power of negation, into technological rationality actually meant that 'advanced industrial culture is *more* ideological than its predecessor.'[14] It was more ideological than early capitalism, according to Marcuse, because ideology had become part of the very process of production. False consciousness was integral to the 'truth' of the logic of technical reason.

The very real interest of his discussion of this point should not lead us to forget the equally significant shortcomings of the social analysis which informed it. Marcuse's adoption of the terms 'industrial society' or 'advanced industrial society' was ambiguous and confusing. He continued occasionally to use the term 'capitalism', and recognized differences between Western industrialism and that of the East European societies.[15] Moreover, in 'advanced industrial society' class relations remained constitutive of the relations of production, however much this might be concealed by the technical administration of the one-dimensional order. But by making the term 'industrial society' the preferred centre point of his analysis, Marcuse undoubtedly moved too readily into the discourse of his opponents. This terminological preference was not merely fortuitous in his case either. Marcuse portrayed a society in which capitalist mechanisms of production no longer supplied the key to explaining its major institutions.

Marcuse's use of the concepts of 'organized capitalism' and 'advanced industrial society' was ambiguous and inconsistent. In shifting between the two, he moved between a Marxist standpoint and that of Max Weber: 'organized capitalism' was dominated by technical reason, or what to Weber was 'formal rationality'.[16] The changes which Marcuse held to have stabilized capitalism, needing now to be analysed as 'advanced industrial society', concealed a shift in theoretical stance concerning the nature of capitalism itself. This unresolved tension – crudely put, a tension between Marx's conception of capitalism as a class society and the Weberian association of capitalism with the rationality of technique – was a main factor introducing inconsistencies in Marcuse's position.

In any case, the term 'one-dimensional society' surely was, and is, a misleading one. I have emphasized that Marcuse saw an immanent contradiction at the heart of the seemingly consensual order he portrayed. But his identification of that contradiction was sharply delimited by its association with the progression of technical reason as the unifying focus of the one-dimensional order. Both 'internally', and in the context of international economic and political relations, the US and the other capitalist societies were more divided and conflictful than Marcuse's analysis suggested. Marcuse sought to stand pluralism on its head. The pluralist political theorists, and the many advocates of the theory of industrial society, portrayed a picture of the capitalist countries seemingly quite contrary to that of Marcuse. For him, the picture was one of increasing, 'totalitarian' conformity; the others argued that the Western societies were becoming more internally differentiated. But the opposition between the two viewpoints was less dramatic than one might imagine. For in agreeing that transformative conflict had been successfully contained, each underestimated the divided and fragmentary character of industrial society; and failed to connect internal sources of tension or antagonism with strains in the world system.[17]

Marcuse's discussion in *One-Dimensional Man* was explicitly based upon the US. As a diagnosis of trends of development in that society, for the reasons I have indicated, it was at best only of limited plausibility. But the presumption that the US, as the technologically most advanced capitalist society, blazes a trail that others are destined to follow should be treated with some scepticism. We should not imagine that there is only one model of 'advanced capitalism', other societies simply lagging behind in respect of moving towards that model.

Technology, freedom, politics

One-Dimensional Man was a radical book in a true sense. Marcuse was above all concerned to sustain a commitment to profound social transformation, and refused to have any truck with palliatives. That a supposedly 'pessimistic' book should have served to contribute to political activism is easy to understand when it is seen in such a light. Not only did Marcuse attack all forms of compromise, he sought to demonstrate how these in fact took on an opposite guise to their apparent one. 'Repressive tolerance', 'repressive desublimation', these terms conveyed Marcuse's diagnosis of the 'internal inadequacies' of one-dimensional culture. The opening sentence of the first chapter of *One-Dimensional Man* set the tone for the whole of the book. In the West, Marcuse proposed, 'a comfortable, smooth, reasonable, democratic unfreedom prevails'.[18]

Marcuse was not, as I have commented previously, a utopian thinker – at least, in the pejorative sense which that term has acquired since Marx treated 'utopian socialism' so dismissively in the nineteenth century. Whatever reservations one might have of the interpretation of Freud which Marcuse adopted, in the context of his philosophical anthropology Marcuse developed a radicalism concerned with issues that were only weakly dealt with in more orthodox forms of Marxism. These were in some part, but only in some part, shared by the others in the Frankfurt School. I shall emphasize here only the issues of sexuality and technology.

The time has long since passed when Marcuse could be identified, as he was by some who had only a casual acquaintance with his writings, as a protagonist of the 'permissive society'. He emerged rather as one of its strongest critics, as is made perfectly clear both in *Eros and Civilization* and in *One-Dimensional Man*. 'Sexual liberation' was explicitly one of his main objects of attack. In this context it is perhaps worth remarking that Marcuse's discussion of sexuality was not as distant from, or opposed to, that of Foucault as might appear.[19] Foucault's view of Freud and Marcuse's 'critical Freudianism' might seem quite irreconcilable, and no doubt in some respects this is the case. But when Foucault argued that, in contemporary Western civilization, rather than liberating ourselves through sexuality we need to liberate ourselves from sexuality, there was more than an echo of Marcuse's thought in what he had to say. The discourse of 'sexuality' and a preoccupation with 'sex' were for both writers a concomitant of, rather than a mode of dissolving, the 'internalized' discipline characteristic of contemporary forms of social organization. In Marcuse's argument, the liberation of the erotic depended upon the transcendence of 'sexuality', seen as an activity separated from the rest of life. The interesting feature of Marcuse's argument was the idea that the liberation of the erotic did not derive from the release from repression as such – as Reich proposed. It could only be achieved by transforming sublimation itself.

On the face of things, Marcuse's attempt to combine a rather orthodox version of Freud with a distinctly unorthodox version of Marx would seem to have been doomed to failure. Marcuse forcibly rejected the 'revisionism' of authors such as Fromm and Horney. According to Marcuse, Freud's theory 'is in its very substance "sociological"'; it followed that 'no new cultural or sociological orientation is needed to reveal this substance.'[20] Marcuse regarded Freud's theory as already pointing to the possibility of the achievement of a non-repressive society. The most troublesome, and most frequently discarded, element of Freud's views by the psychoanalytic revisionists – the death instinct – Marcuse saw as demonstrating the emancipatory potential of Freudian theory. The merging of Eros and Thanatos, in Marcuse's interpretation of Freud, was inherent in human self-development, and closely involved with the active promotion of historical change emphasized by the early Marx. Pleasure was distinct from the 'blind satisfaction of instinct', characteristic of the behaviour of animals. In pleasure, which was generalized, instinct was not exhausted in immediate gratification, but contributed to the self-formation of the individual. This was what Marcuse called a 'sensuous rationality'.[21] Pleasure would not be *released* in the society Marcuse anticipated for the future, but would have *form*. Erotic energy 'would surge up in new forms of cultural creation'. The result, he accentuated: 'would not be pansexualism, which rather belongs to the image of the repressive society . . . To the extent that erotic energy were really freed, it would cease to be mere sexuality and would become a force that determines the organism in all its modes of behaviour, dimensions and goals.'[22]

These ideas retain their provocative character, and contrast interestingly with the outlook of Habermas. Habermas drew extensively upon Freud in formulating his version of critical theory. But his use of Freud appears to be almost wholly 'methodological': psychoanalytic therapy demonstrated how increased autonomy of action could be achieved via the individual's own self-understanding. Habermas gave little indication of how much he accepted of the *content* of Freud's writings. In this respect his appropriation of Freud stands in distinct contrast to that of Marcuse – and this has ramifications for Habermas's later work.

For the conception of an ideal speech situation, interesting as it may be in its own right, remains on a peculiarly cognitive level. What of affect, of sexuality, love, hate and death? Whereas Marcuse's formulation of critical theory was founded upon an abiding concern with these phenomena, Habermas's account provided little way of coping with them conceptually.

From his earliest works, under the influence of Heidegger, Marcuse set himself against the view – which seems to be that of the later Marx, and certainly became strongly established in orthodox Marxism – that nature was merely a means of realizing human purposes. Marcuse's connection with Heidegger – one which, I have suggested earlier, was of more abiding importance for him than some critics have argued – gave his critique of instrumental reason a rather different character from the views of either Horkheimer or Adorno. For all three writers, the succumbing of orthodox Marxism to the sway of instrumental reason was inherently related to the degeneration of socialism into nothing more than an alternative mode of promoting industrialization to that offered by capitalism. However, Marcuse's disavowal of an 'ungrounded' negative dialectics led him to emphasize that critical theory must incorporate a theory of Being. His juxtaposition of 'technics' with 'aesthetics' owed a lot to Adorno; and his preoccupation with technology as a medium of domination in some respects had close affinities with the similar concerns of conservative authors such as Freyer, Schelsky and Gehlen. But the synthesis he worked out differed significantly from all of them. The most obvious element differentiating Marcuse's views from those of these other writers is his emphasis upon the liberating potential of technology itself. He agreed that technical progress and the progress of humanity were certainly not one and the same. But technical advance, and increasing productivity, generated the increasing possibility (even probability) of their own negation. 'increasing productivity in freedom and happiness becomes increasingly strong and increasingly rational.'[23]

As follows from Marcuse's account of the generalizable character of the erotic, this transformation could not merely take the form of the lifting of repression. Certainly in stressing the significance of automation, Marcuse emphasized the importance of altering the character of technology itself, and of overcoming human subordination to the machine. He was fond of alluding to the passages in the *Grundrisse* in which Marx spoke of automation freeing the human being from bondage to production, and instead allowing the individual to become master of the production process. But in what he had to say about the consequences of this process, Marcuse proposed an ontology according to which humanity would again live 'in' nature and not merely 'from' it. Contemporary capitalism preyed upon nature, protecting only certain areas from this destructive attitude: recreation areas, parks, etc. Nature survived here only as repressive desublimation. A drive out to the country at weekends might allow a person to recover from the pressure of work and urban life, but was a poor substitute indeed for the rich, aesthetically rewarding relation between human beings and nature which Marcuse envisaged. Here again, if it was in some part nourished from conservative sources, Marcuse's radicalism surfaced in full force. A recovery and extension of the erotic cathexis of nature, Marcuse argued, would allow human beings to 'find themselves in nature'; nature was to be found as 'a subject with which to live in a common universe'. This would in turn demand breaking through the dominant understanding of the world as commodified time–space: 'Existence [he affirmed] would be experienced not as a continually expanding and unfulfilled becoming but as existence or being with what is and can be. Time would not seem linear, as a perpetual line or rising curve, but cyclical, as the return contained in Nietzsche's idea of the 'perpetuity of pleasure'.[24]

These ideas still have relevance for social theory. To say this, however, is not to endorse them as they stand. It would be surprising if an analysis so open to criticism on a 'substantive' level should prove unobjectionable when read 'symptomatically'. And indeed there are basic shortcomings in Marcuse's thought which cannot be overcome simply by trimming away some of the difficulties or ambiguities in his appraisal of the one-dimensional society.

Marcuse called the contemporary Western liberal democracies 'totalitarian'. In using this term he was well aware of the differences between such societies and those more directly based on terror. 'Bourgeois democracy', he accepted, 'is still infinitely better than fascism.'[25] Such comments, however, are no substitute for an adequate analysis of the political conditions of liberty; and such an analysis is absent in Marcuse's writings. This has consequences both for his interpretation of existing societies, and for his envisaged society of the future. Marcuse's basic attitude towards liberalism was established in some of his early writings, and I do not think it changed a great deal thereafter. Liberalism, according to Marcuse, and the 'bourgeois rights' associated with it, were products of the entrepreneurial capitalism of the nineteenth century. Bourgeois freedoms, always class-biased in any case, declined with the replacement of competitive by organized capitalism. 'Liberalism', Marcuse wrote in 1934, ' "produces" the total-authoritarian state out of itself, as its own consummation at a more advanced stage of development.'[26] Liberalism and fascism, Marcuse continued, were closely affiliated: the real enemy of both was radical Marxian socialism.

This standpoint is fundamentally defective. Rather than providing a basis for political analysis, it avoids it. Political power – as Marcuse made plain in *One-Dimensional Man* – was no more than an extension of the dominance of technological rationality, of the 'power over the machine process'.[27] In the one-dimensional society, bourgeois rights and liberties became of only marginal importance, eroded by the pervasive influence of technical reason. Such a conception ignores the fact that 'bourgeois freedoms' have from the early years of capitalist development provided a stimulus to change for those excluded from them: subordinate groups in society. Marcuse underestimated the significance of struggles to universalize rights and liberties previously effectively the privilege of the few – a forgivable view, perhaps, in Germany in the early 1930s, but not when generalized to 'advanced industrial societies' as a whole. The contemporary capitalist societies are of course in some very basic respects quite different today from those of the nineteenth century. But they have changed in some substantial part as a result of class struggle. In this respect, T.H. Marshall's account of the importance of citizenship rights, when adopted in a modified version, is significant.[28]

One of the most central of Marcuse's themes is that of the relation between technology and emancipation. The transformations in technology which Marcuse anticipated and advocated were *themselves*, in his analysis, the guarantee of freedom. Freedom and servitude were not, in Marcuse's theory, phenomena of politics, or even of power more broadly understood. Freedom, Marcuse repeatedly argued, was to be interpreted in relation to the satisfaction of need. In a society in which the erotic energy of the personality would be freed, the emancipation of the single individual was simultaneously the emancipation of all. Here there lurks and old-established but entirely unsatisfactory doctrine: the domination of persons will cede place to the administration of things, as the foundation of free society. Marcuse, the improbable guru of a novel radicalism, was revealed as a latter-day adherent of an archaic political philosophy, that of Saint-Simon.

8 Garfinkel, Ethnomethodology and Hermeneutics

In the following discussion, I shall connect some of the themes found in the writings of Harold Garfinkel with some developments in European social philosophy. By submitting both to a 'constructive critique' I shall hope to elucidate their importance for contemporary social theory.

The notion of *Verstehen* over the past few decades has been rehabilitated, particularly in the context of the *Geistes-wissenschaften*. In Germany, this has centred upon the work of Hans-Georg Gadamer, which in turn drew extensively upon Heidegger's 'hermeneutic phenomenology'. Gadamer's writings demonstrate clear connections and overlaps with the work of such authors as Winch in Britain and Ricoeur in France.[1] I shall not attempt to single out the distinctive views of such authors, but only to characterize certain notions arising from them – ones that contrast rather radically with Max Weber's version of 'interpretative sociology', which served to introduce the concept of *Verstehen* into English-speaking sociology. More qualifications are in order with respect to 'ethnomethodology' – a term that embraces a number of mutually dissident views. What I have to say is not directed at Garfinkel's programme of practical studies of 'everyday accomplishments', which seems to me at once deeply interesting and poorly elucidated philosophically. All I want to do is to compare, in a critical way, some of Garfinkel's ideas with those emanating from the more abstract traditions of European social philosophy.[2]

I shall argue that a grasp of these themes, and an appreciation of their significance, signals a major break with the erstwhile dominant schools in sociology, according to whom the social sciences can be narrowly modelled upon natural science. An important emphasis of these schools is that sociology is (or can hope to be) *revelatory* in respect of the confusions or misapprehensions of 'common sense'. That is to say, just as the natural sciences seem to have stood in opposition to common-sense views of the physical world, to have penetrated the mystifications of ordinary lay thought, so sociology can strip away the musty errors of everyday beliefs about society. The claimed 'findings' of social research, like the findings of natural science, are frequently resisted or disclaimed by lay people on the basis of what 'common sense shows'. As far as natural science is concerned, such 'resistance' normally takes the form of the refusal to abandon a 'common-sense' belief in the face of findings that contravene it: for example, the clinging to the belief that the earth is flat rather than spherical. Something like this certainly may occur in respect of the claims generated by sociology; but another – almost diametrically opposed – response is common. This is not that social science reports conclusions that people cannot accept because they go against trusted beliefs, but rather that it merely *repeats the familiar* – that it 'tells us what we already know', albeit perhaps wrapped up in a technical language. Sociologists are prone to dismiss this sort of rejoinder to their work rather cursorily, holding that it is the business of social research to check up upon the convictions of 'common sense', which may be right or wrong. But to regard lay beliefs as in principle corrigible in this sense is to treat them as if they were merely adjuncts to human action, rather than integral to it. Lay beliefs are not merely *descriptions* of the social world, but are the very basis of the *constitution* of that world, as the organized product of human acts. Recognition of this point, I shall seek to demonstrate, makes us aware that sociology stands in more complex relation to its 'subject matter' – human social conduct – than natural science does. The natural world is transformed by human activity, but it is not constituted as an object-world by human beings. The social world, on the other hand, is constituted and reproduced through and in human action; the concepts of 'common sense', and the everyday language in which they are expressed, are drawn upon by lay actors to 'make social life happen'.

Let me distinguish five themes that can be discerned in at least some of the writings of those involved with, or close to, 'ethnomethodology'. These by no means exhaust the interest of such writings, but I consider them to be particularly important. First, the theme of the significance of the notion of human *action* or *agency* in sociological theory. Most of the leading schools of sociology, with the partial exception of symbolic interactionism, lack a concept of action. Now this initially seems an odd thing to say, because one of the main figures who influenced Garfinkel, Talcott Parsons, explicitly based his scheme of theory upon an 'action frame of reference', and in his first major work, *The Structure of Social Action*, attempted to incorporate 'voluntarism' as a core component of it. It is sometimes argued that, whereas Parsons began his intellectual career as a 'voluntarist', his theories become more and more deterministic. I think it more accurate to claim that Parsons did not successfully embody such a perspective within his system of theory in the first place. What Parsons did was to treat voluntarism as equivalent to the internalization of values in personality, thereby attempting to relate motivation to the *consensus universel* upon which social solidarity is held to depend. But this has the consequence that the creative element in human action becomes translated into a causal outcome of 'need-dispositions', and the adoption of voluntarism merely a plea for complementing sociology with psychology. Here the actor does indeed appear as a 'cultural dope', rather than as a knowing agent at least in some part the master of his or her own fate. As against the determinism inherent in the sort of approach favoured by Parsons, it is fruitful to place in the forefront the thesis that society is a skilled accomplishment of actors; this is true even of the most trivial social encounter.

Second, the theme of reflexivity. The notion of action, as the writings of philosophers have made clear, is integrally bound up with the capacity of human agents for self-reflection, for the rational 'monitoring' of their own conduct. In most orthodox forms of sociology (including Parsonian functionalism), but not in ethnomethodology, reflexivity is treated as a 'nuisance' whose effects are to be minimized as far as possible, and which is only recognized in various marginal forms, as 'bandwagon effect', 'self-fulfilling prophecies', etc. Moreover, these tend to compress together two aspects of reflexivity: that of the social observer in relation to the theories he or she formulates, and that of the actors whose behaviour he or she seeks to analyse or explain. There is an irony here that ties together these two aspects, or rather the neglect of them, in positivistically inclined forms of social thought. For what is denied, or obscured, on the level of theory – namely, that human agents act for reasons and are, in some sense, 'responsible' for their actions – is implicitly assumed on the level of sociological discourse: that is to say, it is accepted that one has to provide 'reasoned grounds' for the adoption of a particular theory in the face of the critical evaluations offered by others in the sociological community.

Symbolic interactionism is perhaps the only leading school of thought in English-speaking sociology that assigns a central place to agency and reflexivity. G.H. Mead's social philosophy hinges upon the relation of 'I' and 'we' in social interaction and the development of personality. But even in Mead's own writings, the 'I' appears as a more shadowy element than the socially determined self, which is elaborately discussed. In the works of most of Mead's followers, the social self displaces the 'I' altogether, thus foreclosing the option that Mead took out on the possibility of incorporating reflexivity into the theory of action. Where this happens, symbolic interactionism is readily assimilated within the mainstream of sociological thought, as a sort of 'sociological social psychology' concentrated upon face-to-face interaction.

Third, the theme of language. Now language, in the form of the symbol, is obviously stressed within symbolic interactionism, as the term itself indicates. But this is distinct from the standpoint of ethnomethodology, in which language is conceived, not simply as a set of symbols or signs, as a mode of representing things, but as a 'medium of practical activity', a mode of doing things. Language, to use Wittgensteinian terminology, operates within definite 'forms of life', and is routinely used by lay actors at the medium of organizing their day-to-day social conduct. The meanings of utterances thus have to be understood in relation to the whole variety of uses to which language is put by social actors – not just those of 'describing', but also those of 'arguing', 'persuading', 'joking', 'evaluating', etc., etc. I have alluded briefly to the significance of this above. One of its consequences is that ordinary language cannot be ignored by sociological investigators in favour of a wholly separate technical metalanguage which 'clears up' the 'fuzziness' or the 'ambiguity' of everyday speech. Ordinary language is the medium whereby social life is organized *as* meaningful by its constituent actors: to study a form of life involves grasping lay modes of talk which express that form of life. Ordinary language is not therefore just a topic that can be made available for analysis, but is a resource that every sociological or anthropological observer must use to gain access to his or her 'researchable subject matter'.

Fourth, the theme of the temporal and contextual locating of action. I think it would be plausible to say that it is only in respect of societal evolution that orthodox social theory has attempted to build temporality into its analyses. In ethnomethodology, on the other hand, the locating of interaction in time becomes of central interest. In the conduct of a conversation, for example, it is pointed out that participants typically use the conversation reflexively to characterize 'what has been said', and also anticipate its future course to characterize 'what is being said'. The context-dependence or indexical character of meanings in interaction, of course, involves other elements besides that of time. Garfinkel is undoubtedly correct in emphasizing the indexical character of ordinary language communication – and also in seeing this as a basic source of 'difficulty' for orthodox views of the nature of sociological metalanguages.

Fifth, and finally, the theme of tacit or 'taken for granted' understandings. In the active constitution of interaction as a skilled performance, the 'silences' are as important as the words that are uttered, and indeed make up the necessary background of mutual knowledge in terms of which utterances 'make sense', or, rather, sense is made of them. Tacit understandings are drawn upon by actors as ordinary, but unexplicated, conditions of social interaction. The emphasis upon this in ethnomethodology is one of the direct points of connection between it and the forms of European social philosophy I shall turn to in the next section, reflecting Garfinkel's indebtedness to Schutz, thereby linking the former's work to the great traditions of phenomenology such as are exemplified, for example, in Husserl's *Crisis of European Sciences*.

In so far as ethnomethodology shares certain origins, in 'existentialist phenomenology', with the developments in European social thought I shall now go on to mention, it is not particularly surprising that we should be able to discern similarities between them. If these are not immediately apparent it is because the styles of writing in which they are couched are so different, ethnomethodology being mainly oriented to generating an empirical research programme, the other being expressed in the style of abstract philosophy. In approaching the traditions of thought that have breathed new life into the notion of *Verstehen*, it is important to appreciate the contrast which they offer to the earlier phases of development of the *Geisteswissenschaften*, as represented by Dilthey and (in spite of many reservations) Max Weber. In the 'older tradition', *Verstehen* was regarded above all as a *method*, to be applied to the human sciences, in contrast to the sorts of method of external observation employed in the natural sciences. For Dilthey, especially in his earlier writings, the process of understanding was conceived to depend upon the re-experiencing or re-enactment of the thoughts and feelings of those whose conduct was to be understood. That is to say, in some sense or another – which Dilthey increasingly found difficult to specify – in understanding the action of others one mentally 'puts oneself in the other's shoes'. Weber adopted much the same stance, although suspicious of notions such as 're-experiencing' and 'empathy', and rejecting the idea that there was a logical gulf between the methods of the social and natural sciences. Weber's version of interpretative sociology meshed closely with his commitment to what has subsequently come to be called methodological individualism: the thesis that statements that refer to collectivities can always in principle be expressed as the behaviour of concrete individuals.

Both Dilthey and Weber argued that their particular understandings of 'understanding' could be reconciled with the achievement of objective sciences of history (Dilthey) or sociology (Weber). Their views have been sharply attacked by critics who claim that *Verstehen* cannot yield the sort of evidence that would seem to be necessary to 'objective science'.[3] According to such critics, the process of interpretation can be useful as a source of hypotheses about conduct, but cannot be used to test hypotheses thus derived. It is difficult to resist the force of such criticism if *Verstehen* is supposed to be compatible with criteria of evidence characteristic of natural sciences. Moreover, there is a series of other difficulties with Weber's views, of which I shall mention here only two. One is to do with 'empathy', the other with Weber's formulation of 'social action'. Weber wished to distance himself from the view that empathic identification played a major part in understanding the meaning of actions; but that he was unable to do so is illustrated by certain puzzles to which his position gives rise. Thus he supposed that mysticism was 'on the margins of meaningful action', since the behaviour of mystics could only be understood by those who were 'religiously musical'. Let us suppose that some, and only some, social scientists are 'religiously musical': how could they ever communicate their understanding to those who are not? To admit that they could not compromises Weber's views about the possibility of achieving an intersubjectively agreed set of criteria in terms of which an objective 'observation-language' could be established in the social sciences. As against Weber's view, I would say that to call conduct 'mystical' is already in a certain sense to have 'understood it meaningfully': and that 'understanding' is tied to the capacity to describe actions linguistically: to typify them in Schutz's term. There is a series of problems relating to what Schutz calls, rather unhappily, 'objective meaning' that Weber's analysis, concerned only with 'subjective meaning', fails to come to terms with. Weber's preoccupation with subjective meaning was closely bound up with his methodological individualism, since 'meaning' only came into being through the subjective consciousness of actors. It is against this backdrop that Weber distinguished between meaningful action and social action, the latter being the main interest of interpretative sociology, defined as action which was oriented towards others and thereby influenced in its course. In Weber's famous example, if two cyclists who did not see each other coming bumped into one another, this was not a case of social action, since the behaviour of the one did not figure in the subjective orientation of the other. If, having collided, they started quarrelling about who was responsible for the accident, this then became social action. But this formulation, which specified what was social only in terms of the subjective standpoint of actors, does not seem at all satisfactory: it is not easy to apply, and it does not encompass the range of elements that I would wish to claim are 'social'. It is not easy to apply to actual conduct because there are many cases of behaviour in which the other, to whom the action may be said to be oriented, is not present on the scene. What are we to make, for instance, of a man shaving prior to going out for the evening? Is he

orienting his action towards another particular person he antici-
pates meeting later on? The answer is that he may or may not have
another's possible responses clearly in mind while he carries on
the activity; and this is in fact not particularly relevant to the social
character of what he is doing, which is likely to reside more in
conventions or norms of 'cleanliness', etc. Similarly, I want to say
that the action of a cyclist pedalling along the road is already
social, regardless of whether others are in sight or not, in so far as
what the cyclist does is oriented towards, and 'interpretable' in
terms of, the social rules governing traffic behaviour.

In the series of writings to which I have referred previously,
Verstehen is treated not as a method of investigation peculiar to
the social sciences, but as an ontological condition of life in society
as such; it is regarded not as depending upon a psychological
process of 're-enactment' or something similar, but as primarily a
linguistic matter of grasping the content of familiar and unfamiliar
forms of life; to understand others, it is held, is in an important
sense to enter into *dialogue* with them; such understanding cannot
be 'objective' in any simple sense, since all knowledge moves in a
circle, and there can be no knowledge 'free from presuppositions';
and, finally, *Verstehen* is linked to norms of meaning in such a way
as to break free from methodological individualism.

There can be no question of pursuing these very complex ideas
in any sort of detail here, and all I shall try to do is to clarify what
they share with the points of interest in ethnomethodology that I
have distinguished earlier.

To argue that *Verstehen* should be regarded as an ontological
condition of human society, rather than as a special method of the
sociologist or historian, is to hold that it is the means whereby
social life is constituted by lay actors. That is to say, 'understanding' the meaning of the actions and communications of others, as
a skilled accomplishment, is an integral element of the routine
capabilities of competent social actors. Hermeneutics is not simply
the privileged reserve of the professional social investigator, but is
practised by everyone; mastery of such practice is the only avenue
whereby professional social scientists, like lay actors themselves,
are able to generate the descriptions of social life they use in their
analyses. One of the consequences of this, of course, is to reduce
the distance between what sociologists do in their researches, and
what lay actors do in their day-to-day activities. To revert to the

terminology of ethnomethodology, not only is it the case that every social theorist is a member of a society, and draws upon the skills associated with such membership as a resource in his or her investigations: it is equally important that every member of society is a 'practical social theorist'. The predictability of the social world does not just happen, it is 'made to happen' by lay actors.

The centrality of language as the organizing medium of the 'lived-in world' is stressed alike in the hermeneutic phenomenology of Heidegger, Gadamer and Ricoeur, and in the writings of those following the later Wittgenstein in English-speaking sociology. Garfinkel of course drew directly upon Wittgenstein's writings. However, continental philosophers began to emphasize the relevance of Wittgenstein's writings to their own concerns. For while Wittgenstein gave no special technical meaning to *Verstehen*, his later philosophy certainly moved towards recommending that the understanding of actions and communications could only be approached within the practical involvements of definite 'language-games'. Gadamer emphasized that the individual 'lives in and through language', and that to understand a language was to understand the mode of life which that language expressed. In focusing upon the importance of dialogue *between* different forms of life, however, Gadamer went beyond Wittgenstein. The characteristic problem to which Wittgenstein's philosophy seems to lead is: how does one ever get out of one language-game into another? For language-games appear as closed universes of meaning. In Gadamer, on the other hand, the mediation of language-games through dialogue was placed as a beginning point rather than as a conclusion; the emphasis was upon what was involved in grasping the meaning of long-distant historical texts, understanding alien forms of life, etc. It is perhaps not too fanciful to suppose that the prominence of dialogue in Gadamer's philosophy finds something of a parallel, on a much more modest scale, with the prominence of conversation in Garfinkel's work.

The 'circle' in which all knowledge moves is a preoccupation of many different modern philosophies. If one breaks – as in the philosophy of science Popper, Kuhn and others have broken – with the idea of a 'first philosophy', founded upon a bedrock of certainty, one becomes committed to the notion that it is the business of epistemology to make the circle of knowledge a fruitful rather than a vicious one. That is, for example, what Popper tries to do for science by means of his philosophy of conjecture and refutation; and what, from what is in most respects a very different standpoint, the modern phenomenological philosophers seek to do via the notion of the 'hermeneutic circle'. One does not find, in Garfinkel's writings, or in those of others immediately influenced by him, a sophisticated discussion of such matters of epistemology. Such a concern would appear to be foreign to the style of work characteristic of ethnomethodology. None the less, the theme of 'indexicality' is certainly directly relevant to the sorts of issue raised by philosophies that stress the inherent circularity of knowledge – although again on a more minor scale. Some of the similarities are quite easy to see. One of the notions associated with the 'hermeneutic circle' is that in, say, understanding a text, the reader grasps each part through an initial appreciation of the whole; there is thus a constant process of moving from part to whole and back again, whereby an enriched understanding of the whole illuminates each part and vice versa. A similar idea appeared in Garfinkel's discussion of indexicality in conversations, where it was pointed out that a conversation was constantly drawn upon by participants both as a mode of characterizing itself and so as to 'gloss' the meaning of each particular contribution to that conversation. Garfinkel (cf. also Cicourel on 'indefinite triangulation') seems to present a version of the idea that the circularity of knowledge can be fruitfully explored, but did not feel any need to elucidate this on any kind of abstract level; in fact, this idea seems to go along with a defined strain of naturalism in Garfinkel's writings, as expressed for example in the claim that it was the task of ethnomethodology to describe indexical expressions 'free of any thought of remedy'. Such unresolved perplexities seem to underlie the very different directions which the work of those originally influenced in some part by Garfinkel has taken: on the one hand, in the writings of Sacks and Schegloff, towards a naturalistic form of 'conversational analysis'; on the other, in the writings of Blum and McHugh, towards a concern with the abstract ramifications of the 'hermeneutic circle'.[4]

The newer version of *Verstehen* depends upon the thesis that understanding the meaning of either actions or communications involves the application of 'publicly accessible' linguistic categories connected to tacitly known norms or rules. In tracing out some of the connections between this and ethnomethodology, we return to the origins that each party shares in the development of phenomenology after Husserl, in Schutz and in Heidegger. It is highly important to appreciate the degree to which this development, as culminating in hermeneutic phenomenology and linking up to the largely independent evolution of post-Wittgensteinian philosophy, makes a movement away from the original impetus to phenomenology. 'Hermeneutic phenomenology' in the hands of Heidegger and Gadamer breaks with the subjectivism characteristic of the earlier phase of development of phenomenology. (Schutz never managed to complete this break.) From this perspective, as from that of the later Wittgenstein, language is essentially a social or public phenomenon grounded in forms of life: the self-understanding of the individual can only occur in terms of 'publicly available' concepts. A person can only refer to his or her private sensations in the same framework of language as he or she refers to those of others. This is very different from the philosophical schema within which Weber worked, and cuts across the assumptions of methodological individualism, since the locus of the creation of meaning is taken to be the standards or rules of the collectivity rather than the subjective consciousness of the individual actor, the latter in fact presupposing the former. Garfinkel's writings certainly assume the same stance as this, and it is thus quite misleading to represent ethnomethodology, as many critics have been prone to do, as a form of subjectivism.

Several of the ideas mentioned in the foregoing sections are of basic significance to the social sciences; but they cannot be accepted as they stand, within the traditions of thought that have given rise to them: it is as vital to recognize the shortcomings of these traditions as it is to appreciate the signal value of their contributions. The limitations of certain versions of ethnomethodology bear definite similarities to those apparent in the *Verstehen* tradition. In identifying some such shortcomings, however, in the interests of brevity, I shall refer directly only to ethnomethodology.

First, in Garfinkel's writings (and in the writings of most of those who have made use of them at all extensively in seeking to do the sort of 'remedying of constructive analysis' with which Garfinkel himself disclaimed concern), 'accountability' is severed from the pursuance of practical motives or interests. 'Everyday practical activities' refers to much more than the sustaining of an intelligible world. The achievement of an 'ordered' social world has to concern not only its meaningful or intelligible character, but to the meshings – and conflicts – of interests that actors bring to 'accounting processes' and which they endeavour to pursue as part and parcel of those processes. This is one reason, I think, why the reports of conversations that figure in ethnomethodological writings have a peculiarly empty character: conversations are not described in relation to the goals or motives of speakers, and appear as disembodied verbal interchange. Terms such as 'practical accomplishment', etc., that bulk large in ethnomethodological discourse are in this sense not used appropriately. 'Doing bureaucracy', 'doing science', and so on, involve more than merely making such phenomena 'accountable'.

Second, to recognize the force of this comment is to imply that every relation of meaning is also a relation of power – a matter of what makes some 'accounts' *count*. In the most transient forms of everyday conversation there are elements of power that may exist in a direct sense as differential resources that participants bring to the interaction, such as the possession of superior verbal skills, but may also reflect much more generalized imbalances of power (such as class relations) structured into the society as a totality. The creation of an accountable world cannot be explicated apart from such imbalances of resources that actors bring to encounters.

Third, acknowledging the importance of agency in social theory has to be complemented with 'structural' analysis. Ethnomethodological studies are concerned with the production of society, as a skilled accomplishment of lay actors, but much less with its *reproduction* as a series of structures. However, the problem of structural reproduction is also dealt with quite inadequately in orthodox functionalist theory, where it appears in the guise of the 'internalization of values'. To reconcile the notions of agency and structure we must refer to the duality of structure. A speaker who utters a sentence draws upon a structure of syntactical rules in producing the speech act. The rules in this sense generate what the speaker says. But the act of speaking grammatically also *reproduces* the rules which generate the utterance, and which only 'exist' in this way.[5]

Fourth, the term 'common sense' has to be elucidated more carefully than is characteristic of common-sense thought itself.

The 'incorrigibility' of common sense as a necessary resource for social analysis should not blind us to its status as a topic. To 'understand' a form of life is to be able in principle (not necessarily, of course, in practice) to participate in it as a 'competent member'. From this angle, common sense – that is to say, the forms of mutual knowledge shared by the members of a common culture – is a resource that sociologists and anthropologists have to make use of. As a resource such mutual knowledge is not corrigible for the social scientist. The mistake of many of those influenced by ethnomethodological writings is to suppose that there is not another sense of common sense, represented as beliefs that are in principle open to scrutiny in the light of the findings of social science. If common sense is itself set up as a 'topic', the beliefs that are involved, whether about society itself or about nature, are in principle open to rational examination. To study, say, the practice of sorcery in an unfamiliar culture, an anthropologist has to master the categories of meaning whereby sorcery is organized as an activity in that culture. But it does not follow from this that he or she has to accept as valid the belief that sickness can be induced in a victim by means of magical ritual.

9 Habermas on Labour and Interaction

Labour and interaction: innocuous-sounding terms, but ones around which Habermas consolidated some of the main themes in his work. The origins of the differentiation Habermas drew between labour and interaction are to be found in his discussion of the relation between Hegel and Marx – in an analysis which was avowedly indebted to the ideas of Karl Löwith.[1] Habermas's account gave more prominence to Hegel's Jena lectures than is usually acknowledged by Hegel's interpreters, many of whom have regarded these lectures as a transitory phase in the evolution of that thinker's mature philosophy. According to Habermas, the two lecture courses Hegel gave at Jena[2] constituted a distinctive, if incomplete, perspective upon philosophy, which Hegel came to abandon, but which for Habermas marked certain close points of connection between Hegel and Marx (even though Marx did not know of the Jena manuscripts). In the Jena lectures, Hegel treated *Geist*, in the process of its formation, as a phenomenon to be explained. *Geist* was understood in terms of the communication of human beings via categories of meaning comprised in language. Language was the medium of self-consciousness and of the 'distancing' of human experience from the sensory immediacy of the here-and-now. As necessarily implying intersubjectivity, or *interaction*, language had a definite parallel to the significance of *labour* in Hegel's writings. Labour was the specifically human mode of relating to nature: 'Just as language breaks the dictates of immediate perception and orders the chaos of the manifold impressions into identifiable things, so labour breaks the dictates of immediate desires and, as it were, arrests the process of drive satisfaction.'³ Labour and interaction were hence the two key aspects of the self-formative process of human beings in society, or of the development of human culture. In Hegel's Jena lectures, according to Habermas, labour and interaction were presented as irreducible to one another: a matter which became a crucial focus of Habermas's attention in his critique of Marx. Interaction was organized through consensual norms that had no logical connection to the causal processes involved in transactions with nature. This was not to say, of course, that empirically they were two separate realms of human behaviour. All labour was carried on in a social and therefore communicative context.

Even in the Jena period, Habermas accepted, Hegel interpreted labour and interaction in terms of an identity theory: *Geist* was the absolute condition of nature. In other words, Hegel's account of the self-formation of humanity was always an idealist one. While rejecting Hegel's idealism, and although not having access to the Jena lectures, Marx nevertheless was able to appropriate the notions of labour and interaction from Hegel: these appeared in Marx, Habermas said, in the shape of the dialectic of the forces and relations of production.⁴ The progressive development of the forces of production, therefore, manifested the transformation of the world through human labour. The self-formative process, in Marx's writings, no longer expressed the externalization of Spirit, but was rooted in the material conditions of human existence. However, the concept of labour in Marx, Habermas emphasized, remained an epistemological category; nature was only constituted for us through its mediation in human praxis.⁵ Marx presumed that 'nature-in-itself' existed, but this was a kind of counterpart in his thought to the Kantian 'thing in itself': we only directly encountered nature in our practical interchanges with it. This 'preserves', according to Habermas, 'nature's immovable facticity despite nature's historical embeddedness in the universal structure of mediation constituted by labouring subjects'.⁶

Marx's treatment of labour, in Habermas's view, was in some respects a decisive advance over that set out by Hegel. But at the same time it also represented something of a retrogressive step, because Marx did not provide an adequate epistemological support for sustaining the mutual irreducibility of labour and interaction. Marx's scheme of analysis gave a great deal of prominence to interaction, in the shape of the notion of the relations of production. The foundation of subjectivity and self-reflection in communicative frameworks of interaction was not, however, grasped epistemologically by Marx because of the dominant place accorded to the role of labour. This result stemmed from the very success of Marx's repudiation of Hegel's identity theory. Marx's works were thus fundamentally unbalanced, in a way which had major consequences for the later history of Marxism. In his empirical works, Marx always gave considerable weight to the relations of production as well as to the forces of production. Concepts which properly belonged to the former – to interaction in Habermas's terms – especially domination and ideology, thus had a primary role in Marx's empirical writings. But they did not have the philosophical underpinning which labour – the material transformation of the world and of human conditions of existence – enjoyed. Hence Marx's concentration upon material praxis became open to a misleading emphasis: it paved the way for the collapse of interaction into labour on the level of epistemology. According to Habermas, not even Marx fully grasped the implications of this, which helped to push his work in a positivistic direction. In Habermas's words:

> Although he [Marx] established the science of man in the form of critique and not as a natural science, he continually tended to classify it with the natural sciences. He considered unnecessary an epistemological justification of social theory. This shows that the idea of the self-constitution of mankind through labour sufficed to criticise Hegel but was inadequate to render comprehensive the real significance of the materialist appropriation of Hegel.[7]

It is exactly such an epistemological justification which Habermas sought to provide in further expanding upon the distinction between labour and interaction. The collapse of interaction into labour meant that instrumentally exploitable or 'technical' knowledge – the sort of knowledge we use to attempt to control the material world – became regarded as characteristic of the social as well as the natural sciences. All social problems then became seen as 'technical' problems. Technical reason appeared to exhaust the capabilities of human reason as a whole: the defining characteristic of positivism for Habermas. The influence of Horkheimer's and Adorno's *Dialectic of Enlightenment* over

Habermas's thought is evident at this point. Their 'critique of instrumental reason' converged directly with the main political thrust of Habermas's writings (in which the influence of Max Weber also looms quite large): the thesis that increased human control over nature, or over the forces of production, was not at all the same as liberation from domination. The essential difference between Habermas's position and those of the earlier Frankfurt thinkers, a difference explored particularly in the debates between Habermas and Marcuse, is that Habermas rejected the theme that scientific or technical knowledge was itself ideological in its very form. The view of Habermas, which connects his discussion of labour and interaction in Hegel and Marx with his whole conception of knowledge-constitutive interests (today abandoned by Habermas?), was that it was the *universalization* of technical or instrumental reason, as the only form of rationality, which had to be fought against. In Marx's writings, the universalization of technical reason was traced to the epistemological dominance of labour: but the slide of Marxism towards positivism was a characteristic which Marxism shared with a great deal of modern social theory and philosophy as a whole.

Habermas's most systematic early attempt to elaborate the differentiation of labour from interaction appeared in a critical analysis of Marcuse's views on technology.[8] Labour was equated with 'purposive-rational action' (*Zweckrationalität*), which refers, Habermas said, to 'either instrumental action or rational choice or their conjunction'. Instrumental action was action oriented to technical rules, and was founded on empirical knowledge. The technical rules involved in purposive-rational action were formulated on the basis of predictive powers which they allowed. 'Rational choice' here was a matter of deciding between strategies of action, according to the most 'efficient' way of realizing goals or objectives. Interaction, on the other hand, which Habermas equated with 'communicative action', 'is governed by binding *consensual norms*, which define reciprocal expectations about behaviour and which must be understood and recognised by at least two acting subjects'.[9] Communicative action was based on ordinary language communication, and depended upon the mutual understanding of social symbols. The contrast between the rules governing purposive-rational action and those governing communicative action was exemplified by the different character of the sanctions involved in each case. Habermas here echoed a distinction made by Durkheim.[10] Non-compliance with technical rules or strategies was sanctioned by the likelihood of failure in achieving goals; non-compliance with consensual norms was sanctioned by the disapproval of, or punishment by, other members of the social community. To learn rules of purposive-rational action, in Habermas's view, was to learn skills; to learn normative rules was to 'internalize' traits of personality.

The two types of action, Habermas went on to argue, could provide a basis for distinguishing different institutional sectors of society. There were some sectors, among which he listed the economic system and the state, where purposive-rational action was most prevalent. There were others, such as the family and kinship relations, in which 'moral rules of interaction' predominated. This classification could also be applied, Habermas believed, to illuminate overall patterns in the development of societies. In traditional or pre-capitalist societies, the scope of subsystems of purposive-rational action was kept confined by the pervading authority of morally binding frameworks of interaction. Capitalist society, by contrast, was one in which the expansion of subsystems of purposive-rational action was privileged (first of all, as grounded in the expanded reproduction of capital), and progressively acted to erode other institutional forms. Modern science played a major role in this process, especially as science and technological change became more closely integrated. This led directly to the Habermasian themes of the 'scientization of politics' and legitimation crisis:

> The quasi-autonomous progress of science and technology . . . appears as an independent variable on which the most important single system variable, namely economic growth, depends . . . when this semblance has taken root effectively, then propaganda can refer to the role of technology and science to explain and to legitimate why in modern societies the process of democratic decision-making about practical problems loses its function and 'must' be replaced by plebiscitary decisions about alternative sets of leaders of administrative personnel.[11]

The passage from abstract categories of action to a more empirical concern with processes of social development is characteristic of Habermas's style of argument, and comprehensible in the light of his conception of 'epistemology as social theory'. The labour/interaction distinction remains essential to both aspects of Habermas's work in his later writings. Although at first sight the scheme of knowledge-constitutive interests advanced in *Knowledge and Human Interests* and other writings of his earlier period seems to be threefold, it is fundamentally a dichotomous one founded upon the contrast between labour and interaction. The 'interest in emancipation' lacks content, and obtains its existence from the bringing together of nomological and hermeneutic concerns in the critique of ideology. The dichotomous character of Habermas's epistemological ventures is sustained in the format of 'universal pragmatics', in his differentiation of 'theoretical-empirical' from 'practical' discourse, a differentiation that can be superimposed, as it were, upon the labour/interaction and nomological/ hermeneutic distinctions. I shall not be concerned here, however, with these ideas, but shall limit myself to following through Habermas's attempt to use the distinction between labour and interaction to analyse the evolution of societies.

Habermas's later interpretation of social evolution recapitulated some of the elements of his earlier criticisms of Marx. Marx's theory, Habermas reaffirmed, failed adequately to get to grips with communicative action in analysing the development of societies. Under the influence of Luhmann, Habermas was prone to employ terminology associated with systems theory. Marx, he said, located the 'learning processes' associated with social evolution in the sphere of the productive forces (that is, in labour); but learning processes were also to be discerned in 'world views, moral representations, and identity formations' (that is, in interaction). We had therefore to complement the study of the development of the productive forces with that of 'normative structures'. Habermas believed that this could be done without essentially compromising the overall determination of social change by 'economically conditioned system problems'.[12] Habermas's account of the evolution of normative frameworks of interaction was based upon the thesis (advocated also in some form by Durkheim, Piaget and Parsons among others) of a homology between personality and social development. The forms of consciousness, and the stages of their development, of the individual member of society were the same as those characteristic of society as a whole.[13]

According to Habermas, the evolution of societal learning processes could be examined in the following terms. At certain phases of their development, societies met with 'unresolved system problems' which presented challenges to their continued reproduction, and which could not be handled within the existing normative order. Society had then to transform itself, or its continued existence was placed in question. The nature of such a transformation, and whether it occurred at all, Habermas emphasized, were determined not by the system problems, but only by the mode in which the society responded to them, by developing new modes of normative organization. This analysis, he claimed, was still worth calling 'historical materialism'. It was materialist, because problems in the realm of production and reproduction were at the origin of the tensions which provoked system reorganization; and it remained historical because the sources of system problems had to be sought in the contingent development of particular societies. In his account of social evolution, Habermas found archaeological justification for the integral involvement of labour and language with distinctively 'human' society. 'Labour and language', as he put it, 'are older than man and society.'[14]

Having sketched in these ideas, I want to offer a brief critical appraisal of them. I shall concentrate upon some of the more directly 'sociological' difficulties related to the differentiation of labour and interaction.[15] I shall discuss these under three headings. First, it is worth mentioning some conceptual ambiguities involved in the formulation of the distinction. Second, I shall draw attention to certain problems that arise in the case of each concept taken separately. Third, I shall review some implications for Habermas's analysis of institutions.

(1) Some of the ambiguities in Habermas's use of 'labour' and 'interaction' have been pointed out by one of his leading followers.[16] Habermas repeatedly presented the distinction as one referring to two types of action – purposive-rational action on the one hand, and communicative action on the other. One type of action was governed by technical rules, and sanctioned by the likelihood of failure to reach objectives; the other was governed by social norms, and sanctioned by convention or law. The same is the case

for the subdivision he made within the notion of purposive-rational action, between 'strategic' and 'instrumental' action. But none of these was actually a type of action at all, as Habermas was forced to concede. They were, he said in response to this type of criticism, analytical elements of a 'complex'.[17] That is to day, they were ideal-typical features of action, like Weber's types from which they in some part drew their inspiration. All concrete processes of labour, of course, as Habermas emphasized in his discussion of Marx, and as Marx emphasized so forcibly himself, were social: or in Habermas's terms, involved interaction.

But this is wanting to have one's cake and eat it too. It is at best misleading to want to use 'labour' as equivalent to an analytical element of action and at the same time continue to use it in the sense of 'social labour'; and to use 'interaction' similarly as both an analytical element and a substantive type, opposed to 'monologic' or solitary action. I think this confusion stems from an unfortunate *mélange* of ideas drawn from sources which do not really have much in common with one another. These sources are, on the one hand, the Weberian distinction between purposive-rational action and value-rational action (*Wertrationalität*: transmuted considerably by Habermas, however); and on the other, the Marxian differentiation of the forces and relations of production. Weber's distinction was supposed to be an analytical or 'ideal-typical' one, but Marx's was not. Even within the Marxian scheme, 'labour' was not equivalent to 'forces of production', as presumably Habermas would acknowledge. But yet he continued to slur one into the other: to assimilate 'forces of production', 'labour' and 'purposive-rational action'; and to assimilate 'relations of production', 'interaction' and 'communicative action'. These ambiguities or confusions might not matter much if there were purely terminological points at issue, which could be corrected by clearer and more consistent usage. But they appear to me to lead to quite serious conceptual consequences for Habermas's work.

(2) I do not share Habermas's overall standpoint that today epistemology is only possible as social theory, and I do not think, as Habermas does, that the concept of labour remains an epistemological one in Marx. Or at least, it only does so when assimilated to purposive-rational action, which in my opinion is not a justifiable interpretation. Habermas criticized, with some reason, the

expansion of the notion of praxis into a 'transcendental-logical' one, which he thought we found in the works of Marcuse and Sartre. But this sort of usage hardly exhausts the insights of the Marxian notion, if it is interpreted ontologically rather than epistemologically. Rather than attempting to make the idea of labour cover the whole gamut of associations made by Habermas, I would prefer to distinguish labour from praxis, using the former in a more restricted sense and the latter in a more inclusive one. I should regard 'labour', in other words, as 'social labour': as the socially organized productive activities whereby human beings interact creatively with material nature. Labour then remains an intrinsically social activity, among other types of activity or forms of institution. Praxis can be treated as the universal basis of human social life as a whole. Praxis, that is to say, refers to the constitution of social life as regularized practices, produced and reproduced by social actors in the contingent contexts of social life.

The objections that can be raised against Habermas's use of 'interaction' are at least as important as these – perhaps more important, since a goodly amount of Habermas's writing concentrated upon interaction, as the 'neglected' side of the coin in historical materialism. The difficulties with Habermas's concept of interaction seem to me to derive from parallel sources to those relating to the notion of labour. Habermas identified interaction with communicative action, this being governed by consensual norms. His emphasis upon the hermeneutic interpretation of symbols as a methodological demand of social observation, and as the medium of intersubjectivity among the members of society, is quite unobjectionable – indeed, vital to social theory. But to treat interaction as equivalent to 'communicative action' is more than simply misleading, it is mistaken. Although Habermas insisted that interaction was not reducible to labour, I would say that he himself made a triple reduction within the notion of interaction itself. First, it is wrong to treat interaction as equivalent, or reducible, to action. Second, it is wrong to treat action as equivalent, or reducible, to communicative action. And third, it is an error to suppose that communicative action can be examined solely on the level of norms. I doubt that Habermas would accept that he made these reductions when they are thus bluntly stated. But I do not think it difficult to demonstrate that he constantly made these elisions when he wrote about interaction.

Let me develop these points somewhat. As regards the first point, perhaps the easiest way to express the matter is to say that most of Habermas's discussions of interaction did not mention *inter*action at all. To speak of interaction as a type, or even an element of action, is a misnomer. As a consequence, Habermas had little to say about – and proffered few concepts for analysing – the social relations that are constitutive of social systems. This may seem a banal enough observation, but I think it is really rather consequential: for it connects directly with Habermas's severing of the notion of praxis into two. The production and reproduction of social life as praxis involves identifying the mechanisms whereby patterns of interaction are sustained recursively. 'Action theory', as I have tried to show elsewhere, is not the same as 'interaction theory': an adequate account of the constitution of social systems in interaction demands a conception of what I have called the 'duality of structure' in social reproduction.[18]

It might be argued that, if Habermas barely touched upon these issues, this was simply an error of omission, and that the blank space could be filled in without compromising the rest of his ideas. But I think that consideration of the other two points I raised above indicates that this is not so. Interaction is not the same as 'communicative action', because communicative action is only one type of action. As regards this point, a lot hangs on what 'communication' is taken to mean. Again there seems some terminological ambiguity in Habermas here, in so far as he often seemed to equate 'symbolic' with 'communicative'. The first does not necessarily imply, as the second normally does, some sort of intended meaning which an actor wishes to transmit to others. It might plausibly be said that all action involves symbols, but it cannot be maintained that the symbolic elements of action are equivalent to communicative intent. But Habermas quite often appears to argue as though they are, perhaps in some part because of his preoccupation with speech. In so far as he does so, he tends to move back towards the sorts of intentionalist philosophical account of meaning which are incompatible with other of his emphases in his discussions of hermeneutics.[19]

The third point I mentioned above can be put as follows: there is more to interaction than the norms to which it is orientated. Habermas's emphasis upon the normative components of interaction followed plausibly enough from the tendency to slur interaction and communicative action. But the consequence is that his social theory is surprisingly close to the 'normative functionalism' of Parsons. Both accorded primacy to norms in examining social interaction, rather than to power. It might seem surprising to make such a remark, in so far as Habermas's work was presumptively directed to the critique of domination. None the less, I think it is a valid comment. I should want to make the case for arguing that power is as integral a component of all social interaction as norms are.[20] Now Habermas appears to agree with this in so far as domination or power was made one of the three fundamental aspects of social organization linked to the knowledge-constitutive interests in *Knowledge and Human Interests*. But the knowledge-constitutive interest linked to emancipation from domination was, as I have remarked, 'content-less': the critique of domination came to turn upon freedom of communication or dialogue, rather than upon material transformations of power relations. The implications of this, I think, appear rather prominently in Habermas's formulations of the nature of critical theory, which were focused unswervingly upon the uncovering of ideology. Provocative though his formulation of an ideal speech situation is as a counterfactual model for social critique, it operated once more on the level of communication. It gave us no indication of how other problems traditionally associated with disparities of power, such as access to scarce resources, and clashes of material interest, were to be coped with in the 'good society'.

(3) The import of the critical comments I have made so far is that, in some part at least because of problems with the labour/interaction distinction, there is an 'absent core' in Habermas's writings: an adequate conceptual scheme for grasping the production and reproduction of society. This observation can be consolidated, I want to claim, if we look at those segments of his work which concern the institutional organization of society. Here Habermas borrowed in a direct fashion from Parsons's functionalism (as well as from Luhmann's systems theory, or so-called 'functional-structuralism'). Habermas has certainly not been uncritical either of Parsons or of functionalism more generally. But his disquiet with Parsons's theories, as with those of Luhmann, was mainly to do with the logical status of functionalism as an 'empirical-analytic'

inquiry, rather than with the substance of those theories. The values and norms which played such a basic part in Parsons's portrayal of society could not, Habermas argued, be accepted as 'given data' as Parsons assumed. They presupposed hermeneutic procedures of identification, and had to be opened out to the possibilities of ideology-critique.[21]

In other respects, however, Habermas seems prepared to take on board some major elements of Parsonian sociology. Among Parsons's views, there are several which seem to me to be particularly questionable, and more than an echo of these is to be found in Habermas. The views I have in mind are Parsons's 'model of society', which accorded a centrality to values and norms in social integration; the thesis that society and personality were homologous, or 'interpenetrated'; and the significance attributed to 'internalization' in the theory of socialization. Major objections can be brought against all of these. The thesis of the primacy of values and norms in societal integration seems to me to be connected to a point I made previously, the tendency of Habermas to reduce interaction to communication and norms. The model of society which results – if one can judge thus far from what is clearly in Habermas's writings only a tentative approach to problems of social change – seems to embody no account of contradiction, and to underplay the significance of power and struggle in social development. It may be that Habermas will be able to incorporate these in his scheme in a more integral way, but he has not done so thus far. Rather, his discussion moved at the level of 'functional problems' which social systems faced at certain stages in their history. 'System problems', a concept which I am not very comfortable with, are not contradictions; and Habermas has not so far given much indication of just how the identification of such 'system problems' helps explain actual processes of historical change, or active social and political struggle. In lieu of a satisfactory analysis of these issues, I am more struck by the similarity of Habermas's account of social evolution to that offered by Parsons in his *Societies*[22] than I am by its closeness to Marx.

I have strong reservations about the thesis of the homology of society and personality, which became an explicit supposition in Habermas's later writings. Although he recognized the difficulties with this conception viewed phenotypically, one cannot adopt it of course without retaining the general idea that the 'childhood of society' is like the childhood of the individual, the one a more rudimentary version of the other. But the languages of all known 'primitive societies' are as complex and sophisticated as those of the economically advanced societies, and all have rich symbolic or representational contents. The views of Lévi-Bruhl seem to me today to be less compelling than those of Lévi-Strauss.

However that may be, in the present context I am more concerned to criticize the idea of society–personality homology as an analytical postulate of social theory, in which sense it is closely connected to the notion of 'internalization'. These have been pervasive themes of Parsonian sociology, and are again related to the assumption that the value or norm is the key defining characteristic of the social (or of 'interaction'). Parsons's account of the 'internalization' of norms supported the idea that the mechanisms providing for the integration of the individual within society and those integrating society were the same – the moral co-ordination of action through shared values. The very same values we 'internalized' in socialization, and which formed our personalities, were those which cohered the social system. The limitations of this kind of standpoint are pronounced. It further inhibits the possibility of dealing adequately with questions of power, sectional group interest and struggle. But on the level of the society–personality relation it implies a theory of social reproduction which fails to recognize the skilful and knowledgeable character of the everyday participation of actors in social practices. We are led back here, I think, to the demand for a coherent conception of praxis.

10 Foucault, Nietzsche and Marx

A strong current of political conservatism has swept through the West in recent decades. Not only have conservative political parties come to power in a range of countries, but they have done so in a political climate that shows obvious tendencies towards ideological realignment. With the dissolution of Keynesianism, which in the post-1945 period was in some degree accepted by conservative parties as well as by social democratic ones, conservative parties not only swept to power, they did so under the aegis of a revitalized and radical conservatism. It is possible, I think, to exaggerate the long-term import of such a phenomenon. After all, it is only some twenty-five years since the days of the efflorescence of the New Left. If the New Left appears positively old hat, one must not forget the feelings of many at the time – both among those who held strongly hostile attitudes and among its supporters – that profound changes were occurring in the fabric of the industrialized countries. So we should be careful about overgeneralizing in the light of a few years' experience. The social sciences in the post-war period were very much prone to this tendency. On the basis of a decade and a half of rising growth rates, and relatively stable 'consensus politics' in the Western liberal democracies, the most grandiose 'theories of industrial society' were created, projecting an indefinite future of progressive expansion. Most such theories have lacked the historical sense necessary to such ambitious generalization – and have been exposed as having serious shortcomings.

With these reservations in mind, there are important developments in political theory that it would not be wise to ignore. Rather than discussing these in the context of the Anglo-Saxon world, I shall concentrate upon certain aspects of the philosophical 'new conservatism' that achieved a considerable notoriety in France. There is a difference between the new conservatisms of Britain and the US, on the one hand, and the 'new philosophers' in France on the other. The former centred upon the realm of civil society, especially as regarded the influence of monetarism; the political implications have been, as it were, guided by economic theory. The new philosophers, on the other hand, discovered the state, and they discovered power. Their writings have, for the most part, a grandiose character, and they bear the hallmarks of a conversion experience. For the new philosophers were the disillusioned survivors of the 'May events' of 1968, who found themselves not in a world of liberated humanity, but instead in an age of barbarism. They moved from Marx to Nietzsche.

Let us allow Bernard-Henri Lévy to speak for the new philosophers:

> I am the bastard child of an unholy union between fascism and Stalinism. If I were a poet, I would sing the horror of living and the new Gulags that tomorrow holds in store for us. If I were a musician, I would speak of the idiot laughter and impotent tears, the dreadful uproar made by the lost, camped in the ruins, awaiting their fate. If I had been a painter (a Courbet rather than a David), I would have represented the dust-coloured sky lowering over Santiago, Luanda, or Kolyma. But I am neither painter, nor musician, nor poet. I am a philosopher, one who uses ideas and words – words already crushed and macerated by fools. So, with the words of my language, I will do no more than speak of the massacres, the camps, and the processions of death, the ones I have seen and the others, which I also wish to recall. I will be satisfied if I can explain the new totalitarianism of the smiling Princes, who sometimes even promise happiness to their people. [My work] . . . should thus be read as an 'archaeology of the present', carefully retracing through the fog of contemporary speech and practice the outline and the stamp of a barbarism with a human face.[1]

Recognition that the barbaric world of today has 'a human face', really a mere superficial mask of humanity, represents an acknowledgement that the state today claims to act in the name of the people. But the 'human face' of the contemporary state (1) is more than counterbalanced by the increasing concentration of terror in an age of scientism, bureaucracy and high military technology; and (2) is a shallow concealment of a universal institution, the state as co-ordinated power. Now the twentieth century is the century of two devastating world wars; the horrors of Nazism, even the excesses of Stalinism are hardly new. Why the shock of discovery? Why the wholesale abandonment of Marx and the clasping of Nietzsche in such a fervent embrace? No doubt there are reasons particular to France, or to sections of the European left, which were reluctant to admit the realities of Stalinism; Solzhenitsyn's account of the Gulag had more shattering effects in French leftist circles than was the case in Britain or in the US. But I think there were also deeper intellectual factors involved, to do with the intellectual traditions from which Marxism, and Marx's thought also, sprang.

Marxism was a creation of nineteenth-century Western Europe, developed via the critique of political economy. In formulating such a critique, Marx imbibed certain features of the forms of social thought he set out to combat: especially the conception that the modern (capitalist) state was primarily concerned with guaranteeing the rights of private property, against a backdrop of the national and international extension of economic exchange relationships. The classical Marxian texts not only lacked an elaborated theory of the state, they lacked a satisfactory conception of power in a more general sense. Marx offered an analysis of class power or class domination; but the accent here was on 'class' as at the origin of power. Both the state, and, as Marx sometimes said, 'political power', were to be transcended with the disappearance of classes in the anticipated socialist society of the future. There is therefore a certain antithesis between Marx (the radicalization of property) and Nietzsche (the radicalization of power) that provides something of an open door for the disillusioned. The door perhaps only tends to stand open one way – from Marx to Nietzsche – because Nietzsche offers a refuge for those who have lost their modernist illusions without relapsing into complete cynicism or apathy. Few are prepared to endure the mental burden of drawing from both Marx and Nietzsche. Of those who have tried, Max Weber is perhaps the most illustrious example; and he seems, as Fleischmann has remarked, to have ended most close to Nietzsche.[2] Weber's sombre reflections on the state of the world in 1918–19 in 'Politics as a Vocation', in fact, share some echoes with Lévy, even if they lack the flights of rhetoric of which the latter author is fond.

Reference to Max Weber, of course, reminds us that the influence of Nietzsche over social theory is by no means solely a contemporary phenomenon. Indeed there are those, such as Lukács in his book the *Destruction of Reason*, who have regarded Nietzsche as the baleful influence over a rising tide of irrationalism in German thought which culminated precisely in the triumph of fascism. But there is something novel about the resurgence of interest in Nietzsche today. Nietzsche has not before exerted a sway over French intellectual circles; and ideas in some part borrowed from Nietzsche do not only fund a new conservatism.

Rather than discussing the writings of the new philosophers in any detail, I propose to concentrate my attention upon Foucault. Foucault's later writings, those that are primarily preoccupied with power, do of course preserve some of the emphases of his earlier ones. His historical studies are informed by what he called 'genealogy', by which he meant 'a form of history which accounts for the constitution of knowledges, discourses, domains of objects, etc., without having to refer to a subject, whether it be transcendental in relation to the field of events or whether it chase its empty identity throughout history'.[3] Foucault is often bracketed with 'post-structuralism', in spite of his dislike of the term. And one can see some reason for this. Foucault continued, and indeed elaborated upon, the theme of the decentring of the subject that was introduced by Saussure and by Lévi-Strauss. In Foucault's work, the decentring of the subject became both a methodological and, in a certain sense, a substantial phenomenon. History was constituted in epistemes, or more latterly in fields of power, through which human subjects were disclosed; and, in the current age, we were moving away from an era dominated by a particular type of constitution of subjectivity. We were witnessing the 'end of the individual', a phrase which has a poignant contrast with that employed increasingly by Horkheimer and Adorno towards the ends of their lives.

To my mind, Nietzschean themes are strongly prominent in Foucault's later writings, although they are deployed in quite a different (and in some ways much more interesting) way from that of others of his contemporaries in France – even those with whom he has been closely associated, like Deleuze. These themes include not only the all-enveloping character of power, its priority to values and to truth, but also the idea that the body is the surface upon which power impinges. Power, for Foucault, was declaredly the opposite of that haunted and hunted spectre which it appears as in Marxist theory – a noxious expression of class domination, capable of being transcended by the progressive movement of history. Power, said Foucault, was not inherently repressive, not just the capability to say no. If this was all power were, Foucault asked, would we really consistently obey it? Power had its hold because it did not simply act like an oppressive weight, a burden to be resisted. Power was actually the means whereby all things happened, the production of things, of knowledge and forms of discourse, and of pleasure.

The theory of power forms the axis of Foucault's history of sexuality. 'Sexuality', he said, as we understand that phenomenon in contemporary Western society, was a product of power rather than power being repressive of sexuality. Sex had a specific political significance in modern times because it concerned characteristics and activities that were at the intersection between the discipline of the body and control of the population. There are evident connections here with Foucault's account of the origins of the prison, which I find to be his most brilliant work, the focus of most of what he had to say of importance about power. I presume a familiarity with this work, and shall not seek to reproduce its arguments in any detail. According to Foucault, the widespread adoption of the prison in Western societies in the nineteenth century signalled a major transition in fields of power. In the sphere of punishment, incarceration replaced public executions, torturing or other 'spectacles'. A 'double process' of change was involved: the disappearance of the spectacle, and the elimination of pain in favour of the deprivation of liberty and correctional discipline. This epitomized the disappearance of one type of social order, based upon 'the representative, scenic, signifying, public, collective model', and the emergence of another, 'the coercive, corporal, solitary, secret model of the power to punish'.[4]

Discipline and surveillance were key aspects of the prison, according to Foucault; and in his view it was essential to see that these were not peculiar to prisons. On the contrary, they pervaded a range of other organizations that also came to the fore in nine-teenth-century industrial capitalism: factories, offices and places of work, hospitals, schools, barracks, and so on. Discipline, Foucault said, dissociated power from the body, the contrary of traditional practices, in which the body was marked – in the case of punishment, publicly branded in some way. At the same time, the emphasis was placed upon the 'interiorization' of power. Disciplinary power, in Foucault's phrase, was 'exercised through its invisibility'; those who experienced it acquiesced in this new technology of power, and their acquiescence was an essential part of that new technology. It is not difficult in such a context to see how these notions might connect to the analysis of authority that Sennett developed in his work – and I mean here not just the book *Authority*, but earlier work also. By the 'hidden injuries' of class, Sennett meant, I take it, not simply that the 'injuries' of class domination were 'hidden', but that it was in the nature of class domination in contemporary capitalism that it was 'exercised through its invisibility'.

But the invisibility of disciplinary power, Foucault allowed, had a visible counterpart, and sustaining mechanism, in surveillance. The idea that individuals should be constantly 'under obser-vation', he argued, was the natural correlate of discipline, once the latter was manifested externally in regularity of conduct by 'docile bodies'. Thus the type case of the layout of the prison was Bentham's plan of the Panopticon, with its central observation tower. But this was only an 'ideal' form of the physical layout that inevitably accompanied the discipline/surveillance relationship. For disciplinary power involved the specified enclosure of space, the partitioning of space according to specialized criteria of identification or activity. Such spatial sequestration was so much a part of factories, offices and the other organizations I have men-tioned that we should not be surprised to find they all resemble prisons. Perhaps it would not be stretching things too far to say that, for Foucault, it was the prison and the asylum which above all exemplified the modern age, not the factory or place of production as it was for Marx. And this contrast, one might add, in turn expresses Foucault's particular version of the displacement of Marx by Nietzsche.

Now we should not miss the significance of Foucault's work, which in my assessment is perhaps the most important contribution to the theory of administrative power since Max Weber's classic texts on bureaucracy. None the less, it is equally important not to fall too easily under its sway: it is at this juncture I want to begin a series of observations that lead in the end to a rejection of the 'Nietzschean resurgence' in social theory. I want to make several major objections to what Foucault had to say about power, discipline and surveillance; and these will eventually lead us back to issues raised by the perorations of the new philosophers. I believe that the points I shall make have relevance both to social theory as a whole, as it currently exists, and to questions of politics

(1) I think it very important to break with the 'post-structuralist' style of thought in which Foucault stood. Foucault seemed to link the expansion of disciplinary power with the rise of industrial capitalism, but he did so only in a very general way. Like the 'epistemic transformations' documented in his earlier works, the transmutation of power emanated from the dark and mysterious backdrop of 'history without a subject'. Now I accept that 'history has no subject', if that phrase refers to a Hegelian view of the progressive overcoming of self-alienation by humanity; and I accept the theme of the decentring of the subject, if this means that we cannot take subjectivity as a given. But I do not at all accept the idea of a 'subject-less history', if that term is taken to mean that human social affairs are determined by forces of which those involved are wholly unaware. It is precisely to counter such a view that I developed the theory of structuration.[5] Human beings, in the theory of structuration, are always and everywhere regarded as knowledgeable agents, although acting within historically specific bounds of the unacknowledged conditions and unintended consequences of their acts. Foucault's 'genealogical method', in my opinion, continues the confusion which structuralism helped to introduce into French thought, between history without a *transcendental subject* and history without *knowledgeable human subjects*. These are two very different things, however. We must disavow the first, but recognize the cardinal significance of the second – that significance which Marx expressed pithily in the famous observation that human beings 'make history, but not in conditions of their own choosing'.

(2) This first objection has concrete implications for the analyses that Foucault produced of the prison and the clinic. 'Punishment',

'discipline' and especially 'power' itself were characteristically spoken of by him as though they were agents – indeed the real agents of history. But the development of prisons, clinics and hospitals was not a phenomenon that merely appeared 'behind the backs' of those who designed them, helped to build them, or were their inmates. Ignatieff's work on the origins of prisons is in this respect a useful counterbalance to Foucault.[6] The reorganization and expansion of the prison system in the nineteenth century was closely bound up with the perceived needs of state authorities to construct new modes of controlling miscreants in large urban spaces, where the sanctioning procedures of the local community could no longer apply.

(3) Foucault drew too close an association between the prison and the factory. There is no doubt that prisons were in part consciously looked to as models by some employers in the early years of capitalism in their search for the consolidation of labour discipline. Unfree labour was actually sometimes used. But there are two essential differences between the prison and the factory. 'Work' only makes up one sector, albeit normally the most time-consuming one, of the daily life of individuals outside prisons. For the capitalistic work-place is not, as prisons are, and clinics and hospitals may be, a 'total institution', in Goffman's term. More important, the worker is not forcibly incarcerated in the factory or office, but enters the gates of the work-place as 'free wage-labour'. This gives rise to the historically peculiar problems of the 'management' of a labour force that is formally 'free', analysed interestingly by Pollard among others.[7] At the same time, it opens the way for forms of worker resistance (especially unionization and the threat of collective withdrawal of labour) that are not part of the normal enactment of prison discipline. The 'docile bodies' which Foucault said discipline produced turn out very often to be not so docile at all.

(4) In line with his Nietzschean 'hermeneutics of suspicion', by treating the prison as the exemplar of power as discipline, Foucault produced too negative a view of 'bourgeois' or 'liberal freedoms', and of the reformist zeal they helped to inspire. We are all well aware of the Marxian 'hermeneutics of suspicion', which sees liberal freedoms as an ideological cloak for coercive and

exploitative class domination. No one can plausibly deny that the freedom of 'free wage-labour' in the early years of industrial capitalism was largely a sham, a means to the exploitation of labour power in conditions not controlled by the worker. But the 'mere' bourgeois freedoms, those of freedom of movement, formal equality before the law, and the right to organize politically, have turned out to be very real freedoms in the light of the twentieth-century experience of totalitarian societies in which they are absent or radically curtailed. Foucault said of the prison that 'prison reform' was born together with the prison itself: it was part of its very programme. But the same point could be made, and in less ironic vein, about various of the political and economic transformations introduced with the collapse of feudalism. Liberalism is not the same as despotism, absolutism or totalitarianism, and the bourgeois ethos of rational, universalized justice has the same double-edged character as prisons and their reform. With this major difference: prisoners are denied just those rights which the remainder of the population formally possess. Taken together, freedom of contract and freedom to organize politically have helped generate the rise of labour movements that have been both a challenge to, and a powerful force for change within, the political and economic orders of capitalism.

(5) There is a surprising 'absence' at the heart of Foucault's analyses: an account of the state. In Marx, this lack is to be traced to his involvement with political economy. In Foucault, one suspects, it is related to the very ubiquity of power as discipline. The state is what Foucault described as the 'calculated technology of subjection' writ large, *the* disciplinary matrix that oversaw the others. If Foucault did believe this, it is to my mind at best a partial truth. We need not only a theory of 'the state', but a theory of *states*; and this point has implications both 'internally' and 'externally'. 'Internally', it is nonsense to claim that the very existence of 'the state' negates liberal principles. Diffuse talk of the prevalence of power and the unchallengeable might of the state generates a quiescence which is as weakly founded as Marxist chatter about its transcendence.

'Externally', it seems to me of the first importance to follow Tilly and others in emphasizing the association between the rise of capitalism and the state system. Foucault wrote as follows:

> If the economic take-off of the West began with the techniques that
> made possible the accumulation of capital, it might perhaps be said
> that the methods for administering the accumulation of men made
> possible a political take-off in relation to the traditional, ritual,
> costly, violent forms of power, which soon fell into disuse and were
> superseded by a subtle, calculated technology of subjection.[8]

Yet this analysis is misleading, like much talk of the state in
general. There has never been a 'capitalist state', there have
always been capitalist nation-states, in which the internal processes of pacification of which Foucault spoke have been accompanied by a fearsome concentration of the means of violence in
the hands of the state. There are direct relations between the
capitalist labour contract, as a medium of class power, and the
appropriation of the means of violence by the state.[9] The capitalist
labour contract began as a purely economic relation, in which the
employer possessed neither moral sanctions nor sanctions of violence to secure the compliance of the labour force in the work-
place. This 'extrusion' of the means of violence from the labour
contract meant that compliance was secured in substantial degree
through the novel technology of power which Foucault described.
But one could hardly argue that 'costly, violent forms of power'
were thereby done away with, in the context of the relations
between nation-states.

Foucault and those influenced in a more uninhibited way by
Nietzsche were right to insist that power was chronically and
inevitably involved in all social processes. To accept this is to
acknowledge that power and freedom are not inimical; and that
power cannot be identified with either coercion or constraint. But
we should not be seduced by a Nietzschean radicalization of
power, which elevates it to the prime position in action and in
discourse. Power then becomes a mysterious phenomenon, that
hovers everywhere, and underlies everything. Power does not
have a logical primacy over truth; meanings and norms cannot be
seen only as congealed or mystified power. A reductionism of
power is as faulty as is economic or normative reductionism.

Notes

CHAPTER 1   POLITICS AND SOCIOLOGY IN THE THOUGHT OF MAX WEBER

1   Marianne Weber, *Max Weber: ein Lebensbild*, Heidelberg, 1950, pp. 47–8.
2   Max Weber, 'Der Nationalstaat und die Volkswirtschaftspolitik' in *Gesammelte politische Schriften*, Tübingen, 1958, pp. 1–25.
3   Max Weber, *General Economic History*, New York, 1961.
4   Karl Marx and Friedrich Engels, *Werke*, Berlin, 1953, vol. 9, p. 95.
5   The description of Weber's political writings given in this section is necessarily sketchy and somewhat slanted; a more lengthy treatment would take up issues which are largely excluded here. The reader seeking such an account should consult Wolfgang J. Mommsen, *Max Weber und die deutsche Politik: 1890–1920*, Tübingen, 1959.
6   *Gesammelte politische Schriften*, pp. 12, 14.
7   Ibid., p. 18.
8   Ibid., p. 23.
9   Letter to Michels, 1908, quoted in Mommsen, *Max Weber und die deutsche Politik*, p. 392.
10   *Gesammelte politische Schriften*, p. 532. 'In a democracy, the people choose a leader whom they trust; the leader who is chosen then says, "Now shut up and do what I say"'. quoted in Marianne Weber, *Max Weber*, pp. 664–5.
11   Ibid., p. 258. Weber considered the same to be true of the Naumann group; cf. J.P. Mayer, *Max Weber and German Politics*, London, 1956, pp. 45–6.
12   Max Weber, *Gesammelte Aufsätze zur Soziologie und Sozialpolitik*, Tübingen, 1924, p. 409.

13   Ibid., p. 394.
14   All above quotations from Max Weber, *Economy and Society*, vol. III, New York, 1968, pp. 1381–94.
15   For Mommsen's analysis of the influence of these views on Carl Schmitt, cf. Mommsen, *Max Weber und die deutsche Politik*, pp. 404ff. See also Weber, 'Der Reichspräsident', in *Gesammelte politische Schriften*.
16   *Gesammelte politische Schriften*, p. 448.
17   Above quotations all from Mommsen, *Max Weber und die deutsche Politik*, pp. 303, 300, 284.
18   Max Weber, *From Max Weber: Essays in Sociology*, eds H.H. Gerth and C. Wright Mills, New York, 1958, pp. 382, 384. I have slightly amended the translation.
19   Max Weber, *Die Verhältnisse der Landarbeiter im ostelbischen Deutschland*, Leipzig, 1892, p. 798.
20   Quoted in Eduard Baumgarten (ed.), *Max Weber und Person*, Tübingen, 1964, p. 607.
21   Above quotations all from *From Max Weber*, pp. 370–1.
22   *Gesammelte politische Schriften*, pp. 543–4. My translation. A different version appears in *From Max Weber*, p. 124.
23   *From Max Weber*, pp. 384–5.
24   *Economy and Society*, vol. I, pp. 55–6.
25   *From Max Weber*, p. 82.
26   *Gesammelte Aufsätze zur Soziologie und Sozialpolitik*, p. 508.
27   *Economy and Society*, vol. I, p. 239. Amended translation.
28   *From Max Weber*, pp. 83, 89–90. Weber contrasted this, as he often did, with the development of politics in England, 'where parliament gained supremacy over the monarch'.
29   *Economy and Society*, vol. I, p. 243.
30   Max Weber, *Gesammelte Aufsätze zur Wissenschaftslehre*, Tübingen, 1965, p. 64.
31   *Economy and Society*, vol. I, p. 6.
32   Max Weber, *The Methodology of the Social Sciences*, Glencoe, Ill., 1949, pp. 110–11. The polarization between the 'rational' and 'irrational' (in the various senses in which Weber used these terms) tends to preclude a recognition of any distinction between the '*non*-rational' and the 'irrational'.
33   *Economy and Society*, vol. I, p. 244.
34   *From Max Weber*, pp. 293–4. Amended translation.
35   Ibid., p. 142.
36   *Gesammelte politische Schriften*, p. 28.
37   Ibid., p. 470.

38 Quoted in Mommsen, *Max Weber und die deutsche Politik*, p. 118.
39 *Gesammelte politische Schriften*, pp. 280–1.
40 *Economy and Society*, vol. III, pp. 998, 975.
41 Max Weber, *The Protestant Ethic and the Spirit of Capitalism*, New York, 1958, pp. 180–1.
42 Above quotations from *The Methodology of the Social Sciences*, pp. 3, 6, 7.
43 *General Economic History*, p. 252. In traditional China, Weber showed, the absence of a stratum of jurists allowed the 'cultivated' humanism of orthodox Confucianism to become the educational avenue to membership of the state officialdom; similarly, India possessed no group of jurists comparable to those of the West.
44 Max Weber, 'Die drei reinen Typen der legitimen Herrschaft', in Johannes Winckelmann, *Staatsoziologie*, Berlin, 1966, pp. 100–1.
45 Translation as per *The Theory of Social and Economic Organisation*, New York, 1947, p. 392. My parenthesis. This does not mean that bureaucratic officials never use 'initiative', but refers to the moral nature of their 'responsibility': 'to remain outside the realm of the struggle for power – is the official's role'. *Economy and Society*, vol. II, p. 1404.
46 *From Max Weber*, p. 117.
47 In this connection see especially *Gesammelte politische Schriften*, pp. 233–79.
48 *From Max Weber*, p. 116.
49 Georg Lukács, *Die Zerstörung der Vernunft*, Berlin, 1955, p. 488.
50 Quoted in Marianne Weber, *Max Weber: ein Lebensbild*, p. 159.
51 *Gesammelte politische Schriften*, p. 47.
52 Quoted in Mommsen, *Max Weber und die deutsche Politik*, pp. 392–3. This sort of statement has to be read in juxtaposition with Weber's conviction that 'it is a gross self-deception to believe that without the achievements of the Age of the Rights of Man any one of us, including the most conservative, can go on living his life'. *Economy and Society*, vol. III, p. 1403.

CHAPTER 2 MARX, WEBER AND THE DEVELOPMENT OF CAPITALISM

1 George Lichtheim, *Marxism, an Historical and Critical Study*, London, 1964, p. 385.
2 These include the 'Critique of Hegel's Philosophy of Right'; 'Economic and Philosophical Manuscripts'; the complete text of *The*

German Ideology; and other smaller articles, letters and fragments. These were all published for the first time between 1927 and 1932, in *Marx–Engels Gesamtausgabe* (hereafter *MEGA*).

3 Marx did not, of course, use this term, which originated with Engels; but it has become conventional to use it also to refer to Marx's writings on the interpretation of historical development.

4 *A Contribution to the Critique of Political Economy*, Chicago, 1904.

5 David Koigen's *Ideen zur Philosophie der Kultur* (Munich and Leipzig, 1910) was one of the first attempts to stress the importance of the 'young' Marx. In common with most authors who have stressed the divergencies between Marx and Engels, Koigen laid emphasis upon the significance of Hegelian thought upon the whole of Marx's works. But the most influential work along these lines published before *MEGA* was Georg Lukács's *Geschichte und Klassenbewusstsein*, Berlin, 1923. In this article I shall refer to the more accessible French edition: *Histoire et conscience de classe*, Paris, 1960. Lukács was among the first to understand the possibility of assimilating Weber's studies within a truly dialectical Marxist standpoint; cf. especially pp. 142ff and 267ff.

6 In this chapter I shall follow the terminological practice suggested by Rubel, calling those views which I attribute to Marx himself 'Marxian', terming 'Marxist' ideas adopted by professed followers of Marx. I shall similarly use 'Marxism' in a very broad sense to refer generically to the latter group.

7 Cf. Karl Löwith, 'Max Weber und Karl Marx', *Archiv für Sozialwissenschaft und Sozialpolitik*, vol. 67, 1932, part I, pp. 58ff.

8 See, for example, Weber's discussion of bureaucracy and political power in 'Parliament and government in a reconstructed Germany', reprinted as an appendix to the English edition of *Economy and Society*, New York, 1968, vol. 3, pp. 1381–469.

9 The best study of the development of the SPD available in English is Günther Roth, *The Social Democrats in Imperial Germany*, New Jersey, 1963. Cf. also Werner Sombart, *Der proletarische Sozialismus*, Jena, 1924, 2 vols, esp. vol. 1, pp. 333ff, and vol. 2, pp. 9–95. Birnbaum's discussion of the views of Marx and Weber on the rise of capitalism is one of the most incisive analyses which has been made of these issues. But Birnbaum does not separate out the various dimensions which Weber's attack upon 'historical materialism' embraced; consequently, he tends to fluctuate between the conclusions that Weber's work 'made explicit what Marx left implicit' (p. 133), and that Weber considerably modified Marx's theoretical position by refuting the notion that 'ideas are simply reflections of social position and exercise no independent effects on historical development' (p. 134). 'Conflicting interpretations of the

rise of capitalism: Marx and Weber', *British Journal of Sociology*, vol. 4, 1953, pp. 125–41.

10 'Contribution to the critique of Hegel's Philosophy of Right' (1844), in T.B. Bottomore, *Karl Marx, Early Writings*, New York, 1964, pp. 57–9.

11 Cf. also Engels's views as set out in his 'Der Status quo in Deutschland', *Werke*, 4, pp. 40–57.

12 The *Communist Manifesto* announces: 'the bourgeois revolution in Germany will be but the prelude to an immediately following proletarian revolution'.

13 Cf. Marx's article in the *Deutsche Brüsseler Zeitung* of 18 November 1847; *Werke*, 4, pp. 351ff. For a more extended analysis, see Engels, *Germany: Revolution and Counterrevolution*, London, 1933.

14 Cf. Karl Demeter, 'Die soziale Schichtung des deutschen Parlamentes seit 1848', *Vierteljahrschrift für Sozial- und Wirtschaftsgeschichte*, vol. 39, 1952, pp. 1–29. For the attitudes of liberals towards equal suffrage, cf. Walter Gagel, *Die Wahlrechtsfrage in der Geschichte der deutschen liberalen Parteien, 1848–1918*, Düsseldorf, 1958.

15 Particularly significant in separating the development of the labour movement in Germany from that in Britain was the fact that in Germany, until relatively late on, the working class was without the franchise.

16 Eduard Bernstein, *Evolutionary Socialism*, London, 1909 (second edition, London, 1963).

17 It might be pointed out here that the consequences of the German victory of 1870–1 were equally fraught with significance for the sociological perspective of Durkheim.

18 Cf. Wolfgang J. Mommsen, *Max Weber und die deutsche Politik: 1890–1920*, Tübingen, 1959, pp. 103ff; cf. also Raymond Aron, 'Max Weber und die Machtpolitik', et seq., in *Max Weber und die Soziologie heute*, Tübingen, 1965.

19 'Der Nationalstaat und die Volkswirtschaftspolitik', *Gesammelte politische Schriften*, Tübingen, 1958, pp. 1–25.

20 Cf. also Durkheim's analysis of Treitschke in *L'Allemagne au-dessus de tout*, Paris, 1915.

21 Weber made this remark at a meeting of the Verein für Sozialpolitik. See 'Diskussionsreden auf den Tagungen des Vereins für Sozialpolitik', in *Gesammelte Aufsätze zur Soziologie und Sozialpolitik*, Tübingen, 1924, pp. 394ff, and esp. pp. 408–9.

22 'Parliament and government in a reconstructed Germany', p. 1453.

23 Weber also offered a number of technical economic objections to the operation of a planned economy, in the form in which most socialists at that time conceived of such an economy. Cf. *Economy*

and Society, vol. 1, pp. 65–8; and pp. 100–7.

24 'Parliament and government in a reconstructed Germany', p. 1453. For Weber's views on Russia, cf. 'Russlands Übergang zur Scheindemokratie' in *Gesammelte politische Schriften*, pp. 192–210.

25 Cf. 'Das neue Deutschland', *Gesammelte politische Schriften*, pp. 472–5.

26 E.g. Sombart. See, for example, his *Der moderne Kapitalismus*, particularly vol. 1; Sombart of course, even early on in his career, was far from being an orthodox 'Marxist'. On the relationship between Sombart, Marx and Weber, cf. Talcott Parsons, 'Capitalism in recent German literature: Sombart and Weber', *The Journal of Political Economy*, vol. 36, 1928, pp. 641–61; and vol. 37, 1929, pp. 31–51.

27 Cf. Weber's discussion of Stammler's book on historical materialism and law; 'R. Stammlers "Überwindung" der materialistischen Geschichtsauffassung', in *Gesammelte Aufsätze zur Wissenschaftslehre*, Tübingen, 1951, pp. 291–359.

28 Cf. Weber's letter to his mother of 8 July 1884, in *Jügendbriefe*, Tübingen, n.d., pp. 121–2. It is worth noting that Weber was impressed by reading David Strauss's *Das Leben Jesu* (1835) at an early age; the same work had played a prominent part in the development of Marx's views as a member of the 'Young Hegelians'.

29 See Karl Kautsky, *Karl Marx' ökonomische Lehren*, Stuttgart, 1887; and, subsequently, his *Der Ursprung des Christentums*, Stuttgart, 1908.

30 Cf. *The Protestant Ethic and the Spirit of Capitalism*, New York, 1958, esp. pp. 194–8. For an account of the background to Weber's views on religion, see Paul Honigsheim, 'Max Weber: his religious and ethical background and development', *Church History*, vol. 19, 1950, pp. 2–23.

31 Cf. Weber: 'Der Sozialismus', in *Gesammelte Aufsätze zur Soziologie und Sozialpolitik*, pp. 504ff.

32 Cf. Weber's outline of *Erwerbsklassen*, in *Economy and Society*, vol. 1, p. 304.

33 Although this is set out in most detail in his more technical essays on method, Weber's basic epistemological position is formulated in a brilliantly concise fashion in 'Science as a vocation', in H.H. Gerth and C. Wright Mills, *From Max Weber: Essays in Sociology*, New York, 1958, pp. 129–56.

34 See Weber's remarks on Marx's concepts in '"Objectivity" in social science and social policy', in *The Methodology of the Social Sciences*, Glencoe, Ill., 1949, p. 103 and *passim*.

35 Weber discussed the notion of evolutionary 'stages' in some detail in relation to a problem which also preoccupied Marx, and more par-

ticularly Engels: the question of the development of Germanic tribal society in relation to the decline of Rome and the organization of medieval feudalism. Cf. Weber, 'Der Streit um den Charakter der altgermanischen Sozialverfassung in der deutschen Literatur des letzten Jahrzehnts', in *Gesammelte Aufsätze zur Sozial- und Wirtschaftsgeschichte*, Tübingen, 1924, pp. 508–56.

36 The phrase comes from Weber's contribution to a meeting of the German Sociological Association, reported in 'Geschäftsbericht und Diskussionsreden auf den deutschen soziologischen Tagungen', in *Gesammelte Aufsätze zur Soziologie und Sozialpolitik*, p. 456.

37 'Objectivity in social science and social policy', p. 68. Weber nevertheless spoke of the *Communist Manifesto* as 'a scientific achievement of the first rank' in 'Der Sozialismus', pp. 504–5.

38 *Economy and Society*, vol. 1, p. 63. For Weber's earlier formulation of the concept of the 'economic', see 'Objectivity in social science and social policy', p. 64.

39 'Objectivity in social science and social policy', p. 65.

40 Marx, *The Poverty of Philosophy*, Moscow, n.d., p. 92. (The quotation in the text is Weber's version of the Marxian original.) For Weber's distinction between 'economy' and 'technology' see *Economy and Society*, vol. 1, pp. 65–7.

41 'Geschäftsbericht und Diskussionsreden auf den deutschen soziologischen Tagungen', p. 450.

42 *Economy and Society*, vol. 2, pp. 928ff.

43 Collected together as *Gesammelte Aufsätze zur Wissenschaftslehre*, Tübingen, 1968 (third edition).

44 'Science as a vocation', p. 153.

45 Much of the dispute over Weber's objectives in the book stems from neglect of Weber's published replies to his early critics. Cf. his 'Antikritisches zum Geist des Kapitalismus', *Archiv für Sozialwissenschaft und Sozialpolitik*, vol. 20, 1910; and his 'Antikritisches Schlusswort', ibid., vol. 31.

46 The most definite evidence for the continuity of Marx's thought is the draft version of *Capital*. This was published in 1939, but did not become generally available until 1953, as *Grundrisse der Kritik der politischen Ökonomie*, Berlin, 1953. For an analysis of some of the phases in the development of differing 'interpretations' of Marx since the turn of the century, see Erich Thier, 'Etappen der Marxinterpretation', *Marxismusstudien*, 1954, pp. 1–38.

47 'Theses on Feuerbach', in Loyd D. Easton and Kurt H. Guddat, *Writings of the Young Marx on Philosophy and Society*, New York, 1967, p. 402 (Thesis 9).

48 Ludwig Feuerbach, *The Essence of Christianity*, London, 1853.

49 This phrase was, of course, originally used by Engels to refer to

Marx's relation to Hegel. Cf. Engels, 'Ludwig Feuerbach and the end of classical German philosophy', *Selected Works*, London, 1950, vol. 2, p. 350.

50　'Theses on Feuerbach', p. 400 (Thesis 1).

51　'Preface to *A Contribution to the Critique of Political Economy*', in Marx and Engels, *Selected Works*, vol. 1, pp. 328–9.

52　Cf. Thesis 7 in 'Theses on Feuerbach', p. 402.

53　*The German Ideology*, Moscow, 1968, pp. 38–9.

54　Ibid., p. 61.

55　'Theses on Feuerbach', p. 402 (Thesis 6).

56　Cf., for example, 'The Civil War in France', in *Selected Works*, vol. 1, pp. 429–40.

57　*Grundrisse*, pp. 375–413; the relevant sections are mostly included in an English translation of a small section from the work – E.J. Hobsbawm, *Pre-capitalist Economic Formations*, London, 1964; Weber's discussion of Rome is to be found in 'Die sozialen Gründe des Untergangs der antiken Kultur', in *Gesammelte Aufsätze zur Sozial- und Wirtschaftsgeschichte*, pp. 289–311. In the subsequent part of this chapter I do not deal with the discrepancies between Marx's discussion of 'the Asiatic mode of production' and Weber's analysis of China and India. It has often been stated that Weber's views upon the emergence of rational capitalism in the West can only be fully understood in the light of his writings on the various 'world religions'. This is undeniably true. It is, however, quite misleading to regard these writings, as many have, as a form of *ex post facto* experiment which 'tests' the 'independent' influence of ideology upon social development. What Weber showed was that *both* the content of the religious ethics he discussed *and* the specific combination of 'material' circumstances found in Europe, China and India differed. (Thus, for example, Weber laid stress upon the ease of communications in Europe, the peculiar economic and political independence of the European city, plus various other 'material' conditions in terms of which Europe differed from China and India.) These material and ideological factors formed a definite, interrelated 'cluster' in each case: the material conditions could not therefore simply be treated as a 'constant' against which the 'inhibiting' or 'facilitating' influence of religious ideology as a 'variable' could be determined.

58　*Pre-capitalist Economic Formations*, p. 84.

59　*Grundrisse*, p. 740.

60　Marx pointed out also that while the use of money was widespread in antiquity, only in certain trading nations did it become essential to the economy; in Rome, the monetary system came to be fully developed only during the period of the disintegration of the economy. *Grundrisse*, pp. 23–4. Compare Engels's discussion of Rome, in his 'The origin of the family, private property and the state', in *Selected Works*, vol. 2, pp. 270–8.

61 See the discussion of Stirner's *Der Einzige und sein Eigentum* in *The German Ideology*, pp. 143ff.

62 Ibid., p. 151. Weber, on the other hand, stressed that Christianity had always been primarily a religion of the urban artisanate. See *Economy and Society*, vol. 2, pp. 481ff.

63 'Contribution to the critique of Hegel's Philosophy of Right', in *On Religion*, p. 50. Marx only briefly alluded to the significance of the ideological content of Calvinism. (See, for example, *Capital*, vol. 1, p. 79.) Engels, on various occasions, discussed Calvinism at greater length.

64 'Economic and Philosophical Manuscripts', in Bottomore, *Karl Marx*, pp. 168ff.; see also Löwith, 'Max Weber und Karl Marx', pp. 77ff.

65 *Grundrisse*, p. 313. Cf., on the 'universalizing' character of money, Georg Simmel, *Philosophie des Geldes*, Leipzig, 1900. Weber remarked of Simmel's book that 'money economy and capitalism are too closely identified, to the detriment of his concrete analysis' (*Protestant Ethic*, p. 185). Marx also noted the significance of a phenomenon which Weber later discussed at great length – the fact that Roman law played an important role in the formation of bourgeois society. Cf. *Grundrisse*, p. 30; and p. 916.

66 'Economic and Philosophical Manuscripts', p. 171; cf. Avineri, pp. 110–11.

67 *Grundrisse*, pp. 133–4.

68 Marx and Engels, *The Holy Family*, Moscow, 1956.

69 Letter to the editor of *Otyecestvenniye Zapisky*, 1877, *Selected Correspondence*, London, 1934, p. 355. (I have modified the translation.)

70 Marx, of course, realized that political structures could vary to a considerable degree independently of class interests. (See, for example, his letter in *Letters to Kugelmann*, London, n.d., p. 23.) Marx saw that the most developed society in economic terms, England, had a less complex state than Germany or France. The English state, Marx wrote in 1885, was 'an archaic, time-worn and antiquated compromise between the bourgeoisie, which rules over all the various spheres of civil society in reality, but *not officially*, and the landed aristocracy which rules *officially*'. 'Die britische Konstitution', *Werke*, 11, p. 95.

71 Gerth and Mills, *From Max Weber*, p. 47.

72 *Grundrisse*, p. 428. Marx, however, noted that the case of the army and that of the capitalist organization differed in that the professional soldier was not hired in order to produce surplus value.

73 *Anti-Dühring*, Moscow, 1962; *Dialectics of Nature*, Moscow, 1954.

74 The phrase is Lukács's, *Geschichte*, p. 20.

75 Engels, in fact, disclaimed the writings of some of his intellectual disciples who were actually only drawing the logical implication of the main themes of *Anti-Dühring*. His attempt to escape the theoretical impasse to which his views led is given in his statement, 'According to the materialist conception of history, the determining element in history is *ultimately* the production and reproduction in real life. More than this neither Marx nor I have ever asserted.' Engels to Bloch, 21 September 1890, in *Selected Correspondence*, p. 475. Marx had earlier, of course, also felt compelled to comment ironically that he 'was not a Marxist'.

CHAPTER 3   DURKHEIM'S POLITICAL SOCIOLOGY

1 Talcott Parsons, *The Structure of Social Action*, New York, 1937 (second edition, New York, 1949).

2 *Leçons de sociologie*, 1950. Translated into English under the title of *Professional Ethics and Civic Morals*, London, 1957.

3 Compare the treatment of Marx in Erich Thier, 'Etappen der Marxinterpretation', *Marxismusstudien*, 1954, pp. 1–38.

4 See, for example, Marion M. Mitchell, 'Emile Durkheim and the philosophy of nationalism', *Political Science Quarterly*, vol. 46, 1931, pp. 87–106.

5 Cf. my 'Durkheim as a review critic', *Sociological Review*, vol. 18, 1970, pp. 188–91.

6 Parsons's usage of this term is somewhat unusual. See *The Structure of Social Action* (second edition), pp. 60–9.

7 Robert A. Nisbet, *Emile Durkheim*, Englewood Cliffs, N.J., 1965, p. 37. My first parenthesis.

8 See my *Capitalism and Modern Social Theory*, Cambridge, 1971, ch. 14.

9 Parsons, *The Structure of Social Action* (second edition), p. 307 and *passim*.

10 E. Durkheim, *The Division of Labour in Society*, Glencoe, Ill., 1964, p. 228. (I have modified the translation in this and certain other quotations in subsequent parts of the chapter.)

11 E. Durkheim, 'L'individualisme et les intellectuels', *Revue bleue*, vol. 10, 1898, pp. 7–13.

12 In saying this, of course, I do not wish to say that Saint-Simon and Comte were the only important intellectual influences over Durkheim. Other, more immediate influences were Renouvier, Fustel de Coulanges, and Boutroux.
13 'L'individualisme et les intellectuels', p. 7.
14 Ibid., p. 8.
15 Ibid., pp. 11 and 13.
16 Melvin Richter, 'Durkheim's politics and political theory', in Kurt H. Wolff, *Emile Durkheim et al.: Essays on Sociology and Philosophy*, London, 1964, pp. 172ff.
17 See, for example, Simon Deploige, *Le Conflit de la morale et de la sociologie*, Paris, 1911. Durkheim reviewed the book in the *Année sociologique*, vol. 12, 1909–12. For an earlier exchange of letters between Deploige and Durkheim, see the *Revue néoscolastique*, vol. 14, 1907, pp. 606–21.
18 See, above all, E. Durkheim, *L'Evolution pédagogique en France*, Paris, 1969 (first published, in two vols, in 1938).
19 Georges Davy, 'Emile Durkheim', *Revue de métaphysique et de morale*, vol. 26, 1919, p. 189.
20 Marcel Mauss, Introduction to the first edition of *Socialism and Saint-Simon*, London, 1952, p. 32.
21 E. Durkheim, *Moral Education*, Glencoe, Ill., 1961, p. 137.
22 Cf. K. Marx, 'The Civil War in France', in *Selected Works*, Moscow, 1958, vol. 1, p. 542.
23 E. Durkheim, Review of Antonio Labriola's *Essais sur la conception matérialiste de l'histoire*, *Revue philosophique*, vol. 44, 1897, pp. 649 and 651.
24 Ibid., pp. 648–9.
25 Sorel played an important part in this; for his evaluation of Durkheim, see 'Les théories de M. Durkheim', *Le Devenir social*, vol. 1, 1895, pp. 1–26 and 148–80.
26 *Socialism*, p. 283.
27 Ibid., p. 284.
28 'Socialism is to the facts which produce it what the groans of a sick man are to the illness with which he is afflicted, to the needs that torment him. But what would one say of a doctor who accepted the replies or desires of his patient as scientific truths?' Ibid., p. 41.
29 Ibid., p. 285.
30 Ibid., p. 40.
31 Ibid., p. 90. For further discussion of Durkheim's evaluation of Marx, see my *Capitalism and Modern Social Theory*, ch. 13.
32 Ibid., pp. 39–79.
33 Ibid., pp. 70–1.

34 Ibid., p. 71.
35 E. Durkheim, 'La science positive de la morale en Allemagne', *Revue philosophique*, vol. 24, 1887, part 1, p. 38.
36 *The Division of Labour*, p. 227.
37 'Where restitutive law is highly developed, there is an occupational morality for each profession . . . There are usages and customs common to the same order of functionaries which no one of them can break without incurring the censure of the corporation.' Ibid., p. 227.
38 *The Division of Labour*, p. 220.
39 Durkheim, *Professional Ethics and Civic Morals*, pp. 98ff.
40 Ibid., pp. 98 and 99.
41 Ibid., pp. 102–3.
42 *The Division of Labour*, pp. 280–2; also pp. 405–6.
43 *Professional Ethics and Civic Morals*, p. 75.
44 See E. Durkheim and E. Denis, *Qui a voulu la guerre?*, Paris, 1915; and E. Durkheim, *L'Allemagne au-dessus de tout*, Paris, 1915.
45 *L'Allemagne au-dessus de tout*, p. 7.
46 Ibid., p. 5.
47 Ibid., p. 22.
48 Ibid., p. 7.
49 Ibid., p. 45.
50 See especially Robert Nisbet, 'Conservatism and sociology', *American Journal of Sociology*, vol. 58, 1952, pp. 165–75, and *The Sociological Tradition*, London [New York], 1967; and Lewis A. Coser, 'Durkheim's conservatism and its implications for his sociological theory', in Wolff, *Emile Durkheim*, pp. 211–32.
51 Coser, 'Durkheim's conservatism', p. 212.
52 See my *Capitalism and Modern Social Theory*, passim.
53 E. Durkheim, 'Introduction à la morale', *Revue philosophique*, vol. 89, 1920, p. 89.
54 E. Durkheim, *Suicide*, London, 1952, p. 383.
55 E. Durkheim, Preface to the *Année sociologique*, vol. 2, 1897–8, in Wolff, *Emile Durkheim*, pp. 352–3.
56 H. Stuart Hughes, *Consciousness and Society*, New York, 1958, p. 285.
57 *L'Evolution pédagogique en France*.
58 Ibid., p. 323.
59 *Moral Education*, p. 10.
60 E. Durkheim, *Sociology and Philosophy*, London, 1953, p. 72.
61 'To be free is not to do what one pleases; it is to be master of oneself.' E. Durkheim, *Education and Sociology*, Glencoe, Ill., 1956, p. 89.

62 'The dualism of human nature and its social conditions', in Wolff, *Emile Durkheim*, p. 327.

63 *Professional Ethics and Civic Morals*, pp. 47–8.

64 *The Division of Labour*, p. 226.

65 E. Durkheim, *Montesquieu and Rousseau*, Ann Arbor, 1960, p. 33.

66 E. Durkheim, 'Deux lois de l'évolution pénale', *Année sociologique*, vol. 4, 1899–1900, pp. 65–95.

67 Ibid., p. 650.

68 Ibid., pp. 67–8.

69 Ibid., p. 69.

70 Ibid., pp. 88 and 93.

71 *Professional Ethics and Civic Morals*, pp. 82–3.

72 Ibid., p. 87.

73 Ibid., p. 89.

74 Ibid., pp. 96 and 106.

75 Ibid., p. 106.

76 Ibid., p. 51.

77 Ibid., p. 56.

78 E. Durkheim, *The Rules of Sociological Method*, London, 1964, p. 121.

79 *Suicide*, p. 360. There are major unresolved difficulties in Durkheim's writings on this point, however, analysed in ch. 4.

80 'The dualism of human nature and its social conditions', p. 339.

81 Coser, 'Durkheim's conservatism', pp. 211–12. Cf. Parsons, '[Durkheim] was almost wholly concerned with what Comte would have called "social statics" ', *The Structure of Social Action* (second edition), p. 307.

82 Coser, 'Durkheim's conservatism', p. 212.

83 *The Division of Labour*, p. 377.

84 *Montesquieu and Rousseau*, p. 59.

85 *The Rules of Sociological Method*, p. 47.

86 Review of Deploige, p. 327.

87 *The Division of Labour*, p. 29.

88 Cf. ch. 6.

89 *Professional Ethics and Civic Morals*, pp. 50–1.

90 Ibid., p. 78.

91 For background material on Weber's conception of the state, see my *Politics and Sociology in the Thought of Max Weber*, London, 1972.

92 Parsons, *The Structure of Social Action* (second edition), p. 341.

93 The publication of Marx's early writings, however, made it apparent that this thesis of Durkheim's was erroneous, at least as applied to Marx. Marx was primarily concerned with the alienative dominance

of economic relationships under capitalism: the regulation of the market was to Marx a means, not an end. See my *Capitalism and Modern Social Theory*, ch. 15.

94 *Professional Ethics and Civic Morals*, p. 213.
95 'A limitation to the right of disposal is in no way an attack on the individual concept of property – on the contrary. For individual property is property that begins and ends with the individual.' Ibid., pp. 216–17.
96 *The Division of Labour*, pp. 374 and 377.
97 Robert Wohl, *French Communism in the Making, 1914–1924*, Stanford, 1966, p. 9.

CHAPTER 4   DURKHEIM AND THE QUESTION OF INDIVIDUALISM

1 Perhaps the best of the earlier studies of Durkheim is Roger Lacombe, *La méthode sociologique de Durkheim*, Paris, 1926.
2 'La science positive de la morale en Allemagne', *Revue philosophique*, vol. 24, 1887, 3 parts.
3 Cf. ch. 3.
4 *De la division du travail social*, Paris, 1960, p. xliii. (All translations are mine.)
5 Ibid., p. 396.
6 'L'individualisme et les intellectuels', *Revue bleue*, vol. 10, 1898, pp. 7–13, translated in S. Lukes, 'Durkheim's "Individualism and the Intellectuals"', *Political Studies*, vol. 17, 1969.
7 *L'Evolution pédagogique en France*, Paris, 1938, republished 1969. See, for example, pp. 322–3.
8 *Sociologie et philosophie*, Paris, 1924, p. 106.
9 The term 'anomie' first appeared in Durkheim's writings in his review (1887) of Guyau's *L'Irréligion de l'avenir*. The latter author used the term, however, in a sense closer to Durkheim's conception of moral individualism.
10 'Suicide et natalité: étude de statistique morale', *Revue philosophique*, vol. 26, 1888, pp. 446–63.
11 See my *Capitalism and Modern Social Theory*, Cambridge (UK), 1971, chs 8 and 15; and my Introduction to *Emile Durkheim: Selected Writings*, Cambridge, 1972.
12 Parsons, however, makes too much of this. See Talcott Parsons, *The Structure of Social Action*, Glencoe, Ill., 1949, pp. 350–3.
13 *Les Règles de la méthode sociologique*, Paris, 1950, p. 8.
14 Ibid., p. 7.

15 *Sociologie et philosophie*, pp. 60–2.
16 *Le Suicide*, Paris, 1930, p. 411.
17 'Le dualisme de la nature humaine et ses conditions sociales', *Scientia*, vol. 15, 1914, pp. 206–21, translated in K. Wolff, *Emile Durkheim et al.: Essays on Sociology and Philosophy*, London, 1964.
18 See 'The suicide problem in French sociology', pp. 322–32.
19 *Le Suicide*, p. 8.
20 *De la division du travail social*, p. 399.
21 This is, of course, reinforced by other aspects of Durkheim's methodology which I do not discuss in this chapter: such as the 'rule' that 'an effect can only have one cause.'
22 This is the aspect given most prominence by Parsons. See especially *The Social System*, London, 1951, p. 39.
23 Introduction to *Emile Durkheim: Selected Writings*.
24 See, for example, *Sociologie et philosophie*, pp. 56–7.
25 *De la division du travail social*, p. 327.

CHAPTER 5   COMTE, POPPER AND POSITIVISM

1 The influence of Saint-Simon over Marx is a matter of some controversy in itself. For a systematic treatment, see Georges Gurvitch, 'La sociologie du jeune Marx', in *La Vocation actuelle de la sociologie*, Paris, 1950.
2 Herbert Marcuse, *Reason and Revolution*, London, 1955, p. 341.
3 *Cours de philosophie positive*, vol. 1 (*Philosophie première*), Paris, 1975, pp. 21ff.
4 Ibid., p. 21.
5 Ibid., pp. 28–9.
6 Ibid., vol. 2 (*Physique sociale*), p. 139.
7 Ibid., pp. 139–40.
8 Cf. John Stuart Mill, *Auguste Comte and Positivism*, Ann Arbor, 1961, pp. 125ff.
9 *Cours de philosophie positive*, vol. 1, pp. 44ff.
10 See Herbert Spencer, *Reasons for Dissenting from the Philosophy of M. Comte*, Berkeley, Cal., 1968; Mill comments on this, *Auguste Comte*, pp. 5ff.
11 Durkheim and Fauconnet, 'Sociologie et sciences sociales', *Revue philosophique*, vol. 55, 1903.
12 Mill, *Auguste Comte*, p. 59.
13 Durkheim, *The Elementary Forms of the Religious Life*, New York, 1965, pp. 170ff; (with M. Mauss), *Primitive Classification*, London, 1963.

14   Durkheim, *The Rules of Sociological Method*, London, 1964, p. 14.
15   Ibid., pp. 48ff.
16   *Cours de philosophie positive*, vol. 2, pp. 16ff.
17   Ernst Mach, *The Analysis of Sensations*, Chicago, 1914, pp. 37ff.
18   Mach, *Erkenntnis und Irrtum*, Leipzig, 1917, p. vii.
19   *The Analysis of Sensations*, p. 369.
20   Cf., for example, Victor Kraft, *The Vienna Circle*, New York, 1953.
     Mach's theories also attracted the attention of prominent literary
     figures. Hofmannsthal, the poet, attended Mach's lectures, believing
     that if the world consisted only of our sensations, it could be de-
     scribed more directly and thoroughly in poetry than in science.
     Robert Musil began his career as a philosopher, actually writing a
     doctoral thesis on Mach, before turning to the novel form.
21   A.J. Ayer et al., *The Revolution in Philosophy*, London, 1956.
22   Stephen E. Toulmin, 'From logical analysis to conceptual history', in
     Peter Achinstein and Stephen F. Barker, *The Legacy of Logical
     Positivism*, Baltimore, 1969, pp. 31ff. Carnap later wrote on this
     point, 'when we were reading Wittgenstein's book in the Circle, I
     had erroneously believed that his attitude towards metaphysics was
     similar to ours. I had not paid sufficient attention to the statements
     in his book about the mystical, because his feelings and thoughts in
     this area were too divergent from mine'.
23   Herbert Feigl, 'The origin and spirit of logical positivism', in
     Achinstein and Barker, *Legacy*, p. 5.
24   Cf. Carnap's Preface to the second edition of *The Logical Structure
     of the World*, London [Los Angeles], 1967.
25   A.J. Ayer, 'Editor's introduction', in *Logical Positivism*, Glencoe,
     Ill., 1959, p. 8.
26   Carnap, *The Logical Structure of the World*.
27   Carnap, 'Psychology in physical language', in Ayer, *Logical Positiv-
     ism*, p. 197.
28   Cf. Richard von Mises, *Positivism, a Study in Human Understand-
     ing*, Cambridge, Mass., 1951, pp. 80ff.
29   Richard Bevan Braithwaite, *Scientific Explanation*, Cambridge,
     1968, p. 51.
30   Cf. Carnap, 'The methodological character of theoretical concepts',
     in Herbert Feigl and Michael Scriven, *The Foundations of Science
     and the Concepts of Psychoanalysis*, Minneapolis, 1956.
31   Herbert Feigl, 'The "orthodox" view of theories: some remarks in
     defence as well as critique', in M. Radner and S. Winokur, *Minne-
     sota Studies in the Philosophy of Science*, vol. 4, Minneapolis, 1970.
32   Carl G. Hempel and P. Oppenheim, 'Studies in the logic of expla-
     nation', *Philosophy of Science*, vol. 15, 1948.

33 Hempel, 'Deductive-nomological vs. statistical explanation', in Herbert Feigl and Grover Maxwell, *Scientific Explanation, Space, and Time*, Minneapolis, 1962.

34 Hempel, 'The function of general laws in history', in *Aspects of Scientific Explanation*, New York, 1965, pp. 240–1.

35 Otto Neurath, 'Sociology and physicalism', in Ayer, *Logical Positivism*, p. 283; see also Neurath, *Foundations of the Social Sciences, International Encyclopaedia of Unified Science*, vol. 2, Chicago, 1944.

36 Neurath, 'Sociology and physicalism', p. 299.

37 Paul F. Lazarsfeld and Morris Rosenberg, 'General introduction', in *The Language of Social Research*, New York, 1955, pp. 2ff.

38 Ernest Nagel, *The Structure of Science*, London [New York], 1961, p. 484.

39 Ibid., pp. 468–9.

40 Hans L. Zetterberg, *On Theory and Verification in Sociology*, Totawa, 1966.

41 Ibid., pp. 46ff.

42 Ibid., pp. 81 and 85.

43 Ibid., pp. 102–3.

44 Hempel, 'The logic of functional analysis', in *Aspects of Scientific Explanation*.

45 Ibid., p. 317.

46 Ibid., p. 325.

47 Popper, 'Science: conjectures and refutations', in *Conjectures and Refutations* [New York, 1968], London, 1972, p. 37.

48 Thomas S. Kuhn, *The Structure of Scientific Revolutions*, Chicago, 1970, p. 126.

49 Cf. Kuhn, 'Reflections on my critics', in Imre Lakatos and Alan Musgrave, *Criticism and the Growth of Knowledge*, Cambridge [New York], 1970, p. 248.

50 Max Weber, *The Methodology of the Social Sciences*, Glencoe, Ill., 1949, pp. 13ff.

51 Cf. my *Politics and Sociology in the Thought of Max Weber*, London, 1972.

52 Max Horkheimer, *Eclipse of Reason*, New York, 1974, p. 5.

53 Horkheimer, 'Der neueste Angriff auf die Metaphysik', *Zeitschrift für Sozialforschung*, vol. 6, 1937.

54 Jürgen Habermas, *Knowledge and Human Interests*, London, 1972, pp. 43ff.

55 Max Horkheimer and Theodor W. Adorno, *Dialectic of Enlightenment*, New York, 1972.

56 Adorno et al., *The Positivist Dispute in German Sociology*, London,

1976 (first published in German in 1969).

57   Popper, 'The logic of the social sciences', in Adorno et al., *The Positivist Dispute*, p. 102.

58   Habermas, 'Analytical theory of science and dialectics', in Adorno et al., *The Positivist Dispute*, p. 142.

59   William W. Bartley, *The Retreat to Commitment*, London, 1964.

60   Cf. Habermas, *Knowledge and Human Interests*, pp. 301ff.

61   Hans Albert, 'Behind positivism's back?', in Adorno et al., *The Positivist Dispute*, pp. 246ff. Cf. also Albert, *Traktat über kritische Vernunft*, Tübingen, 1968.

62   Popper, 'Reason or revolution?', in Adorno et al., *The Positivist Dispute*, p. 299.

63   Lakatos, 'Falsification and the methodology of scientific research programmes', in Lakatos and Musgrave, *Criticism and the Growth of Knowledge*, pp. 106ff; cf. Lakatos, 'Changes in the problem of inductive logic', in *The Problem of Inductive Logic*, Amsterdam, 1968.

64   Kuhn, 'Reflections on my critics', pp. 256ff.

65   Lakatos, 'Falsification', p. 121. Cf. also footnote 4, p. 122 and p. 137, where 'verification' is reintroduced, albeit reluctantly.

66   Dudley Shapere, 'Notes toward a post-positivistic interpretation of science', in Achinstein and Barker, *Legacy*.

67   See, for example, W.O. Quine, *From a Logical Point of View*, Cambridge, Mass., 1953; *Word and Object*, Cambridge, Mass., 1960; *Ontological Relativity and Other Essays*, New York, 1969; Hesse, *The Structure of Scientific Inference*, London [Los Angeles], 1974.

68   Cf. Pierre Duhem, *The Aim and Structure of Physical Theory*, Princeton, N.J., 1954; *To Save the Phenomena*, Chicago, 1969.

69   Hesse, *The Structure of Scientific Inference*, pp. 175ff.

70   Ibid., pp. 4–5.

71   Cf. my *New Rules of Sociological Method*, London, 1976, pp. 142ff.

72   Cf. Kuhn, 'Second thoughts on paradigms', in F. Suppe, *The Structure of Scientific Theories*, Urbana, Ill., 1974.

73   Hans-Georg Gadamer, *Truth and Method*, London [New York], 1975, pp. 55ff.

74   Theodore Abel, 'The operation called *Verstehen*', *American Journal of Sociology*, vol. 54, 1948; Carl Hempel, 'On the method of *Verstehen* as the sole method of philosophy', *The Journal of Philosophy*, vol. 50, 1953.

75   Abel, 'The operation called *Verstehen*'.

76   Cf. my *New Rules of Sociological Method*, pp. 148ff.

77   Abel, 'The operation called *Verstehen*'.

78 For a definition of 'determinism' here, see my *New Rules of Sociological Method*, p. 85.
79 Talcott Parsons, *The Structure of Social Action*, Glencoe, Ill., 1949.
80 *New Rules of Sociological Method*; Alfred Schutz, *The Phenomenology of the Social World* [Evanston, 1967], London, 1972.
81 The idea of 'structure', of course, appears in many varying contexts in modern thought. There are obvious contrasts between the mode in which the term is used in 'structural-functionalism' on the one hand, and 'structuralism' on the other.
82 Cf. the analysis offered in my 'Functionalism: *après la lutte*', *Studies in Social and Political Theory*, London, 1979, pp. 96–129.

CHAPTER 6 'POWER' IN THE WRITINGS OF TALCOTT PARSONS

1 Thus Mills, in Parsons's view, showed a 'tendency to think of power as presumptively illegitimate; if people exercise considerable power, it must be because they have somehow usurped it where they had no right and they intend to use it to the detriment of others'. 'The distribution of power in American society', in *Structure and Process in Industrial Societies*, Glencoe, Ill., 1960, p. 221.
2 Ibid., p. 220.
3 Parsons stressed that this analysis of power marked a shift from the views set down in *The Social System*, where he stated he still accepted the 'traditional' (that is, the 'zero-sum') conception. This meant that his view of what constituted 'political science' had also changed; whereas previously in *The Structure of Social Action* he accepted the idea that political science was a synthetic discipline, it now became seen as a relatively autonomous analytical discipline on a par with economics.
4 'On the concept of political power', in *Structure and Process in Industrial Societies*, p. 237.
5 'Authority, legitimation and political action', in *Structure and Process in Industrial Societies*, p. 181.
6 'On the concept of political power', p. 250.
7 'Some reflections on the place of force in the social process', in Harry Eckstein, *Internal War*, Glencoe, Ill., 1964. This typology obviously links up with the functional subsystems of society. As in most of Parsons's schemes involving the four 'functional subsystems', a regressive set of subclassifications is possible for each of the four 'media' of interaction. In the case of 'influence', for example, the pattern would look like this:

(I = integration; GA = goal attainment; A = adaptation; PM = pattern maintenance)

	I	GA	A	PM
Types of 'media'	Influence	Power	Money	'Commitments'
	↓			
	GA	A	I	PM
Types of influence	'Political' influence	Fiduciary influence	Influence based on 'differential loyalties'	Influence 'oriented to norms'

8 'Some reflections on the place of force in the social process', p. 52.

9 Ibid., pp. 63ff.

10 Hans H. Gerth and C. Wright Mills, *From Max Weber*, New York, 1958, p. 180.

11 Parsons claimed these concepts 'bridge the gap between the normative and factual aspects of the system in which they operate'. 'On the concept of influence', *Political Opinion Quarterly*, vol. 27, 1963, p. 45.

12 *Societies: Evolutionary and Comparative Perspectives*, Englewood Cliffs, N.J., 1966, p. 115.

13 Cf. Parsons's comment: 'We can say that the primary function of superior authority is to clearly define the situation for the lower echelons of the collectivity. The problem of overcoming opposition in the form of dispositions to non-compliance then arises from the incomplete institutionalization of the power of the higher authority holder.' 'On the concept of political power', p. 243.

14 Ibid., p. 254.

15 Parsons always recognized in principle the essential linkage between values and interests. See, for example, the discussion in one of his earliest articles: 'The place of ultimate values in sociological theory', *International Journal of Ethics*, vol. 45, 1935, pp. 282–316. In a much later publication, Parsons remarked, presumably with reference to Lockwood: 'I do not think it is useful to postulate a deep dichotomy between theories which give importance to beliefs and values on the one hand, and to allegedly "realistic" interests, e.g. economic, on the other. Beliefs and values are actualized, partially and imperfectly, in realistic situations of social interaction and the outcomes are *always* codetermined by the values and the realistic exigencies.' 'Authority, legitimation and political action', reprinted in *Structure and Process in Industrial Societies*, p. 173. There is clearly a sense in which 'values' are prior to 'interests': to have an 'interest', an individual or group must have some kind of selective

motivation, which presumes in turn some kind of 'value'. But this is very different from saying that in an *explanatory* sense values are necessarily prior to interests. And this is precisely what the whole of Parsons's theory is predicated upon. Parsons's recognition of the role of non-normative interests did not lead to a systematic theoretical treatment of the interaction of values and interests. The point is that not only are the 'outcomes in realistic situations of social interaction' codetermined by values and 'realistic exigencies', but that the latter play an (often crucial) part in the *formation* and degree of 'actualization' of values.

CHAPTER 7 THE IMPROBABLE GURU: RE-READING MARCUSE

1 Herbert Marcuse, *An Essay on Liberation*, Boston, Mass., 1969, p. viii.
2 Some of these appeared in translation much later, in Marcuse, *Negations*, Boston, Mass., 1968, and in other sources. Certain early essays remain untranslated, but are readily available in the reprinted edition of the *Zeitschrift für Sozialforschung*, Munich, 1980.
3 For an analysis which makes this particularly clear, see David Held, *Introduction to Critical Theory: Horkheimer to Habermas*, London, 1980. Held remarked that, 'Of all the members of the Frankfurt School, Marcuse's life-long relation to his early work and political ambitions is perhaps the most consistent' (p. 73). For Marcuse's 'Heideggerian version' of Marx, see 'Contributions to a phenomenology of historical materialism', *Telos*, vol. 4, 1969 (originally published in 1928).
4 Marcuse, *Reason and Revolution*, New York, 1960, p. viii.
5 Marcuse, *One-Dimensional Man*, Boston, Mass., 1966, pp. x–xi.
6 Ibid., p. 21.
7 Cf. on this point Marcuse's essay, first published in 1941, on 'Some social implications of modern technology', reprinted in Andrew Arato and Eike Gebhardt (eds), *The Essential Frankfurt School Reader*, Oxford, 1978.
8 *One-Dimensional Man*, p. 3.
9 Marcuse, *Eros and Civilization*, Boston, Mass., 1961, p. x.
10 *One-Dimensional Man*, pp. 131ff.
11 Ibid., p. 158.
12 Ibid., p. 231.
13 *An Essay on Liberation*, p. 4.
14 *One-Dimensional Man*, p. 11.

15   Cf. Marcuse, *Soviet Marxism*, London, 1958, p. xi and *passim*.
16   Marcuse's critical assessment of Weber, it should be noted, turned more than anything else upon the assertion that what Weber saw as the formal reason of bureaucracy, and as the inevitable concomitant of contemporary society, was actually capable of radical transformation. He accepted the general thrust of Weber's analysis of 'rationalization', while disputing its inescapable character. See 'Industrialization and capitalism in the work of Max Weber', in *Negations*.
17   Cf. my Postscript to the second edition of *The Class Structure of the Advanced Societies*, London, 1981.
18   *One-Dimensional Man*, p. 1.
19   Michel Foucault, *The History of Sexuality*, vol. 1, London, 1978.
20   *Eros and Civilization*, p. 4.
21   Ibid., p. 208.
22   Marcuse, *Five Lectures: Psychoanalysis, Politics and Utopia*, London, 1970, p. 40.
23   Ibid., p. 17.
24   Quotations from *Counterrevolution and Revolt*, p. 60; and *Five Lectures: Psychoanalysis, Politics and Utopia*, p. 41.
25   Marcuse, Habermas, et al., 'Theory and politics', *Telos*, no. 38, 1978–9, p. 148.
26   'The struggle against liberalism in the totalitarian view of the state', in *Negations*, p. 19.
27   See esp. pp. 3ff in that work.
28   See 'Class division, class conflict and citizenship rights', in *Profiles and Critiques in Social Theory*, London, 1982.

CHAPTER 8   GARFINKEL, ETHNOMETHODOLOGY AND HERMENEUTICS

1   Hans-Georg Gadamer, *Wahrheit und Methode*, Tübingen, 1960; Peter Winch, *The Idea of a Social Science*, London, 1958 (new edition, London, 1970); Paul Ricoeur, *De l'interprétation: essai sur Freud*, Paris, 1965.
2   Most of the views in this chapter are discussed in a more detailed way in my *New Rules of Sociological Method*, London, 1976.
3   Theodore Abel, 'The operation called *Verstehen*', *American Journal of Sociology*, vol. 54, 1948; Ernest Nagel, 'On the method of *Verstehen* as the sole method of philosophy', *The Journal of Philosophy*, vol. 50, 1953.
4   Emmanuel A. Schegloff and Harvey Sacks, 'Opening up closings',

Semiotica, vol. 8, 1973; Alan Blum, *Theorising*, London, 1974; Peter McHugh et al., *On the Beginning of Social Enquiry*, London, 1974.
5   Cf. *New Rules of Sociological Method*, pp. 118ff.

CHAPTER 9   HABERMAS ON LABOUR AND INTERACTION

1   See Habermas, 'Remarks on Hegel's Jena *Philosophy of Mind*', *Theory and Practice*, London, 1974, p. 168; Karl Löwith, *From Hegel to Nietzsche*, New York, 1967.
2   *The Philosophy of Mind* and *System of Morality*.
3   'Remarks on Hegel's Jena *Philosophy of Mind*', p. 159.
4   Ibid., p. 168.
5   Habermas, *Knowledge and Human Interests*, London, 1972, pp. 28–34.
6   Ibid., p. 34.
7   Ibid., p. 45.
8   'Technology and science as "ideology" ', in *Toward a Rational Society*, London, 1971. This essay also makes plain the significance of certain ideas of Max Weber for Marcuse and Habermas.
9   Ibid., pp. 91–2.
10 Durkheim distinguished between what he called 'utilitarian', or technical, and 'moral' sanctions. In the latter, the sanction was defined socially, in the former by objects and events in nature. Emile Durkheim, 'Determination of the moral fact', in *Sociology and Philosophy*, London, 1953.
11 'Technology and science as "ideology"', p. 105.
12 Habermas, 'Historical materialism and the development of normative structures', in *Communication and the Evolution of Society*, Boston, Mass., 1979, pp. 97–8.
13 Habermas made various qualifications to this assertion, however. See ibid., pp. 102–3, 110–11.
14 'Toward a reconstruction of historical materialism', in *Communication and the Evolution of Society*, p. 137.
15 See 'Habermas's critique of hermeneutics', in *Studies in Social and Political Theory*, London, 1977.
16 Thomas McCarthy, *The Critical Theory of Jürgen Habermas*, London, 1978, pp. 24–6.
17 Habermas, 'A postscript to *Knowledge and Human Interests*', *Philosophy of the Social Sciences*, vol. 3, 1973.
18 As I have tried to do in *Central Problems in Social Theory*, London, 1979, *passim*.
19 Cf. my *New Rules of Sociological Method*, London, 1974, pp. 68–9

and 86–91.

20   *Central Problems in Social Theory*, pp. 88–94.
21   Habermas, *Zur Logik der Sozialwissenschaften*, Frankfurt, 1970, pp. 170ff.
22   Talcott Parsons, *Societies: Evolutionary and Comparative Perspectives*, Englewood Cliffs, N.J., 1966.

CHAPTER 10   FOUCAULT, NIETZSCHE AND MARX

1   Bernard-Henri Lévy, *Barbarism with a Human Face*, New York, 1980, p. x.
2   Eugene Fleischmann, 'De Weber à Nietzsche', *Archives européennes de sociologie*, vol. 5, 1964.
3   Michel Foucault, *Power, Truth, Strategy*, Sydney, 1979, p. 35.
4   Foucault, *Discipline and Punish: The Birth of the Prison*, London, 1977, p. 131.
5   *Central Problems in Social Theory*, London, 1979.
6   Michael Ignatieff, *A Just Measure of Pain*, London, 1978.
7   Sidney Pollard, *The Genesis of Modern Management*, London, 1965.
8   Foucault, *Discipline and Punish*, pp. 220–1.
9   *A Contemporary Critique of Historical Materialism*, London, 1981.

Index

Merton, R.K. 2
metaphysics, condemnation of 136,
138, 140, 147–8, 149, 153, 221–2
methodological falsificationism
(Lakatos) 181–2
methodological individualism 41,
116–17, 123, 128, 238, 239, 240,
243
Michels, Robert 49
Mill, John Stuart 144, 145, 190,
283nn8,10
Mills, C. Wright 199–200, 225,
274n33
Mises, Ludwig von 155
modernity 12, 13
Mommsen, Wolfgang J. 15, 52, 53,
269n5
money
Marx and Weber and 72, 73–4,
276n60
power analogous to, in Talcott
Parsons 200–2, 203–4, 210,
212–13
Montesquieu, Charles Louis de
Secondat, Baron de la Brède et
de 5, 109, 139, 145
Moore, G.E. 151
moral, separation from rational 42
see also values
moral authority, Durkheim and 80,
81, 82, 83, 87, 89–90, 94, 98,
104–7, 120, 122
moral individualism (Durkheim) see
individualism
Mosca, Gaetano 75
motivation 195–6
see also action; intentionality
Musil, Robert 284n20

Nagel, Ernest 161–3, 164, 196
nationalism
German 59
mystical, of Durkheim 78
Weber and 23, 30, 52, 53–4, 63, 64
nation-state, Weber and see under
nationalism
natural sciences see science(s)
naturalism
Durkheim and 146
Garfinkel and 242

Popper and 178
nature
in Hegel and Marx 229, 246–7
Marcuse and 229–30
Naumann group 269n11
Neurath, Otto 151, 154, 155, 156,
159–60, 175
New Left 216, 259
Nietzsche, Friedrich Wilhelm 52, 55,
230
influence on 'new philosophers' in
France 260–8
Nisbet, Robert A. 79, 94, 280n50
normative functionalism see
functionalism
norms
interaction and 247, 249–50, 251,
252, 254, 255, 256, 257, 258
Verstehen and 242–3
see also internalization; values

objective science, understanding
and 238
see also positivism
occupational associations
(corporations), Durkheim
and 89, 90, 91, 98, 101–2, 103–4,
110–11, 112
One-Dimensional Man
(Marcuse) 216–32
comments on 224–6
leading themes 217–24
technology, freedom and politics
in 226–32
operationalism 160
Oppenheim, P. 158
ordinary-language philosophy 11,
155, 177, 221
organic solidarity (Durkheim) 79, 81,
82, 100, 101, 118–19, 129

Panopticon 264
paradigm 1, 171–3, 181, 186–7, 188
Pareto, Vilfredo 75
parliamentary democracy, system 61
Weber and 25–7, 50, 64
Parsons, Talcott 1–4, 5, 78, 94, 113,
195, 235, 251, 256–8, 282n12,
283n22
on power 199–215